DISTANT ECHOES

OBSERVATIONS ON THE NOCTURNAL

by

James Bengel

For Sandy

with love, thanks and hope

With special thanks to Ti
For being there

FOREWORD

"Everything you have done in your life has brought you to exactly where you are right now."

A dear friend who is a Buddhist monk taught me this years ago; it is a lesson I realize anew every day. The words everything and exactly offer the lessons of mindfulness: of paying full attention to life itself.

Everything: all you have understood and misunderstood, loved, refrained from loving, given, taken, let be. Everything.

At the heart of you is all you have done to be exactly where you are. Exactly. That is, your life is not an accident. There are no coincidences. Your universe unfolds exactly as it does because of everything you have done.

In other words, you make your life. To understand this is to realize you are sacred. That life is sacred.

Artists who live in this knowledge imbue their creative gifts with it to present the spirit of that truth in some new way. Life is exquisitely beautiful.

James is one such artist. He does this on a daily basis. All those things that have shaped his life come together with his photographic expertise to capture the soul of whatever he is seeing. His photos are not about technical correctness--even if they are technically correct. Nor are they about the rules of composition--though they are well composed. They are about the splendid beauty of life. In this book, they are about the ineffable beauty (even when it's painful) of night as he so often lives it.

These photos are about James as much as they are about the world he sees. They are also about so many of us who have lived in the strange other world of night, where things become simpler at the same time they become more mysterious, where solitude is unavoidable regardless of the size of the crowd, where purpose seems pointless. Indeed, sometimes night is the sharpest send-up of all we find meaningful. (Perhaps that is why the ancient bards slept by day and wrote by night.)

These photos are as inviting as they are challenging. They invite us to stand where stood the man with the lens in these moments of clear vision. They ask us to say what we see even at the risk of having the conversation with ourselves alone and to let that be. We are here for one reason: we chose to be here.

Sandy L. Carlson
Woodbury, Connecticut
April 2010

CONTENTS

ABOUT *DISTANT ECHOES*

"I think there's a book in that. Your book."

Going from submitting seventeen syllables to a poetry prompt to compiling an entire book might seem like a leap to you. It certainly seemed like one to *me* when my good friend Sandy Carlson suggested it. I confess, I was skeptical. Sandy never was. And for that reason alone, this is as much her book as it is mine. Without her, it would never have existed.

INSOMNIA

> Which dream was the dream?
> The perfect day, or the night
> It interrupted?

Distant Echoes began as a photo essay of the nighttime world and the people in it. Not simply images of the physical, this is an attempt to capture what happens "when you climb inside what creates the sleeplessness". That question led to something more than a simple collection of photographs. As the project evolved, it took on a different character and I began to add prose or poetry where it fit. The resulting combination hopefully brings the concept to life in a way that neither medium alone would.

Every project, no matter whose name it bears, owes much to many people. So many, in fact, that I cannot possibly name them all here. I have been blessed with friends from (quite literally) all over the world who have offered me the validation and encouragement to undertake this endeavor. Daryl Edelstein in Manhattan, Carmi Levy in London (Ontario), Anna Larsson in Karlstad (Sweden), Robin Epstein in Tel Aviv, Deepak Amembal in Mumbai, Mary Tomaselli in New York, Maggie Ginsberg-Schutz and Lisa DeWayne, both in the Wisconsin wilderness somewhere. The list could fill several pages. They and so many others have freely and consistently given their encouragement, friendship and insight. A simple "Thank you" seems woefully inadequate. That doesn't mean I'm not going to say it anyway. Thank you all. Whether you had a hands on role in the actual production of the book or not, you provided the underpinnings upon which it is built.

I must acknowledge two very special people without whom I could not have – or at least *would* not have – gone forward with the project. First, I have to thank Ti Conkle of Fairbanks, Alaska for her undying support and occasional reality check. When I needed an honest opinion, I knew I could count on hers – even if it wasn't what I wanted to hear. Her help along the way was of inestimable value. Ti, you're amazing girl. And I couldn't have made it the last few miles without you.

Finally, more than anyone else, I owe an incalculable debt of gratitude to Sandy Carlson of Woodbury, Connecticut. A noted author, poet, photographer and teacher in her own right, she is the inspiration that took this book from a nebulous "someday-idea" to a concrete "now-reality". Without her unending patience, guidance, encouragement and support throughout the process, the project never would have reached fruition. Friend, editor, collaborator, muse; you have been all of these and much, much more Sandy. I owe you more than I could ever sufficiently express in a few sentences. The world would be a much better place if everyone could be lucky enough to have a Sandy Carlson in his life. Thank you for showing me the things that are possible, my friend. May happiness visit you in abundance. No one deserves it more.

James Bengel
Raleigh, North Carolina
March 2010

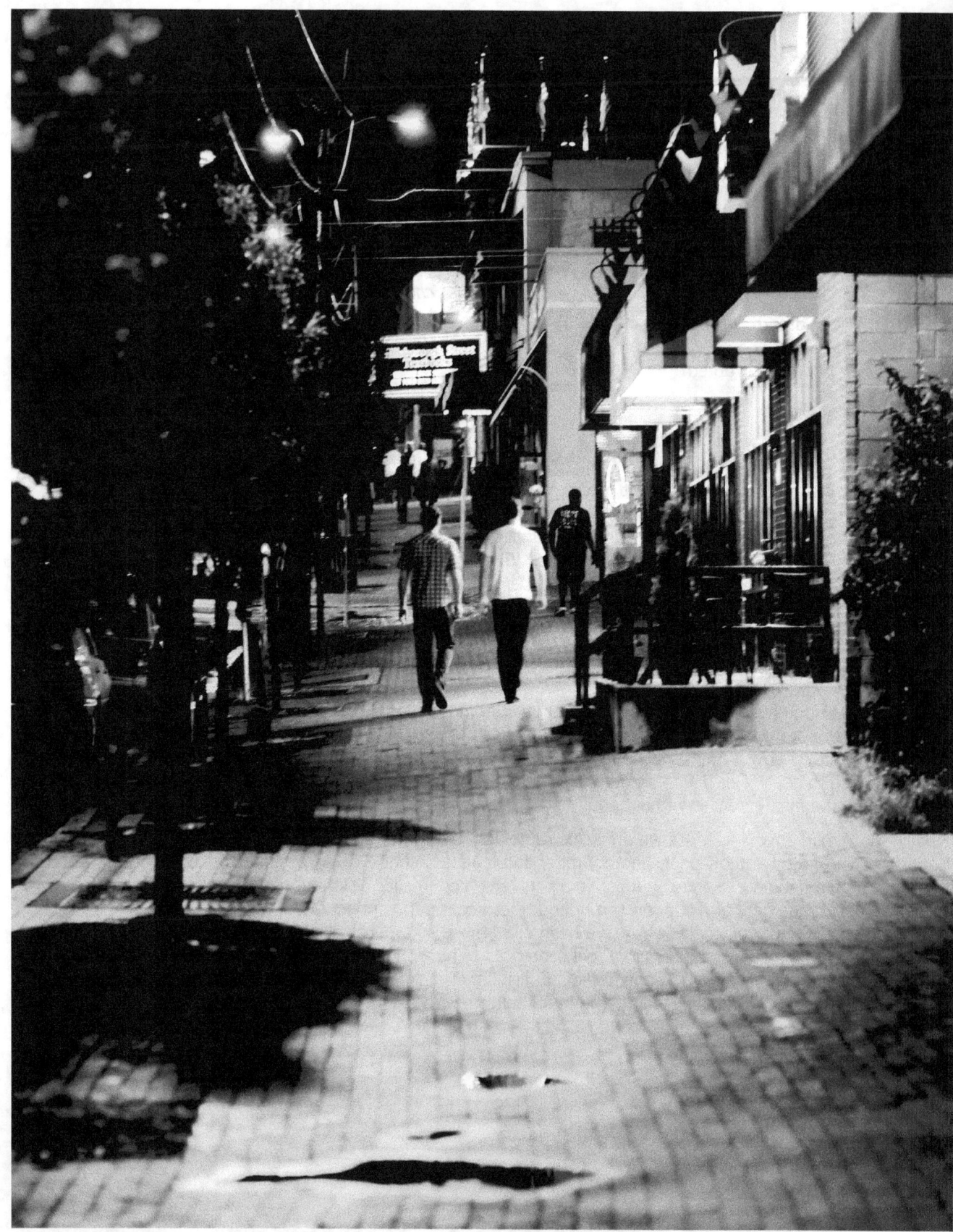

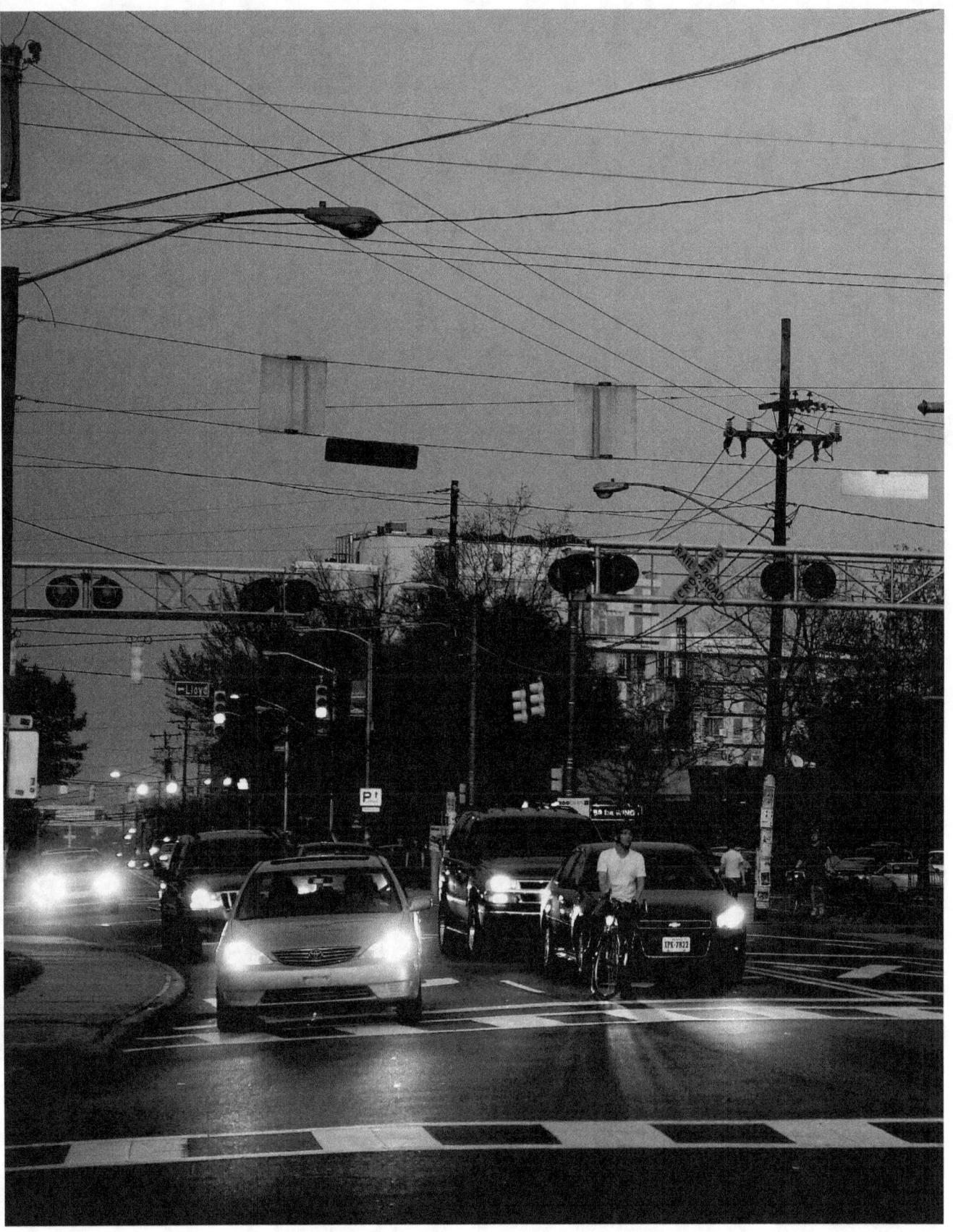

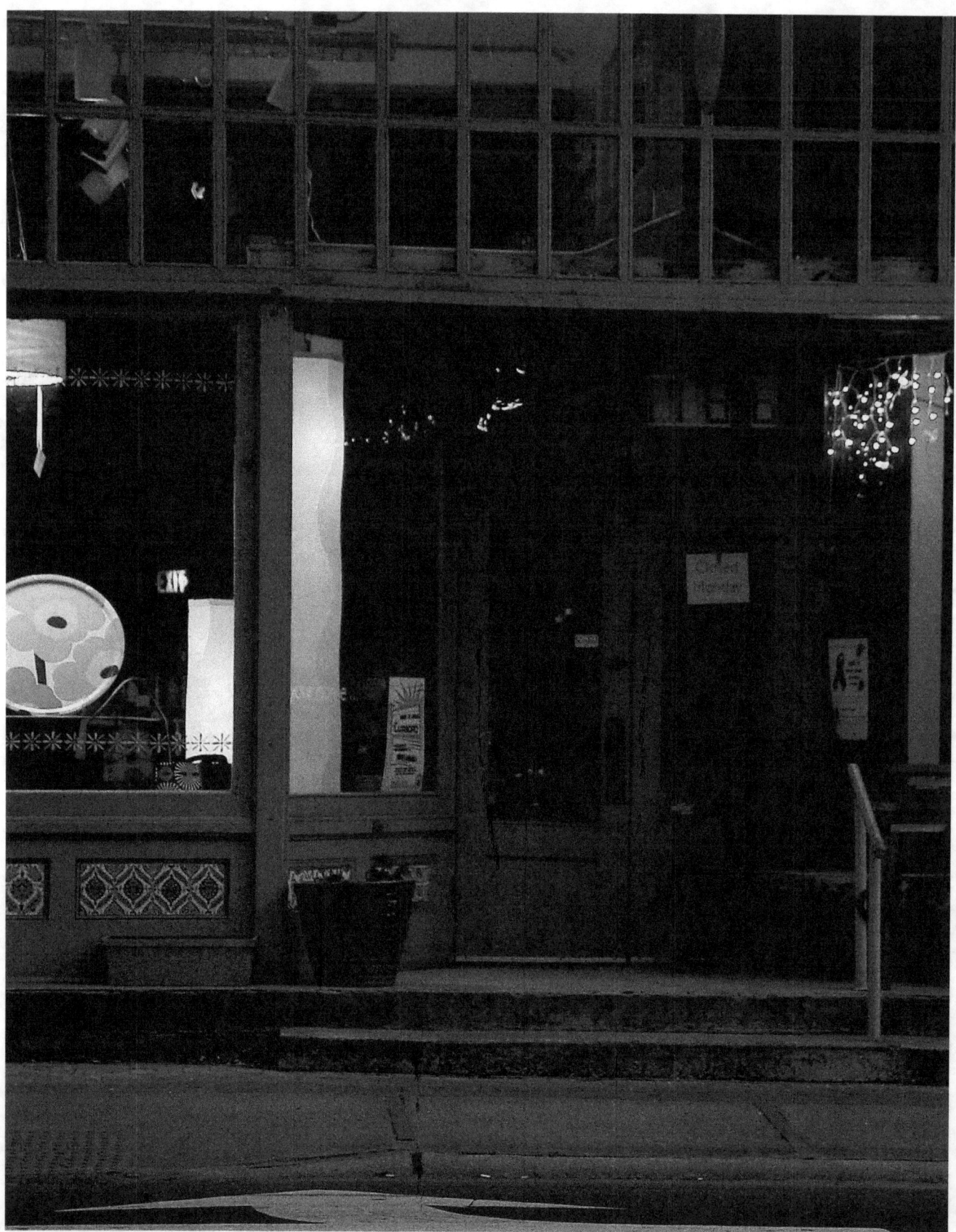

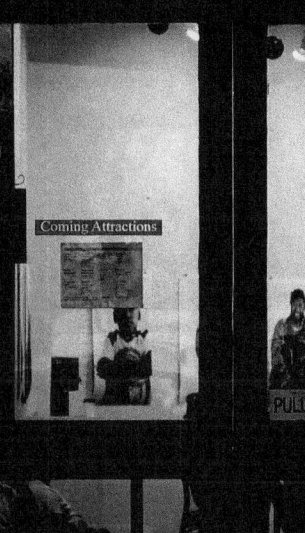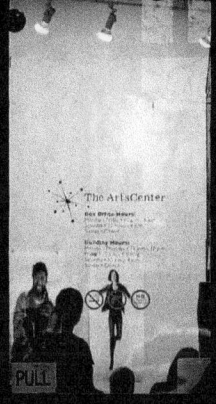

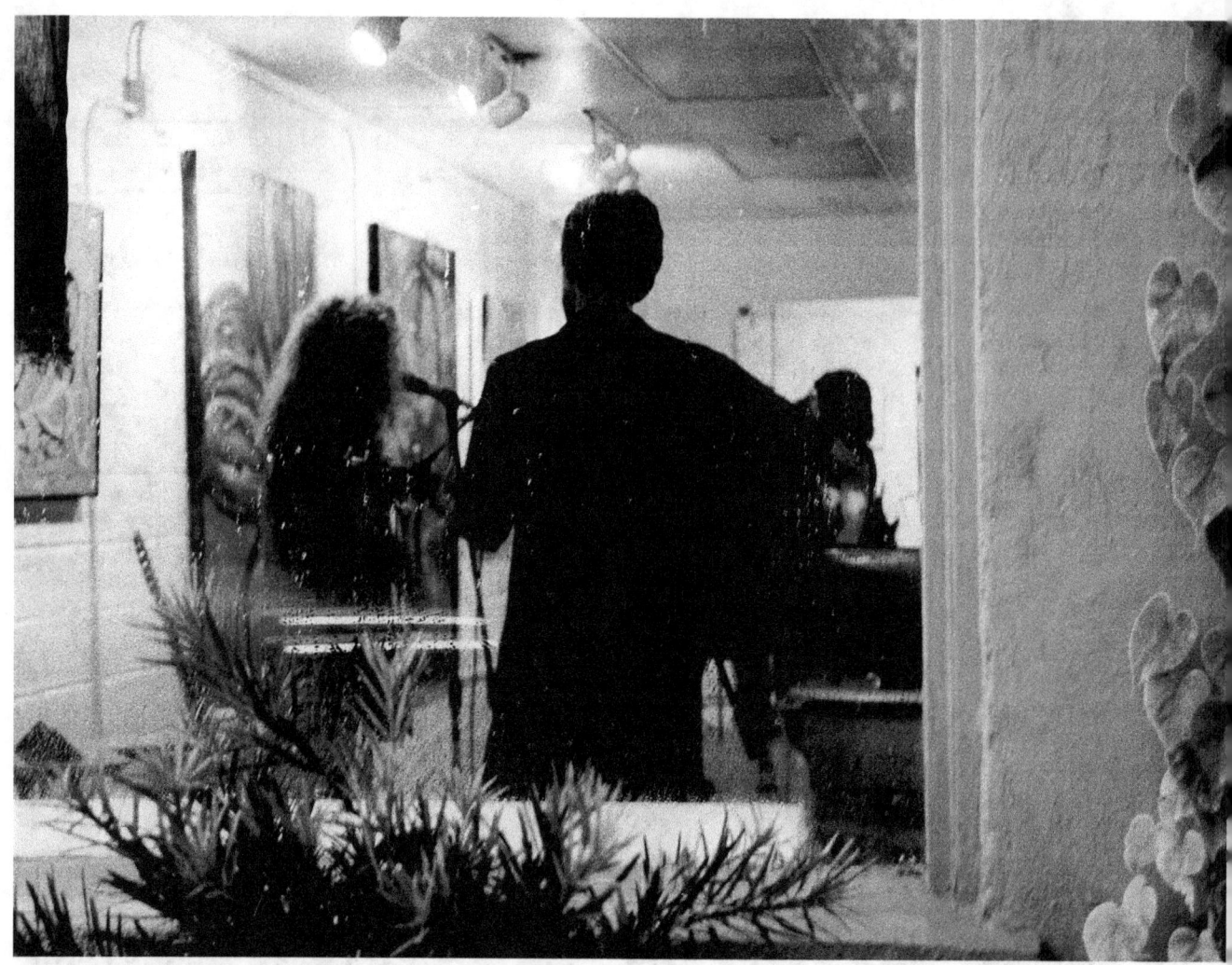

Through My Window

You asked me once
What you would see if
You looked through my window
Some night or other

I wondered then (and now)
Why would you do that?
Stand outside in the cold, looking in?
You are welcome here.

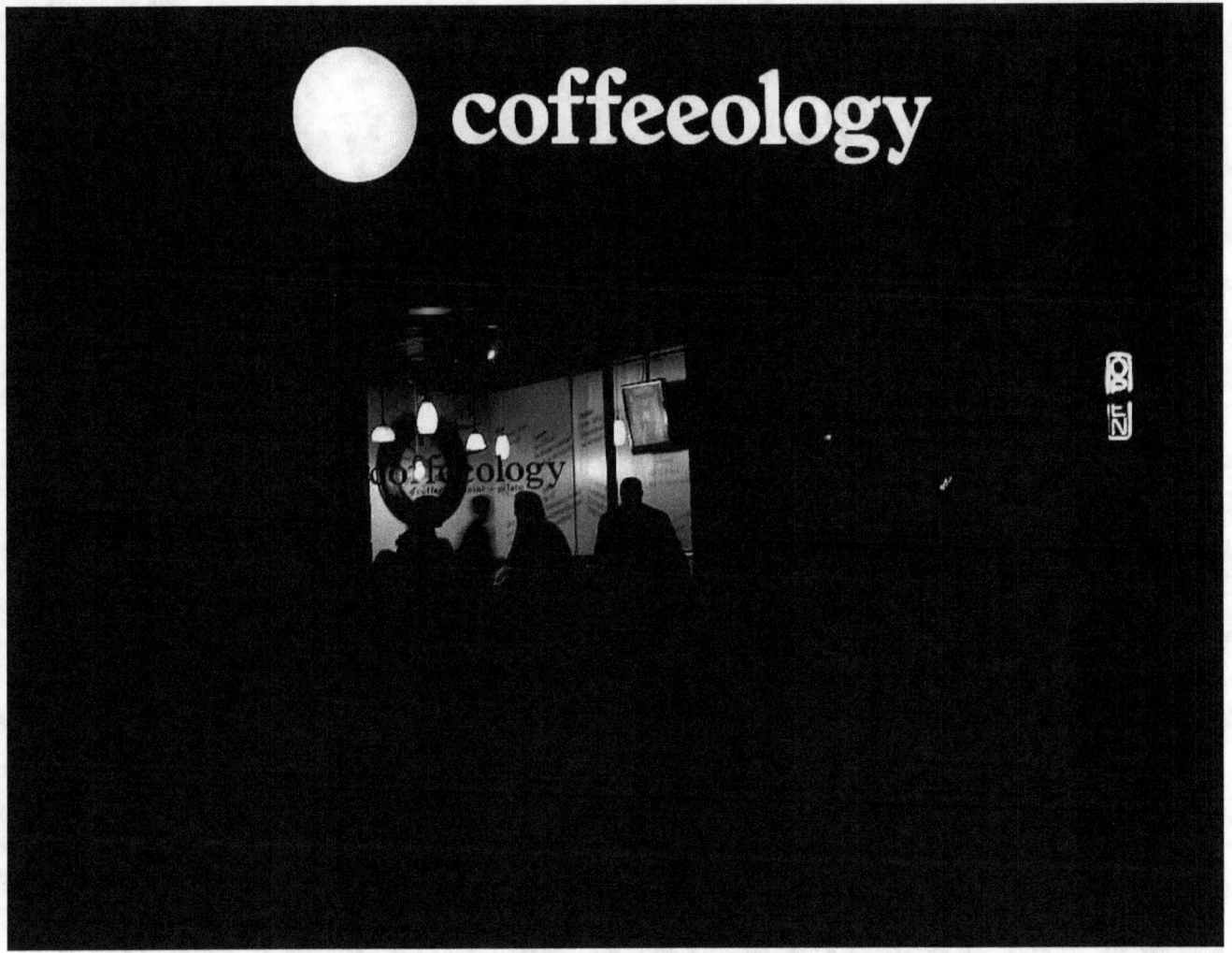

SILENT RESPONSE

I want so much to say
So much
But what need is there?
You know my heart already
You wrote its story
In your own heart's blood
In a time before you even knew me.
A lifetime ago perhaps
You penned my heart's story
In the language of
Crows, and rabbits and squirrels
And of fireflies and mosquitoes.

These dark mornings
When sleep takes its leave
Hours before I would have it depart

I stand steeped in
The sleep of nature
Where nothing stirs
Not even the squirrels.
The ultimate stillness unbroken
Except for my restless heart.
It's in these chilled, damp moments
That the silence speaks loudest
And it is deafening.

I want so much to say
So much
But what need is there?
You know. You've always known.

11

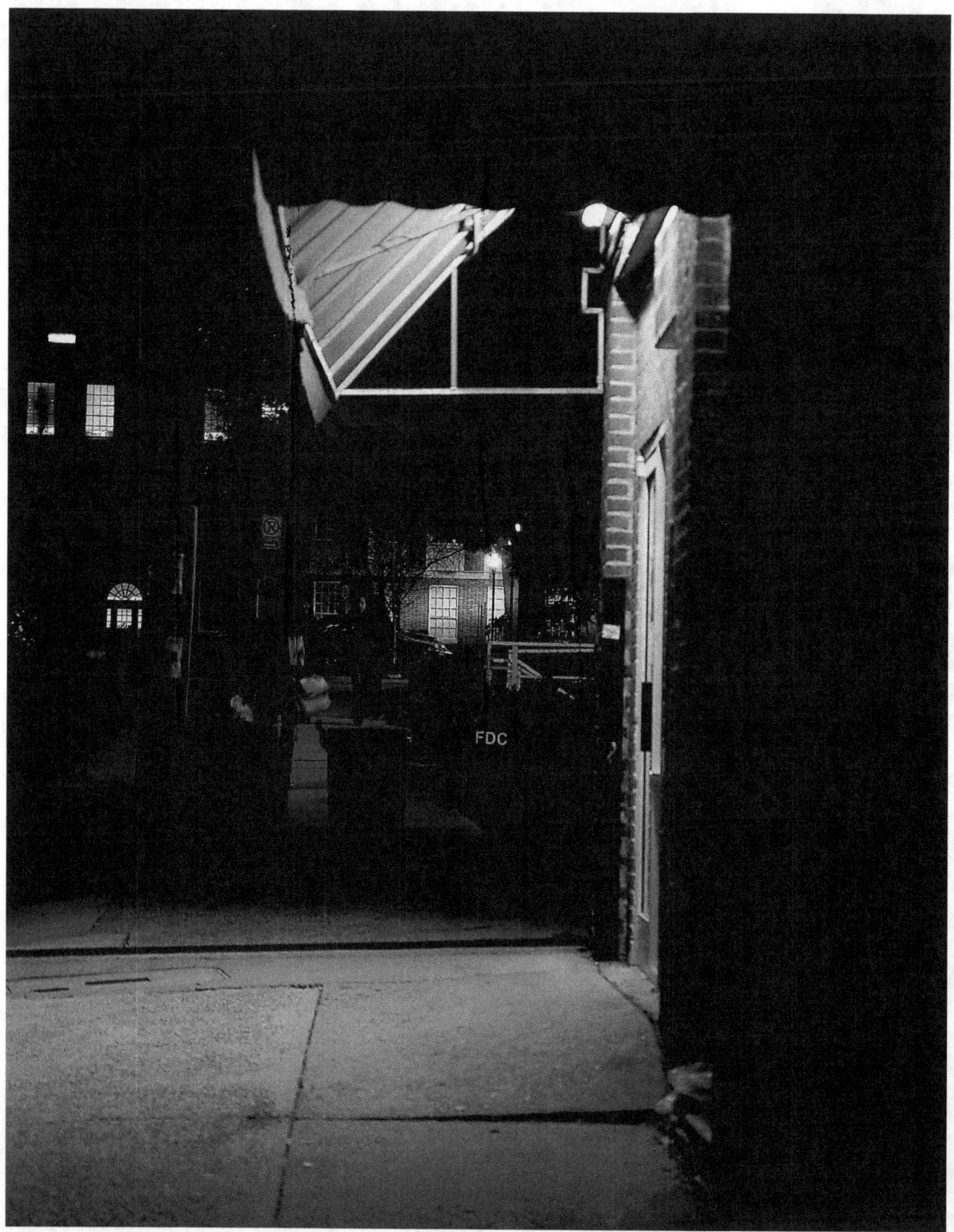

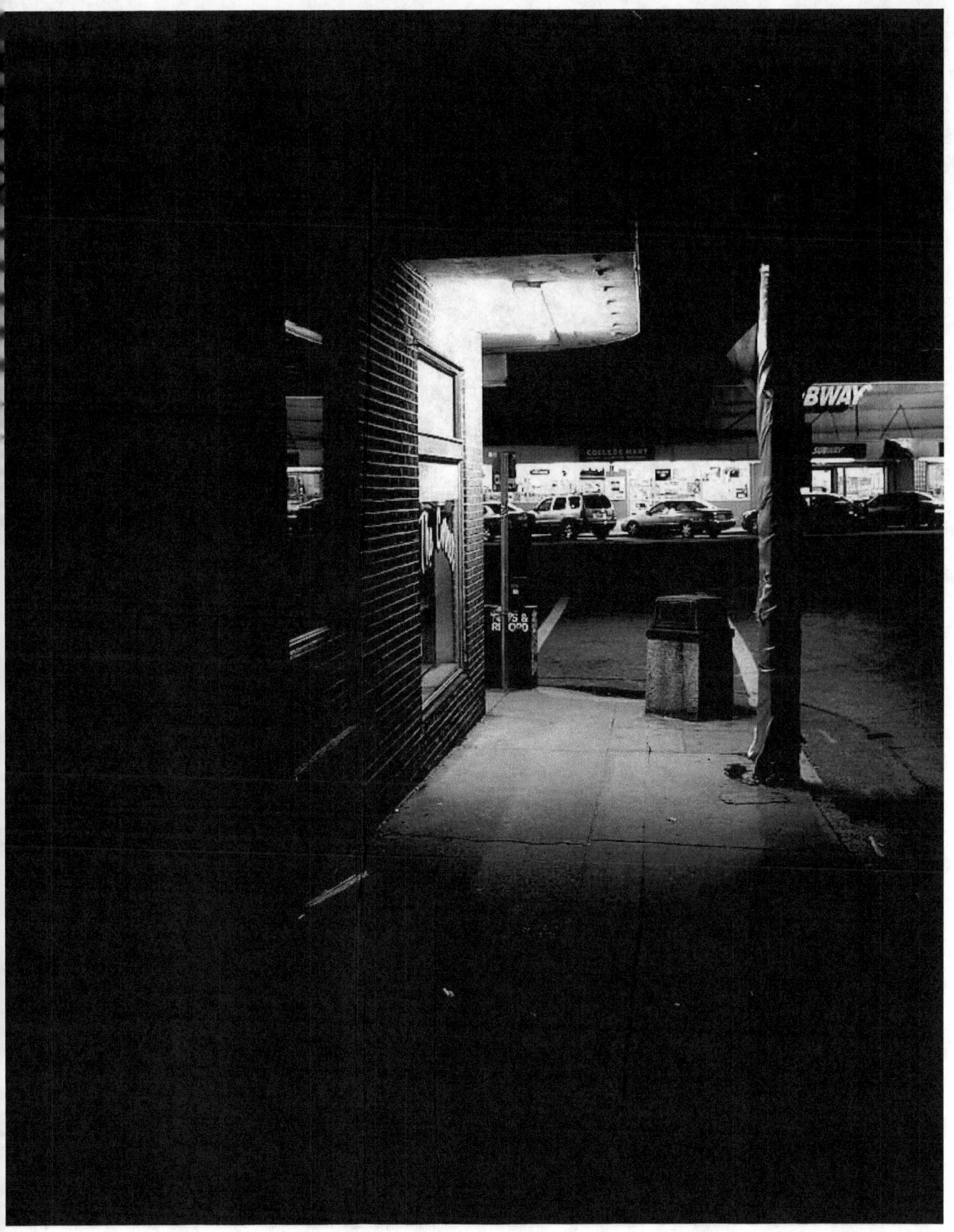

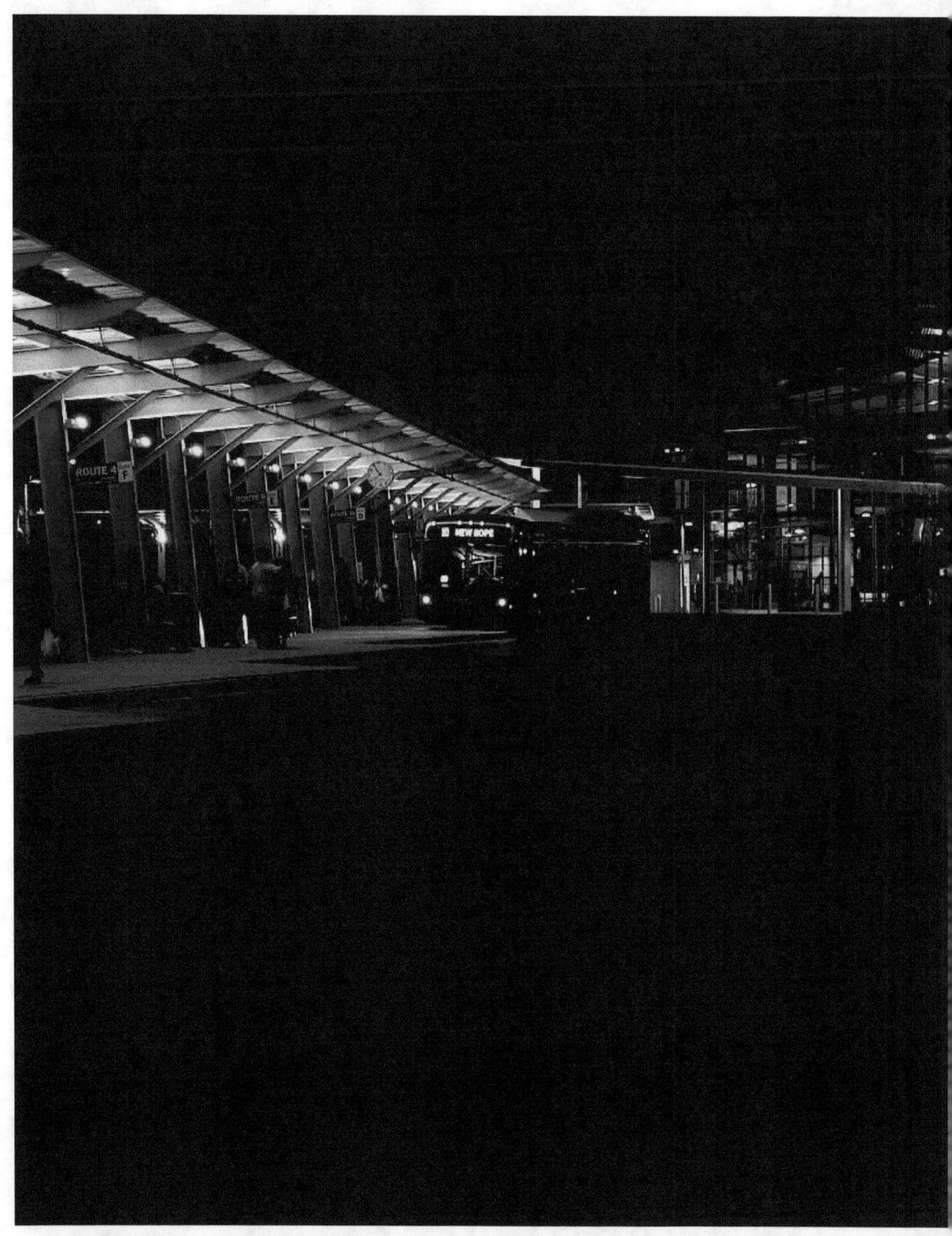

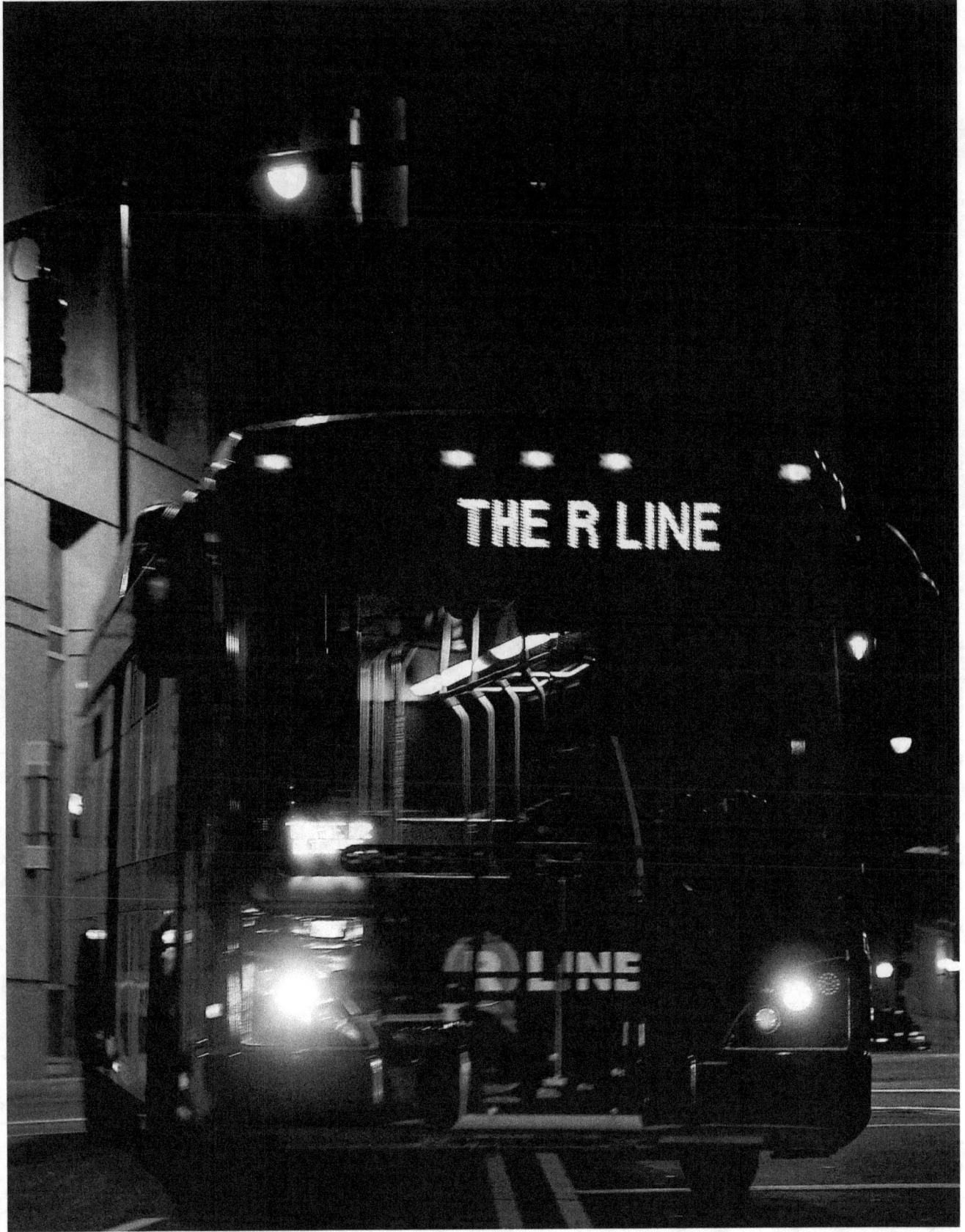

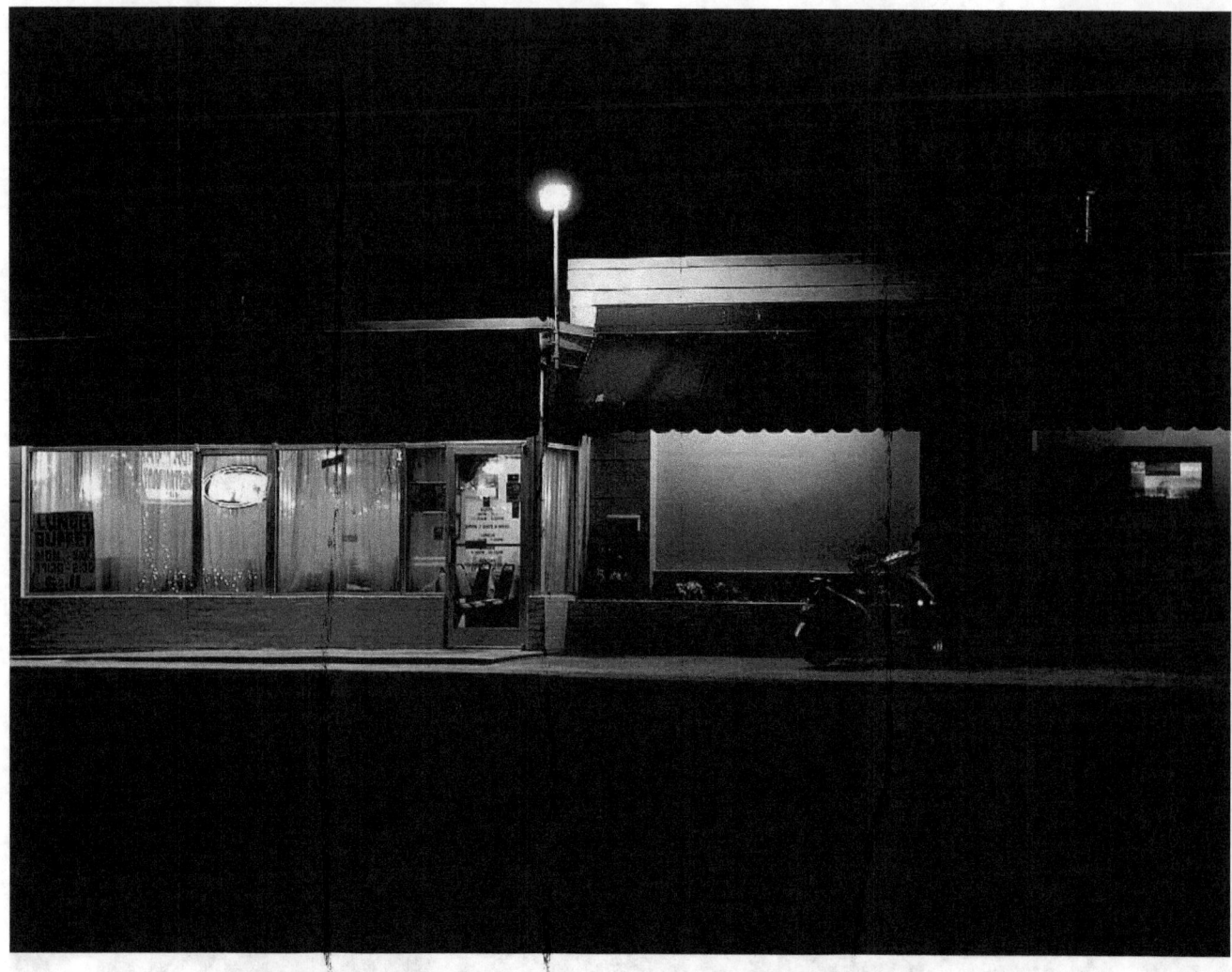

THE ROYAL CAFE

Inside
An old man sits
Toying with the
Mortal remains
Of chicken biryani
Drains his glass
And thinks of a long ago
When he was young
And she was beautiful
And nothing stood
Between them
And the horizon.

Outside
A younger man walks
Toying with the
Mortal remains
Of a memory
Crushes his thin black cigar

And thinks of Hemingway
And how she loved
His story of the cafe
And nothing seemed
Impossible or
Out of reach.

Crossing the space
Between the now and then
Between the in and out
Two souls
One loss
One grief
One pain.
Night draws Her curtain
Around and between them
Shrouding both
And nothing seems
Right at all.

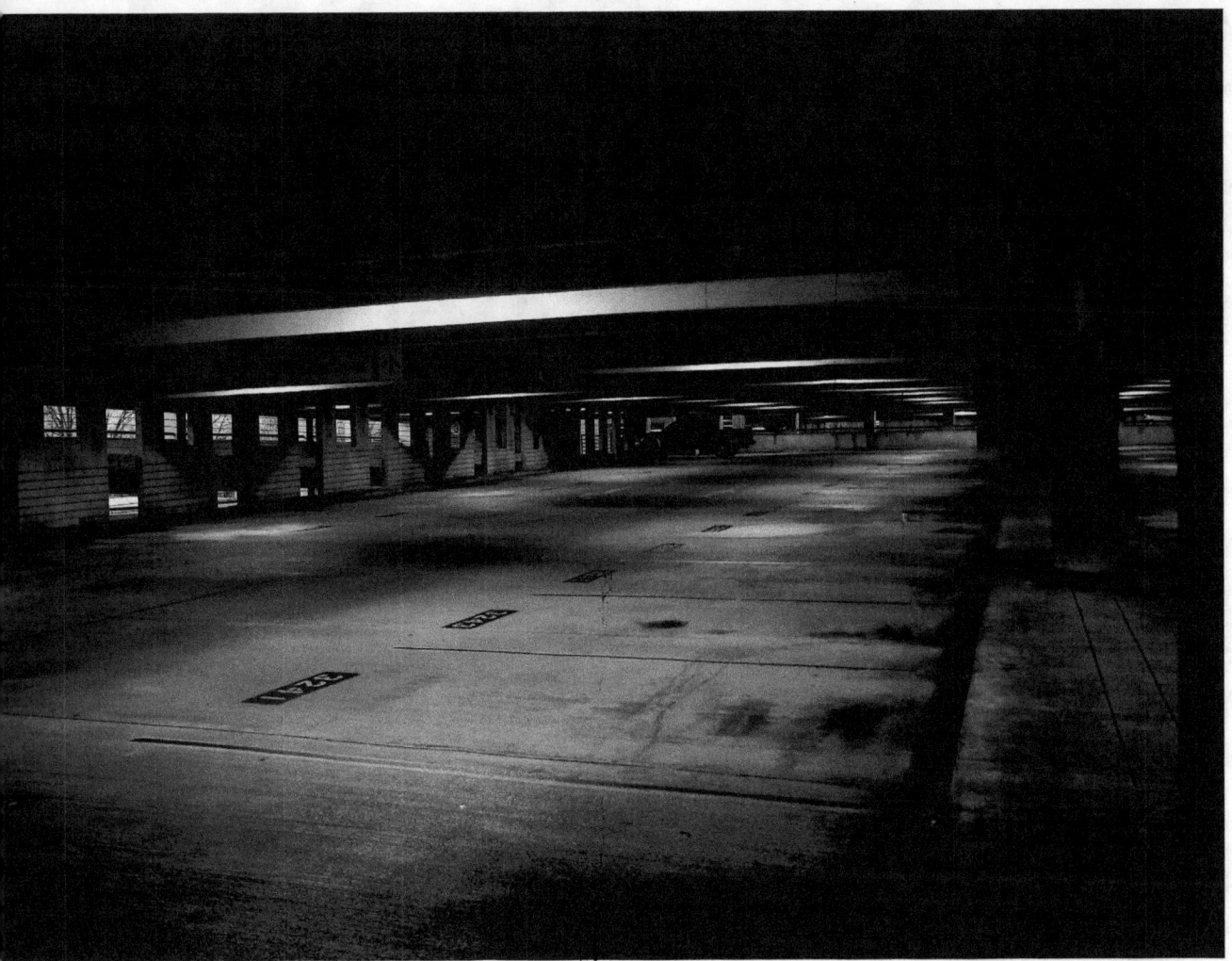

ON SCARS

My right knee
Wears a shiny crescent
(A smile from my angle)
Where no hair grows

A leftover, a gift of sorts
From a long-ago summer afternoon
A gravel drive, and the gnarled root
Of an ancient pecan tree

A reminder of the time
When that wizened old tree
Stuck out his foot
In front of me

Spilled me to the rocks
Loosing a freshet
Of sticky, crimson copper
That painted my hands

Once the sutures were removed
A young boy's red badge of courage
Became a young man's curiosity
Became an old man's lesson

The young boy of eight years
Howled at the pain inflicted
By the sharp point of granite
Piercing flesh on its way to bone

The young man of twenty years
Wondered at the lack of feeling
In a place that had once
Been the locus of such pain

The old man of fifty years
Recognizes that however grave the injury
The scar left behind feels no pain.
It feels nothing at all.

I know a thing or two about scars.

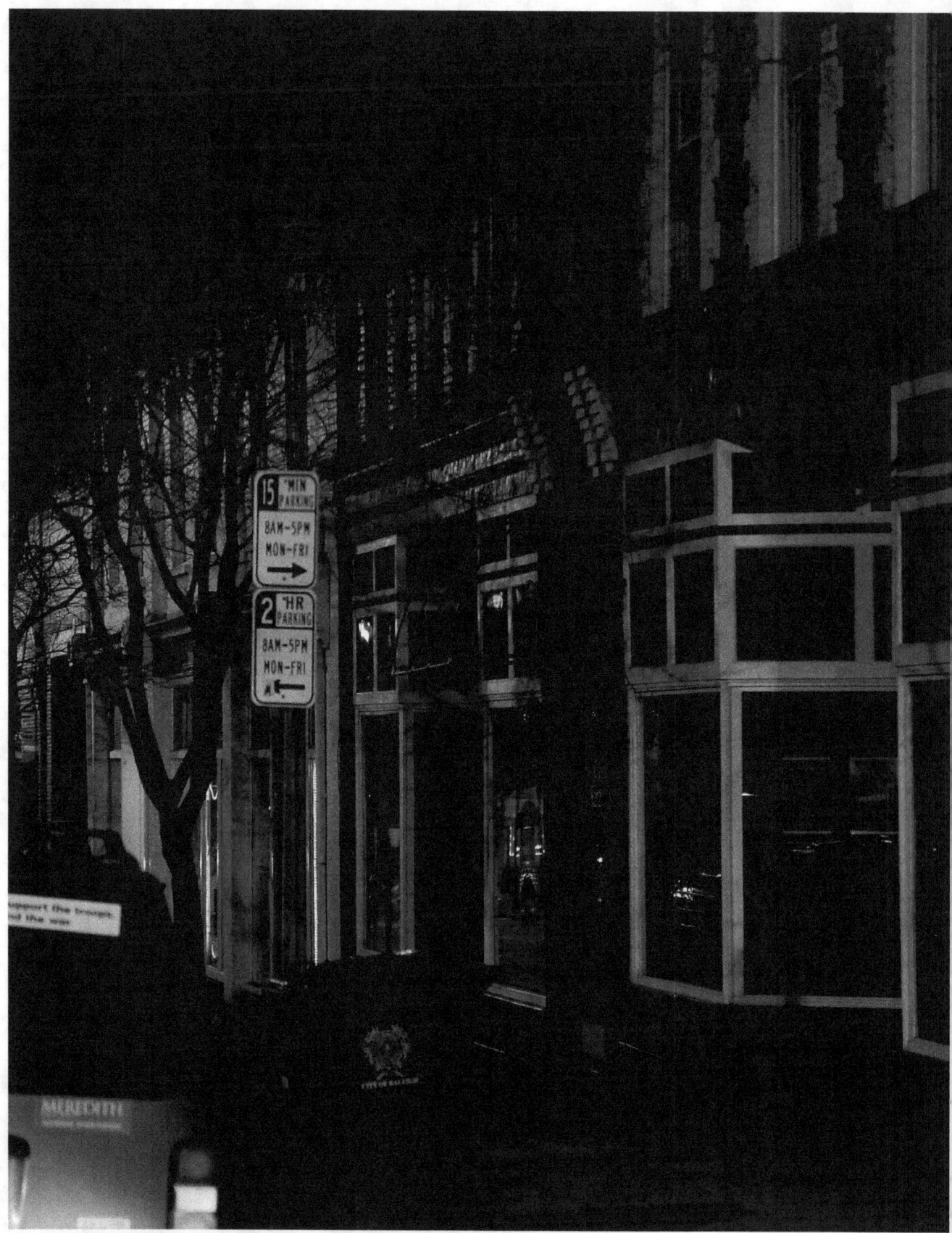

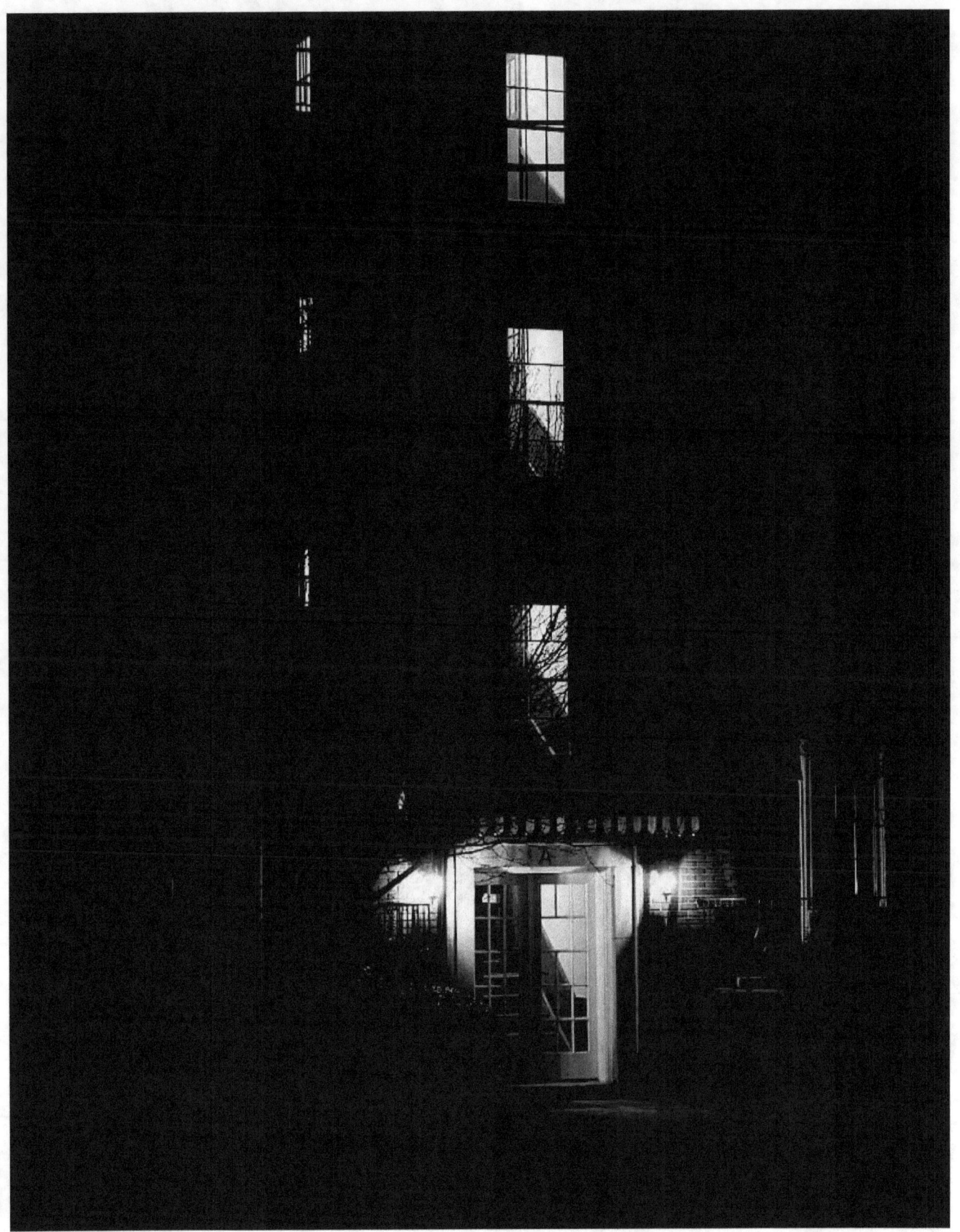

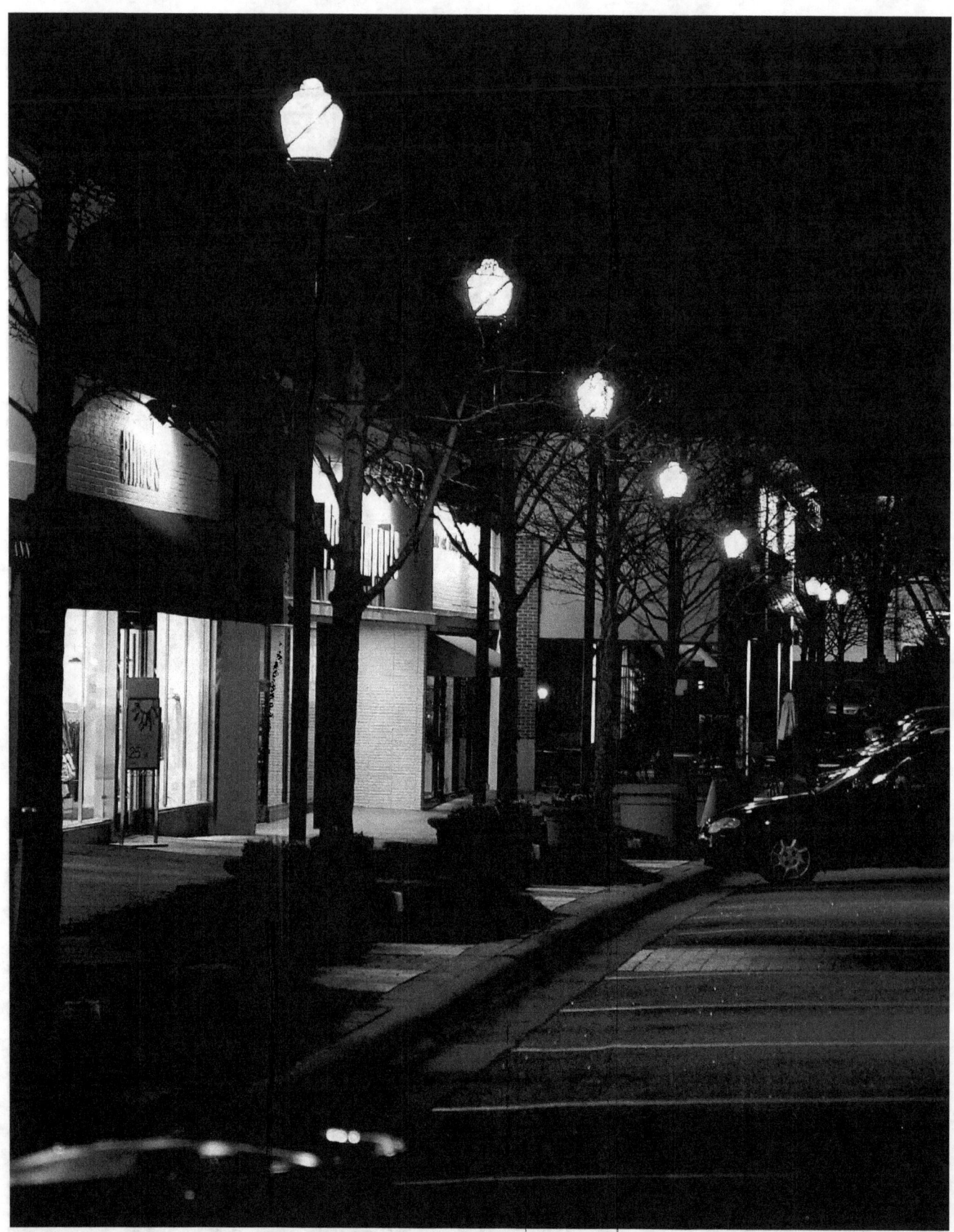

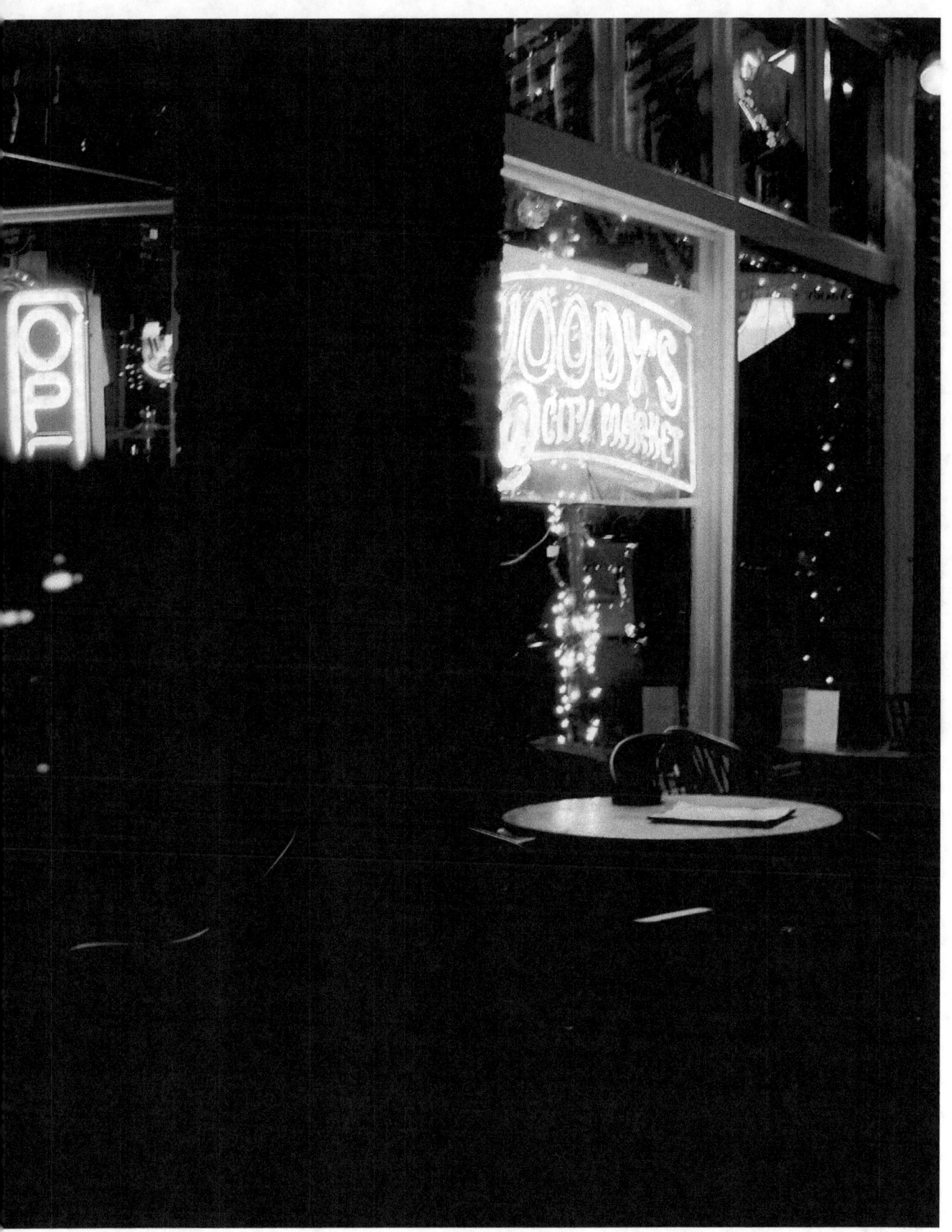

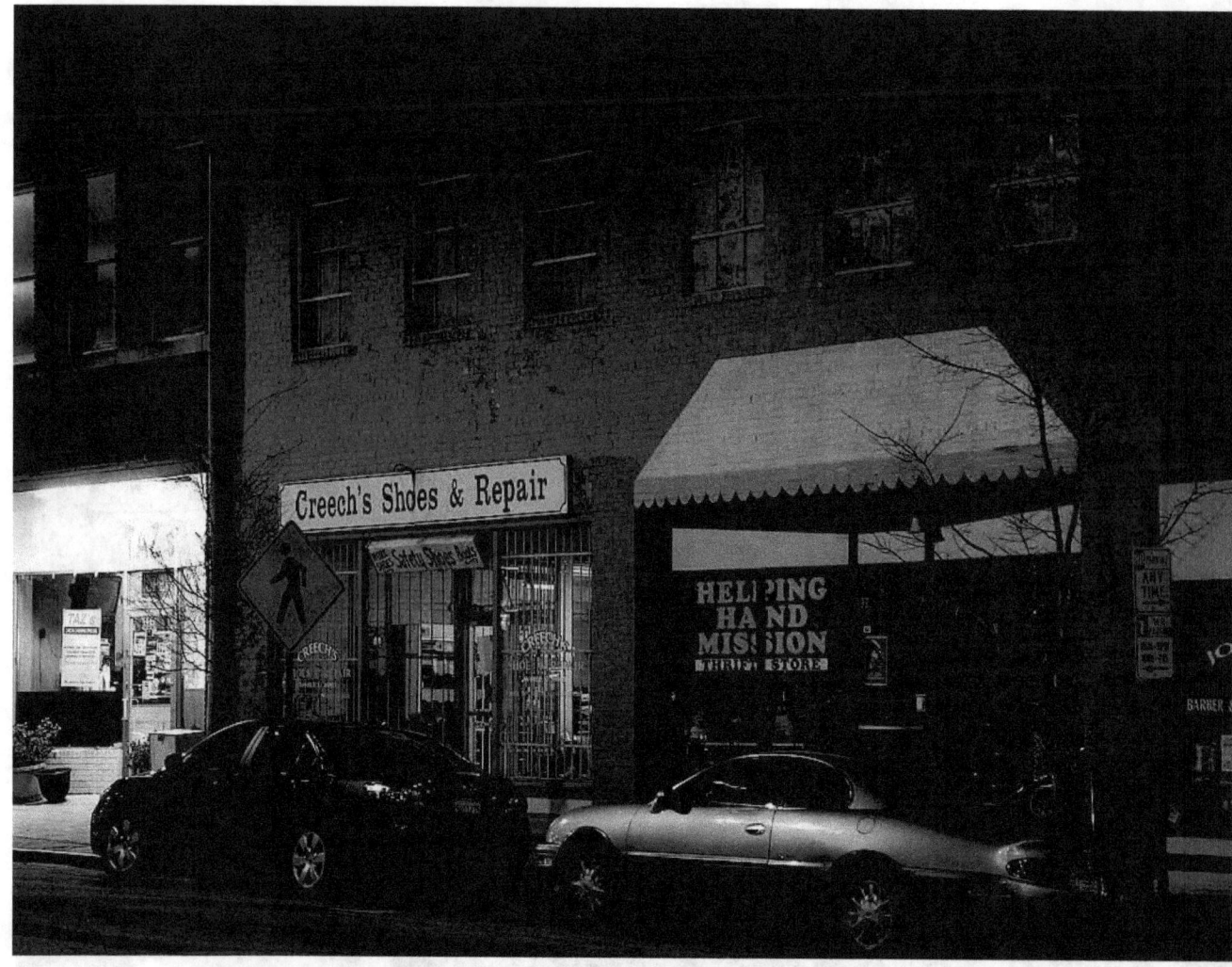

THE TIME BEFORE

When they were young
Nothing seemed impossible
The horizon held hope
Of a long life
Children with curly hair
A lazy dog in the yard
That was the time before

No easy road
But one walked well
Walked happily
The layoff meant
A better job
A blessing they called it
That was the time before

The children never came
Nobody's fault, just not meant to be
They had each other
And that was enough

They learned the art
Of wanting what they had
That was the time before

A spot in a picture
Darker than the rest
Probably nothing
Best not to worry
It can only make things worse
Faith and trust they said
That was the time before

The spot grew, took root
Like a malevolent weed
Sucking the life force
From both of them
Her body, his soul
Both withering
This too, is the time before

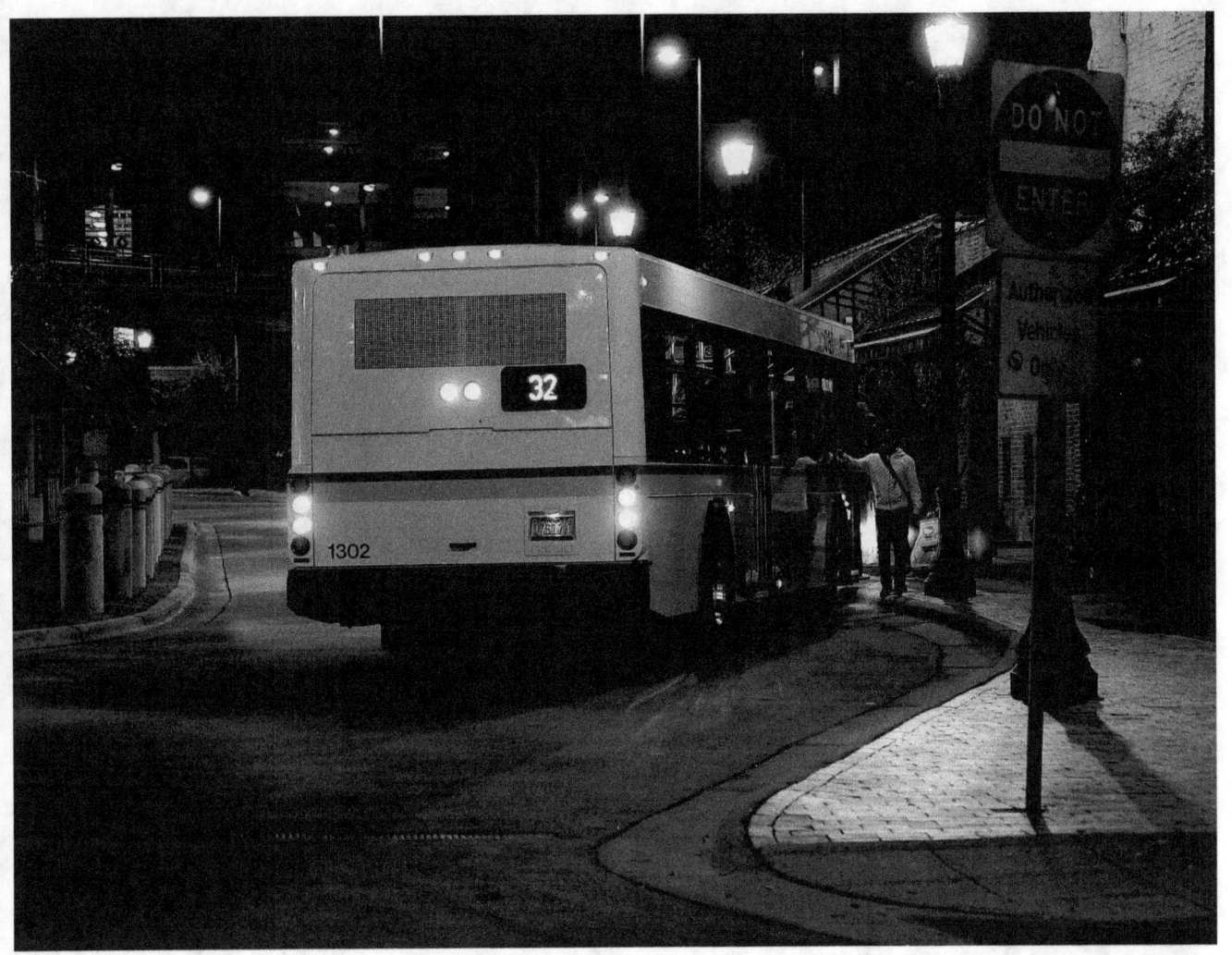

THE VOICE

Following my own tracks
Around the city
One day bleeding into
The vacuum of the day before
A numbing sameness
Of rocking somnolent motion
And the steady thrum of ennui
Reassuring me that Things
Are as they should be
Things are ordered and neat
All Things in their places
Why then, this persistent voice
Of promise that whispers
"Go. Believe. Take Things on Faith.
　　　Dare.
　　　　　To.
　　　　　　　Be."

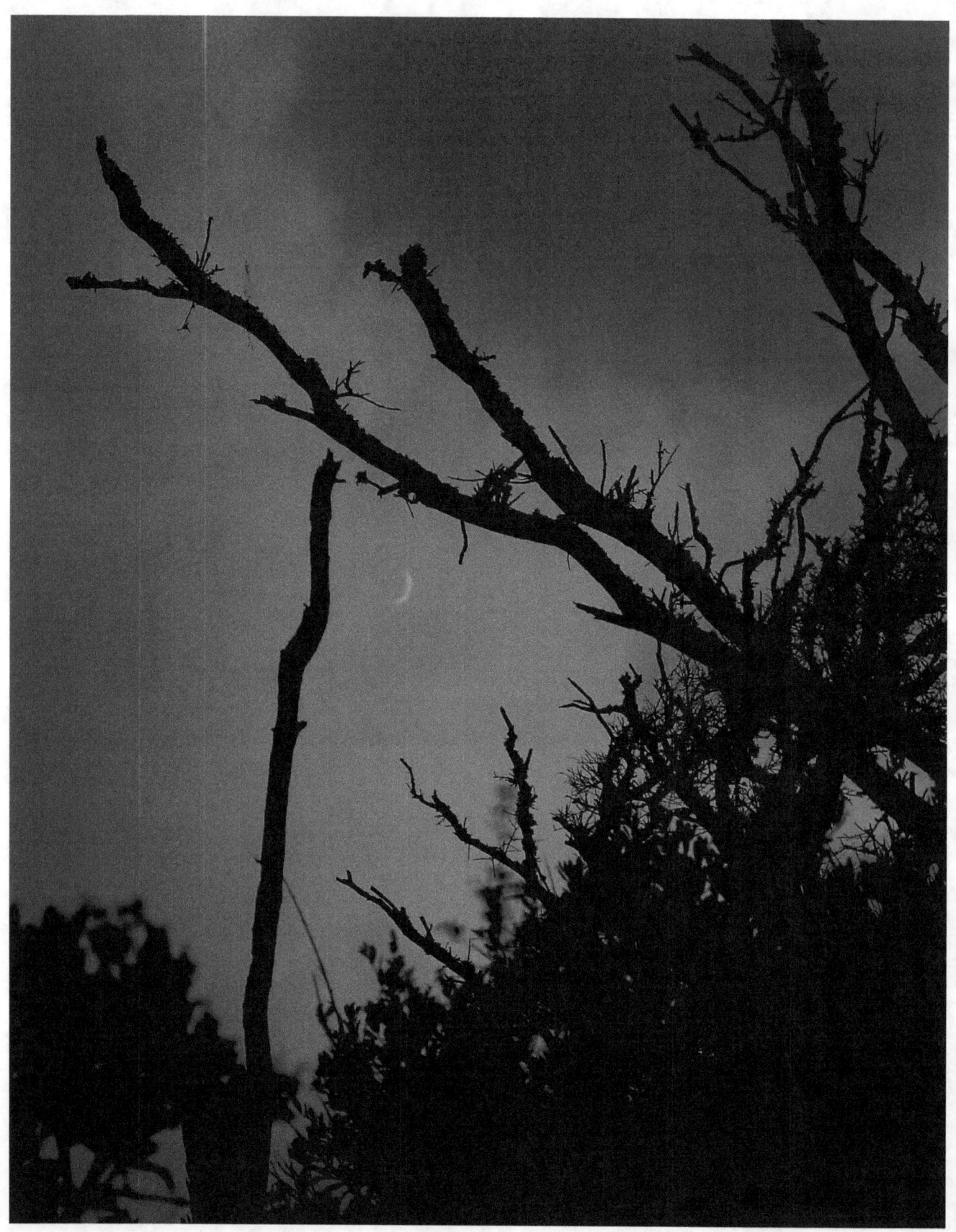

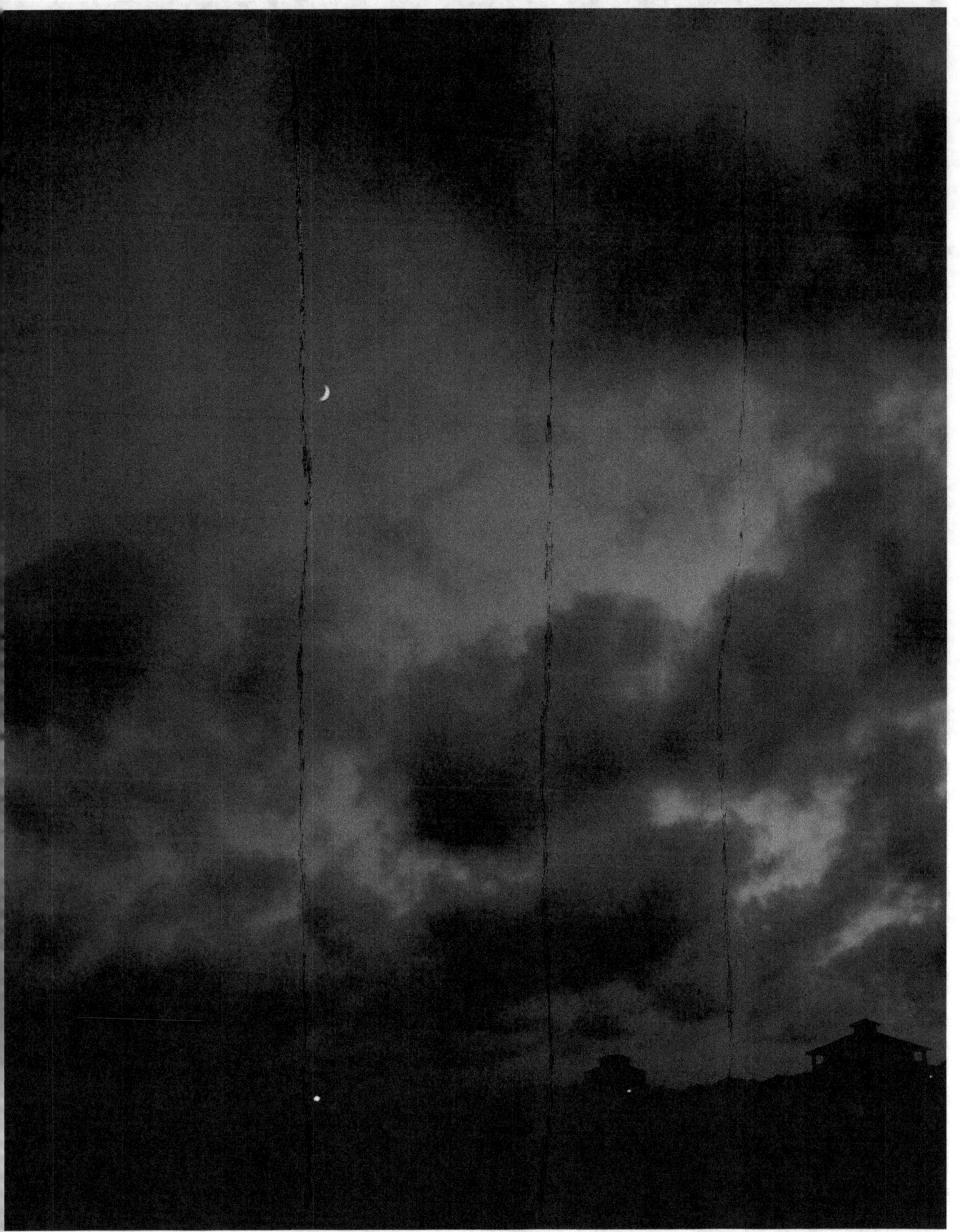

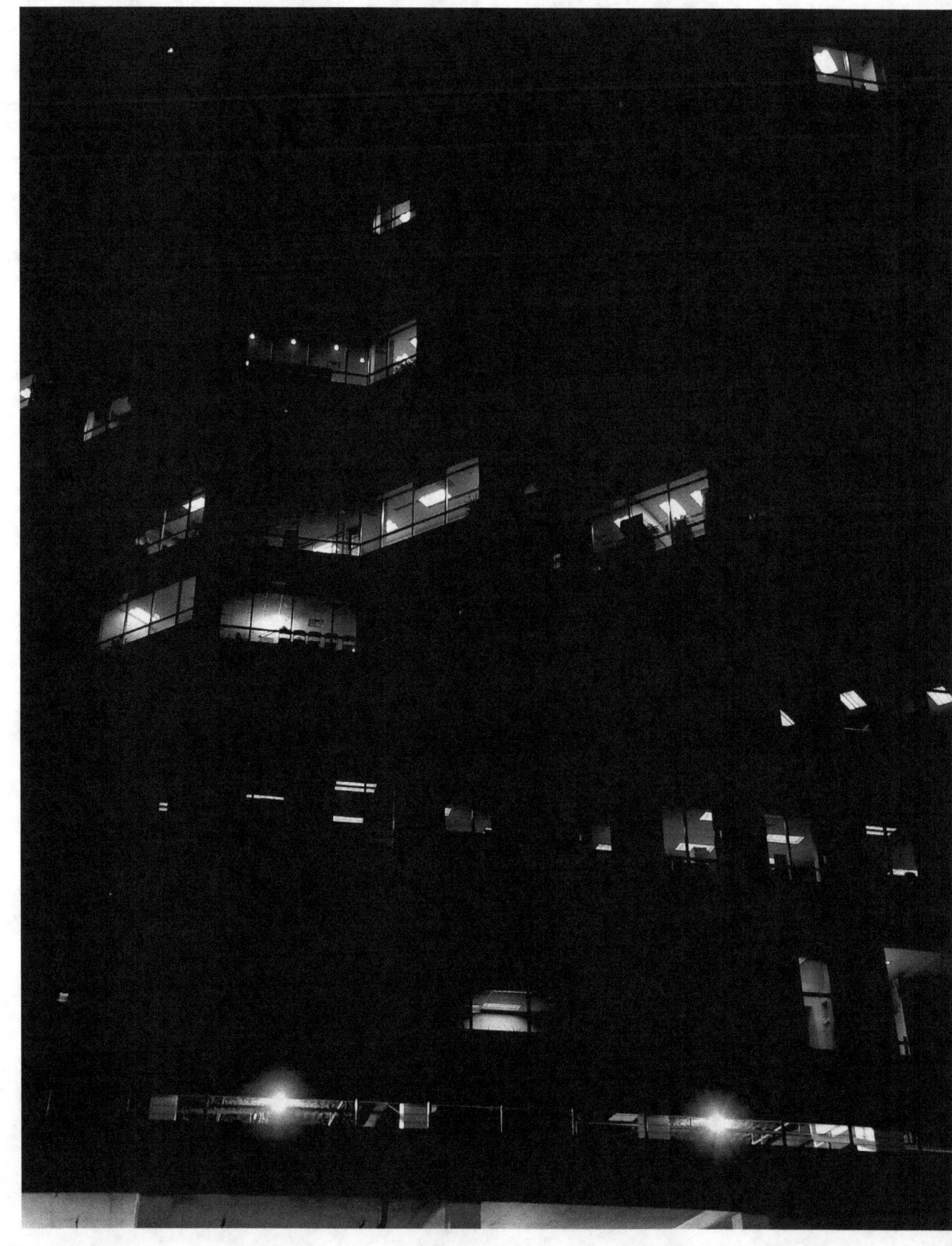

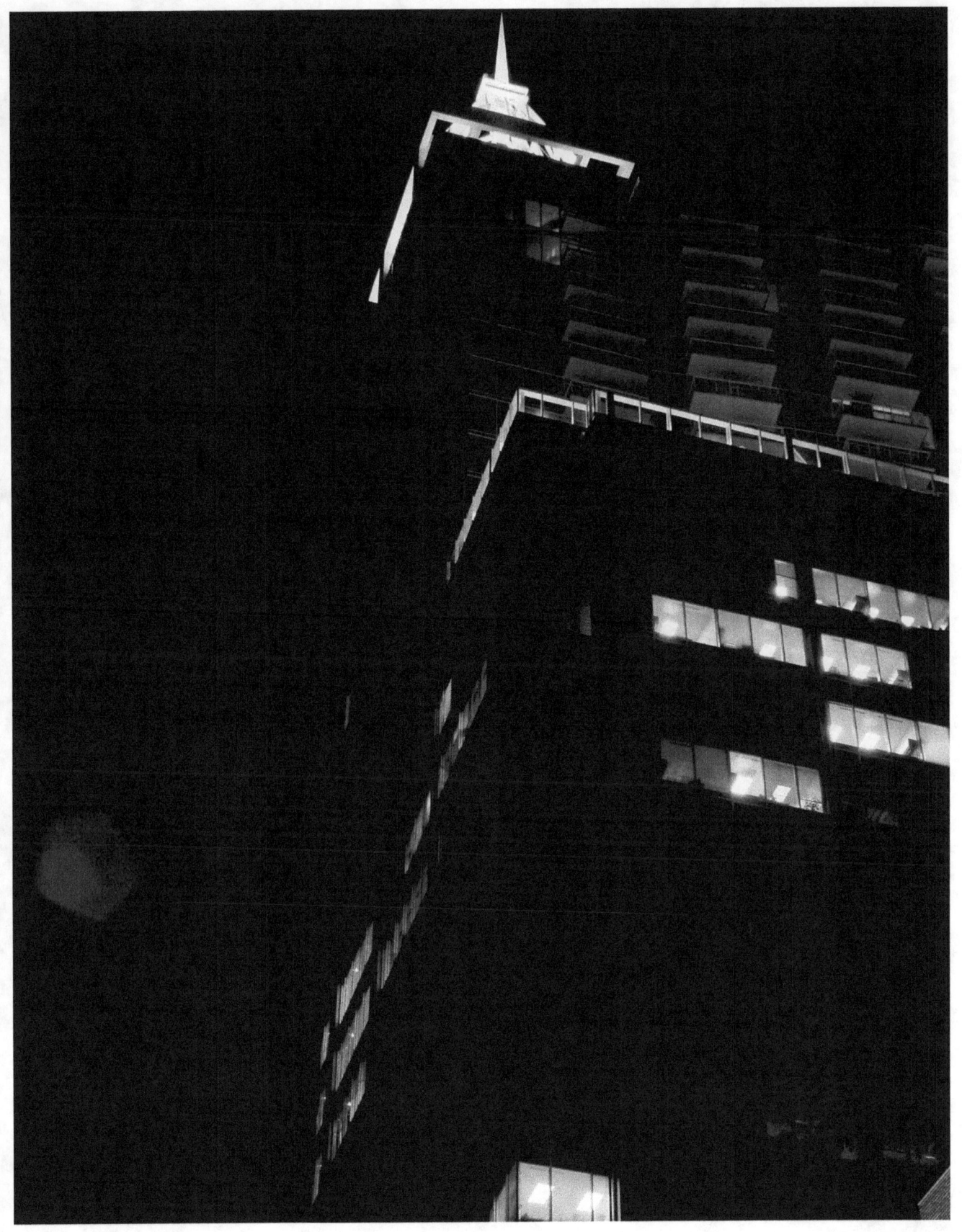

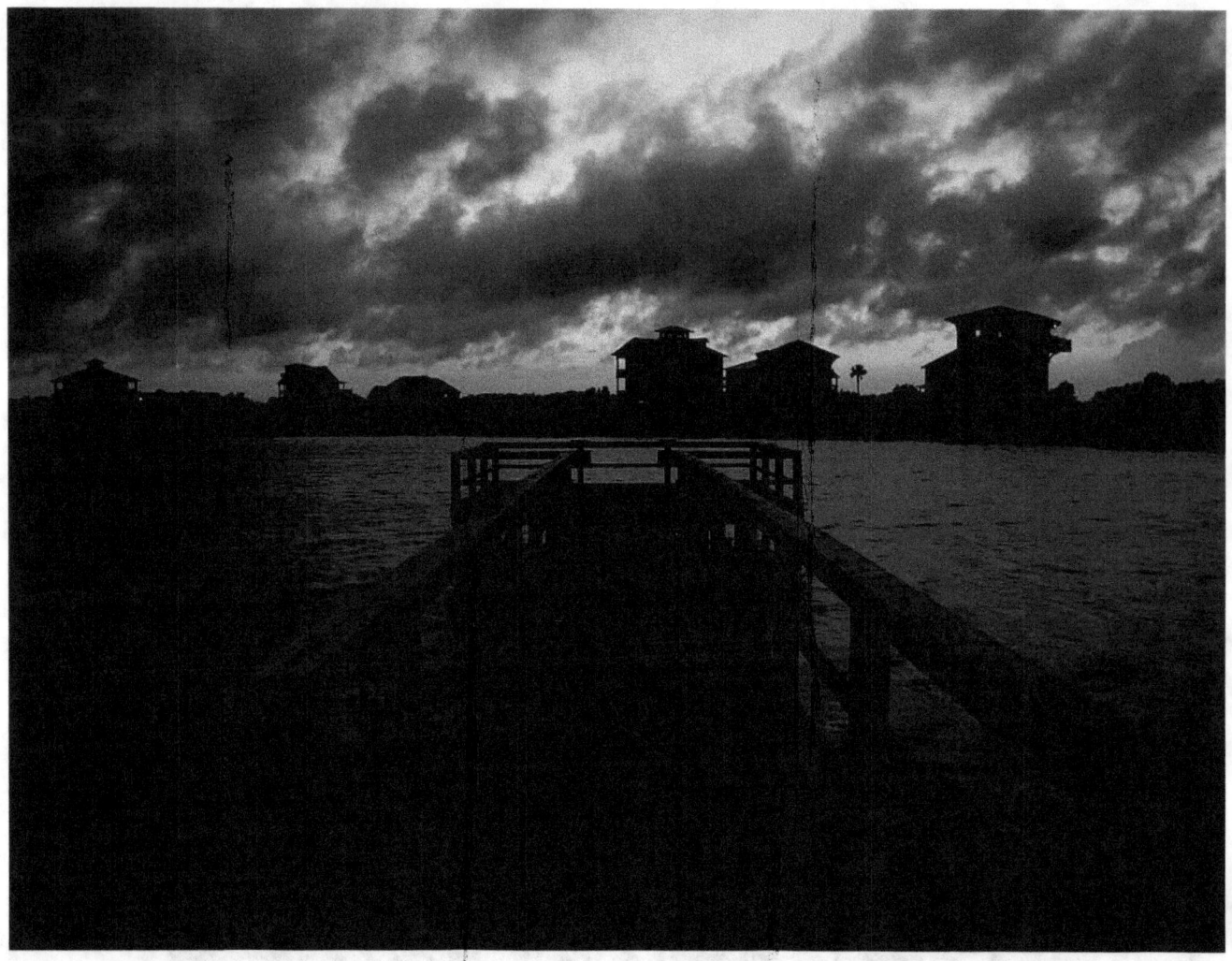

SHIPWRECKED

Adrift on a trackless sea,
Anchorless, rudderless,
Unmasted and floundering.
With neither the energy
Nor the will,
To stitch together enough sail
To hobble to a safe anchorage.

I sailed right into the teeth of the storm,
Eyes wide open.
Unflinching, Dauntless.
Trusting that my ship was
The equal of the gale
Never doubting
That I would reach the far shore.

Here and now
I wonder. I doubt.
I follow the line
On the map that brought me here
And question everything
I thought I knew.
Maps don't tell the full story.

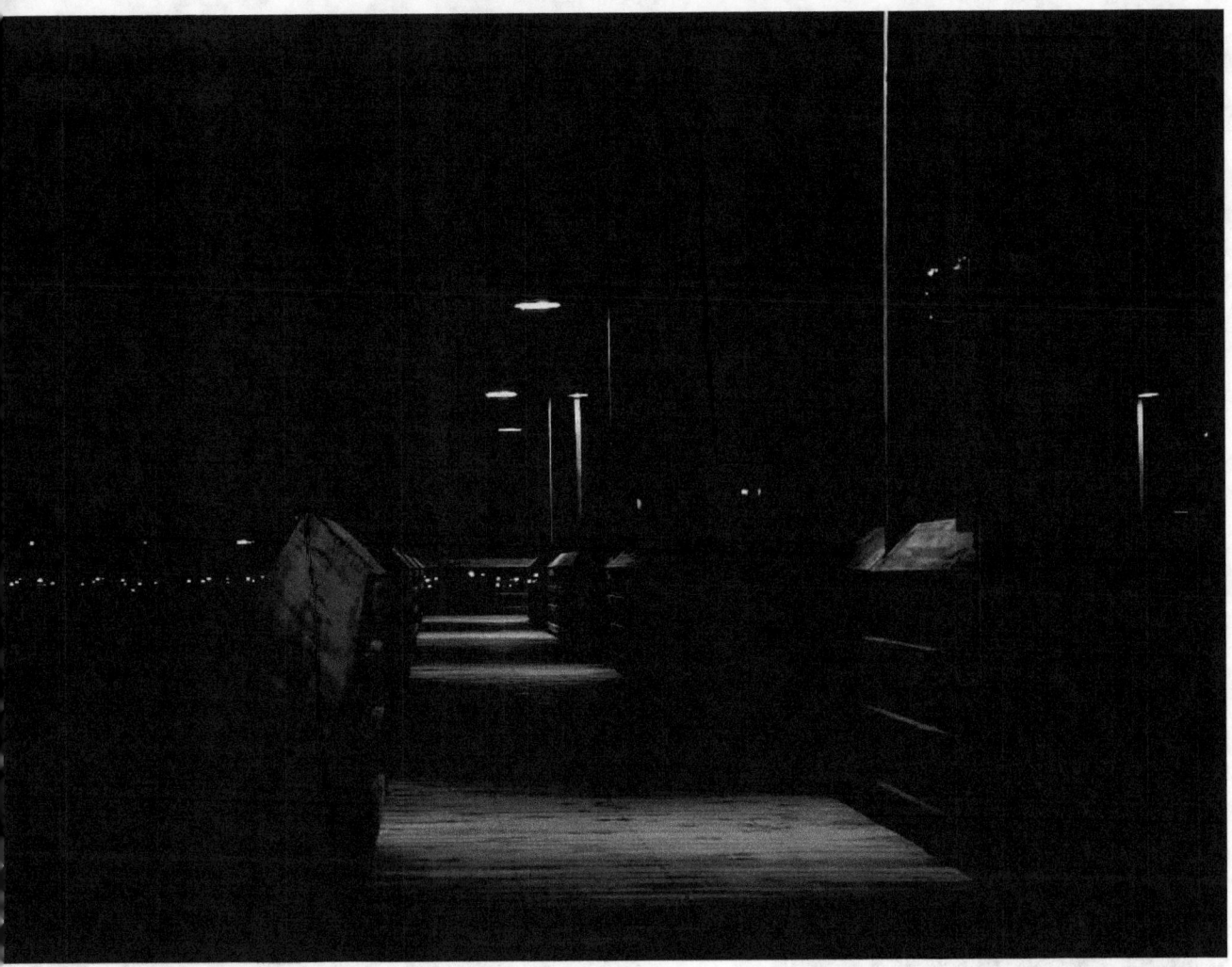

HESITATION (I)

Between there and here, a river runs
Too wide to jump, too swift to swim
Hiding rocks and snares
And the detritus of a thousand wrecks
The bridge across is narrow
And none too sturdy
You hesitate,
Not knowing if it will bear your weight
And hope I understand.

I have seen the wonders on this side
The beauty of a landscape of believing,
In simple things
I want to say, "It's alright, take my hand.
Don't look down, just follow me.
I know the way."
I hesitate,
Not sure the words will come out right
And hope you understand.

But you will cross or not
In your own time,
On your own terms,
And in your own place,
As it must be.
As it was for me,
As it is for us all.
We hesitate,
All of us for our own reasons
That only we understand.

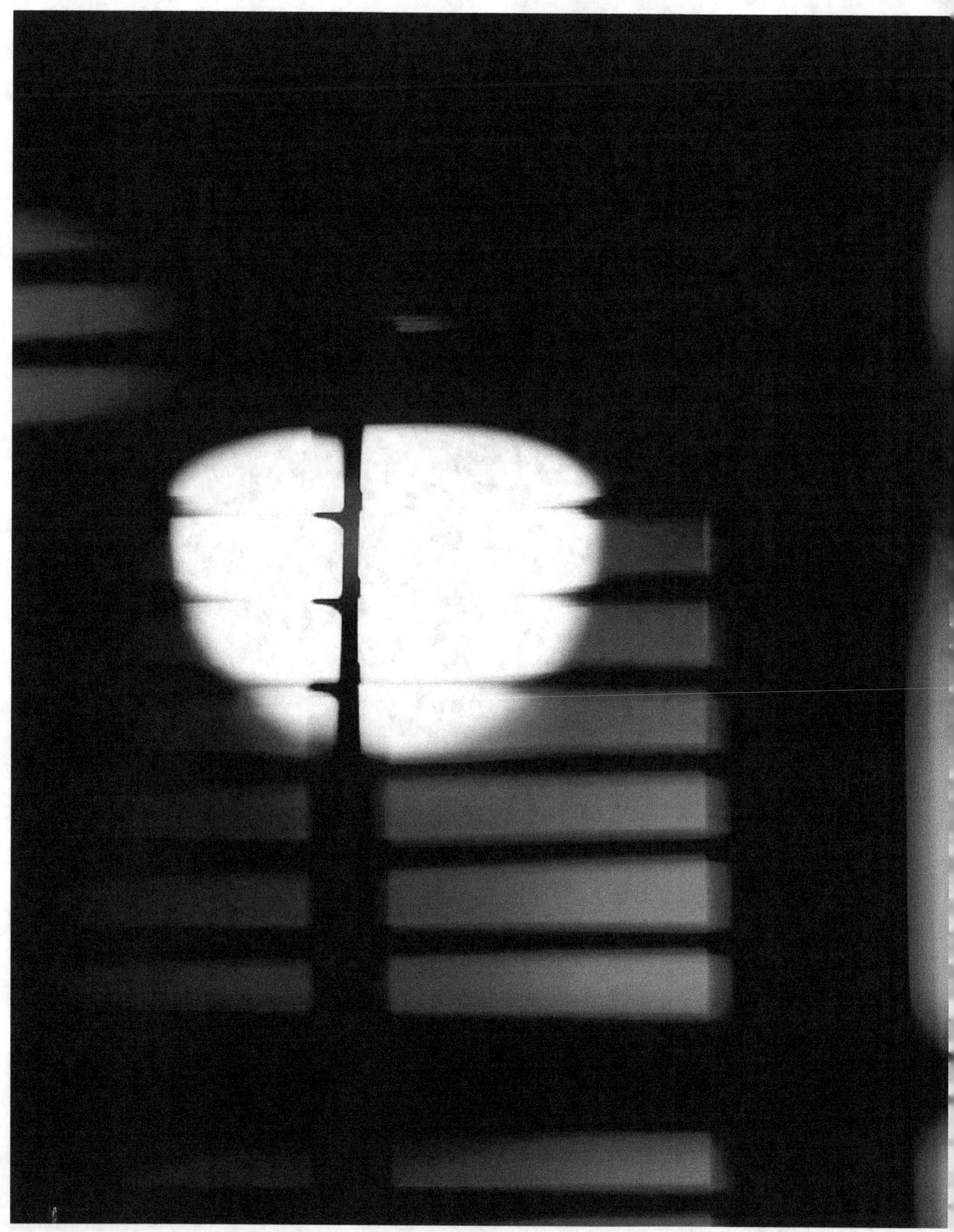

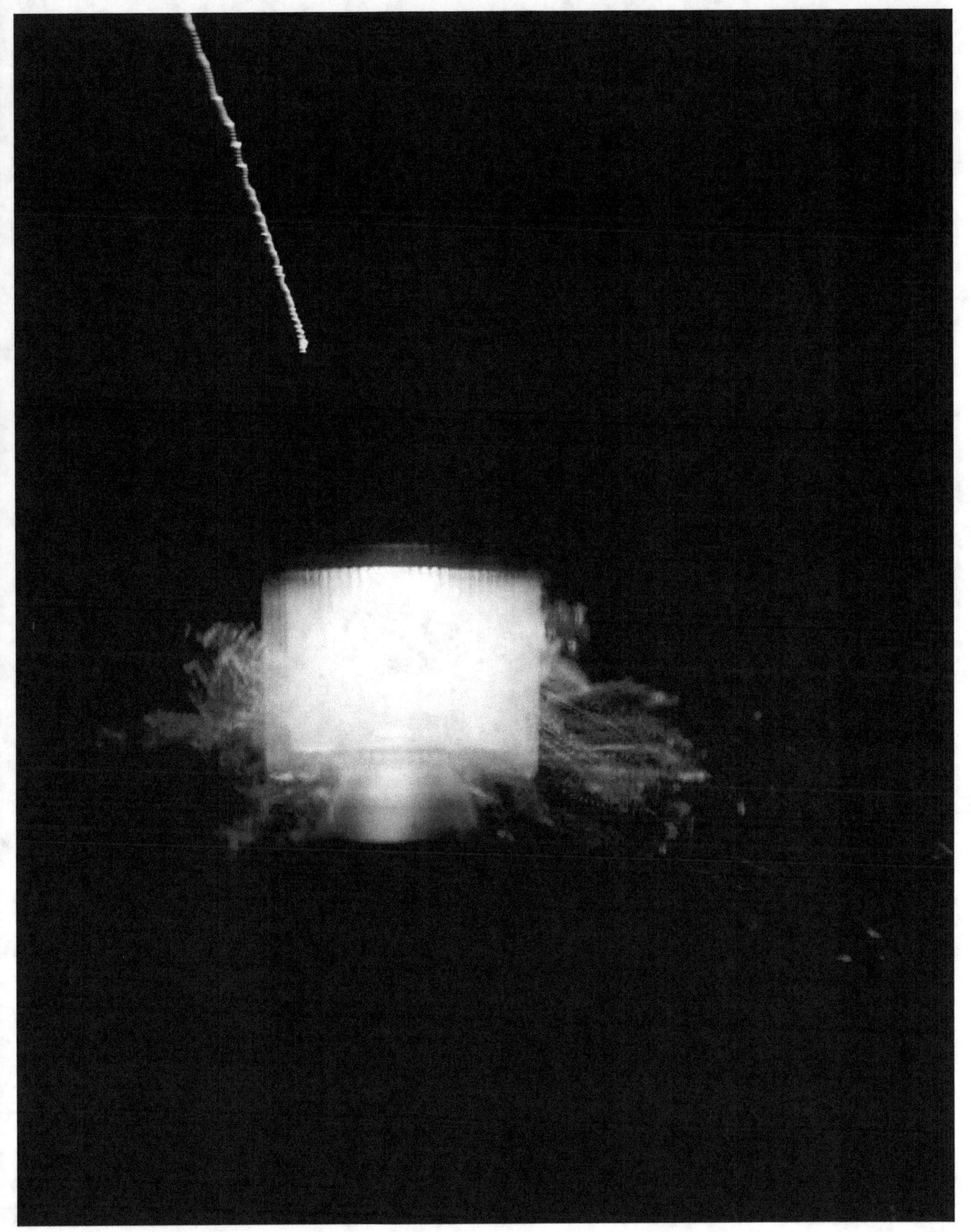

31

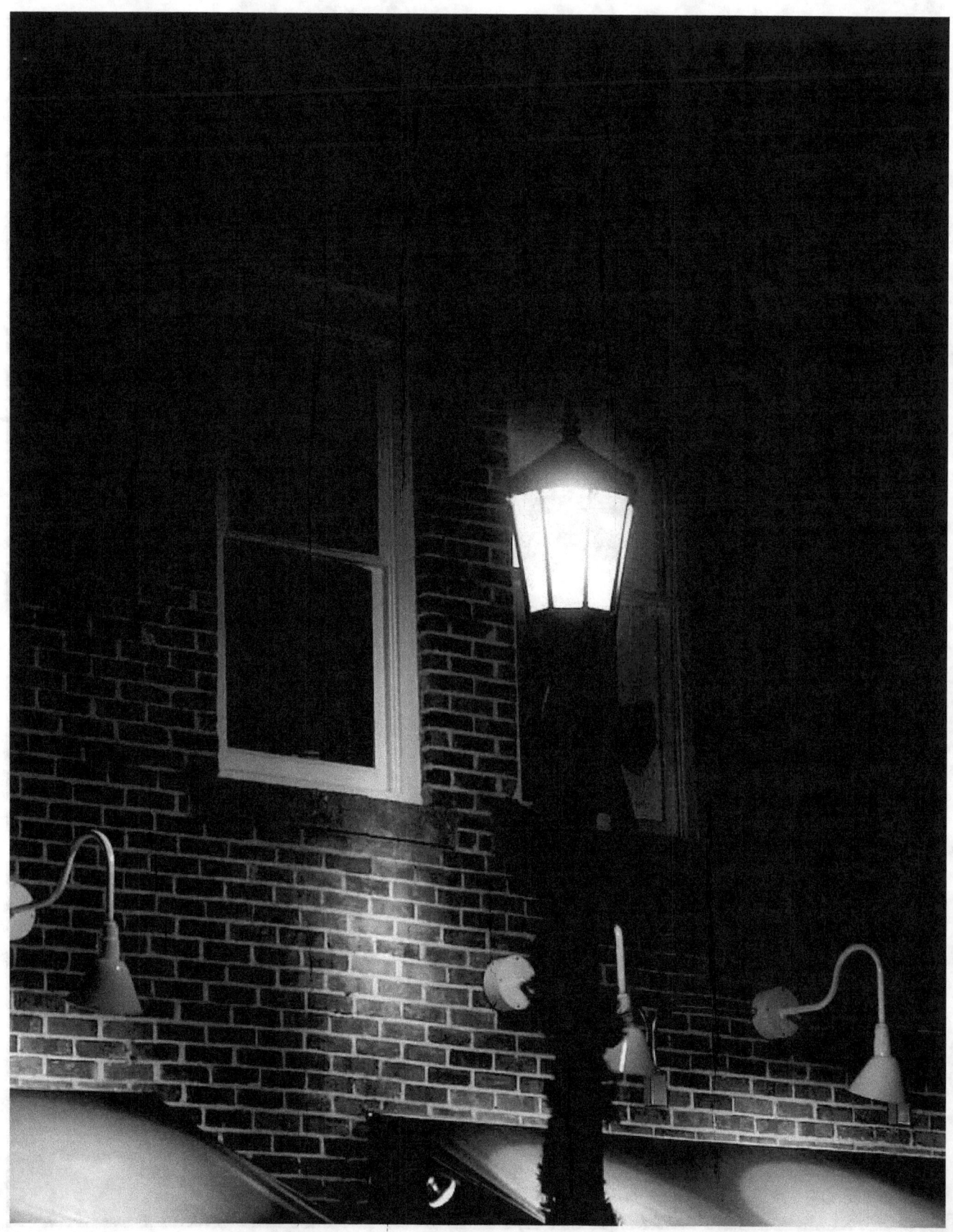

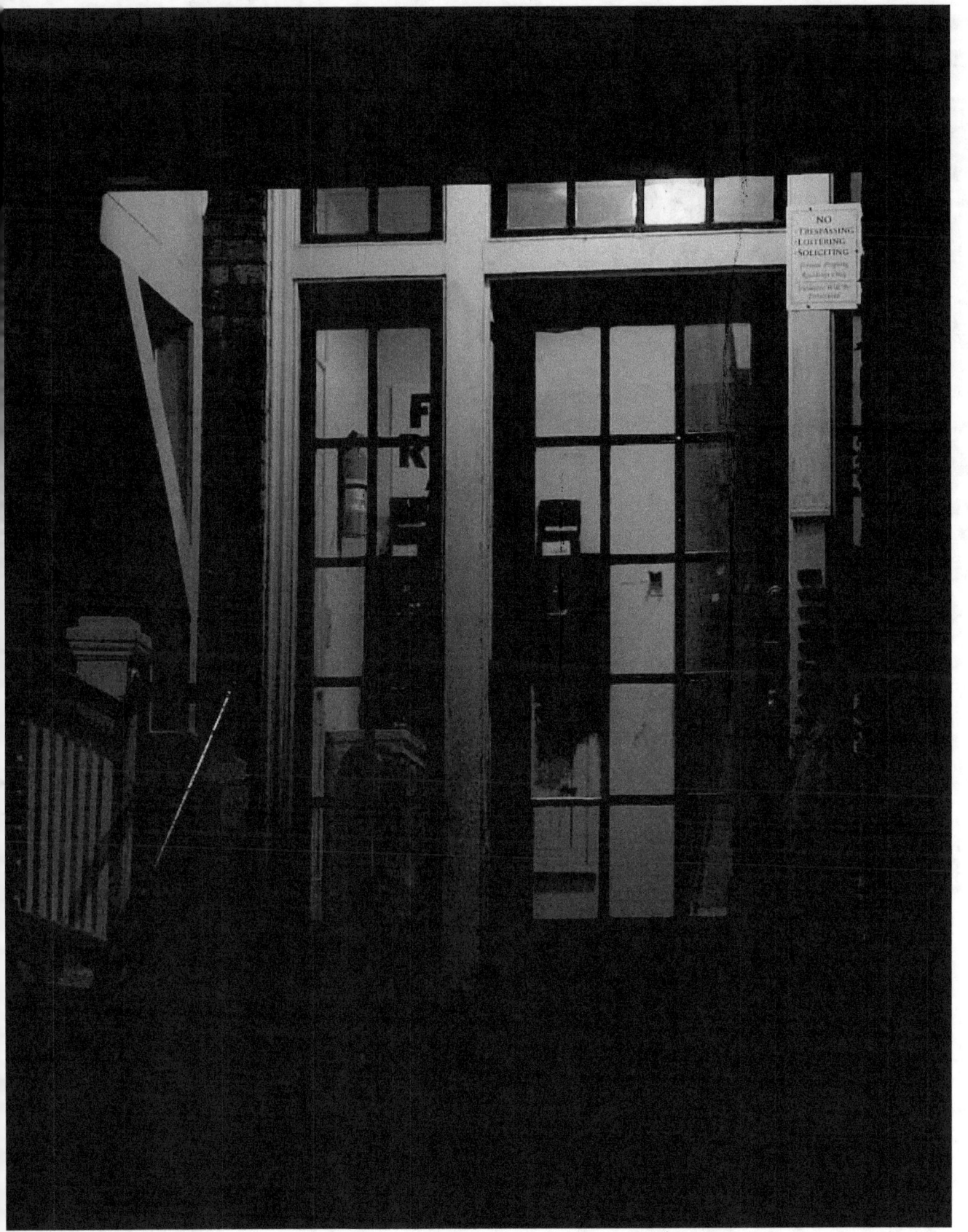

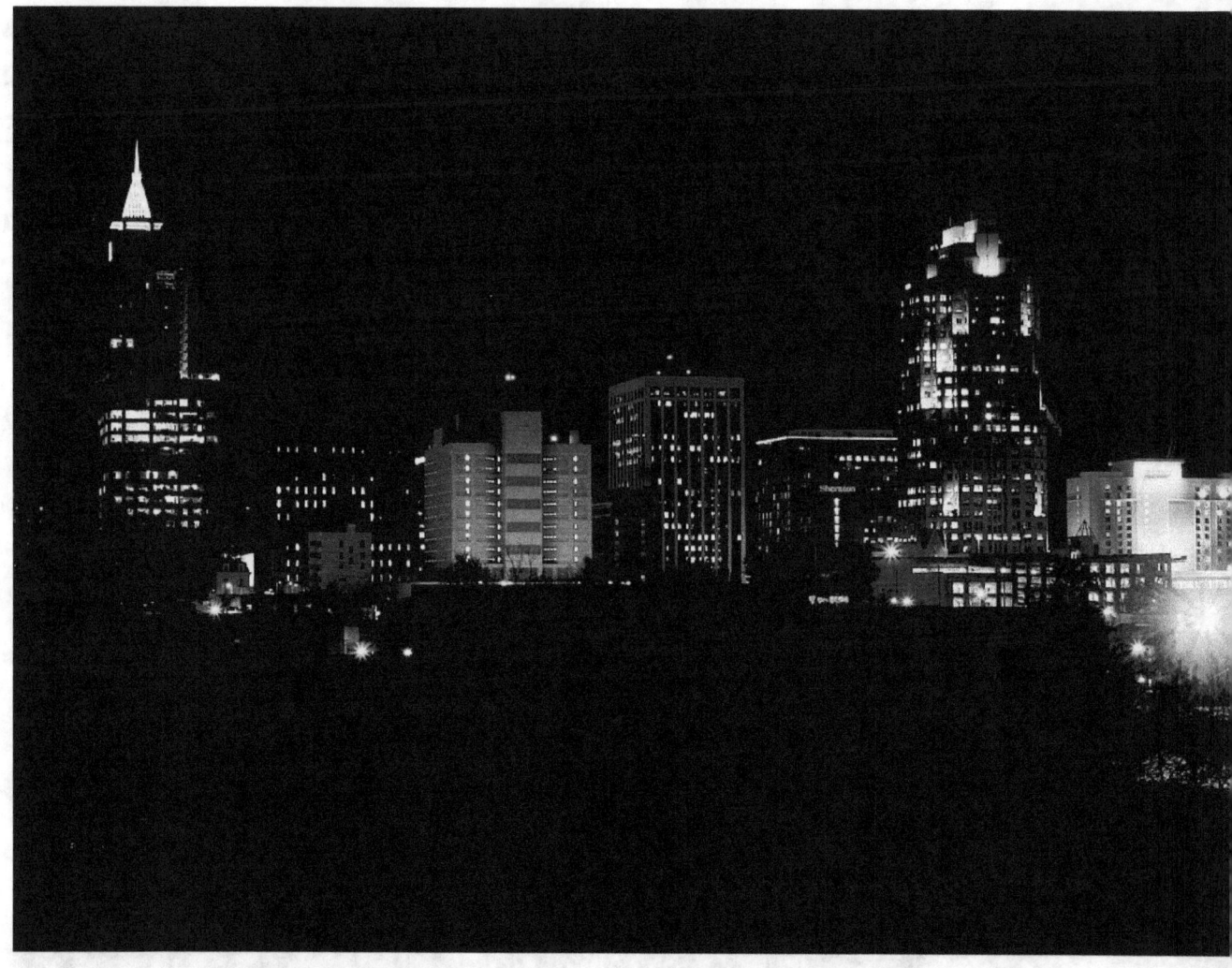

MY END OF THE SKY

Are the stars different
At your end of the sky?
Does the moon come closer to you
Than to me?
Are we so far apart
That the very skies themselves
Take a different form?
I hope, at your end of the sky,
The days are warm,
The evenings cool and fragrant
Brimming with promise
I hope, at your end of the sky,
You are smiling
Living
Loving
Happy

My end of the sky
Is very different
I speak to it
It listens with indifference
If it listens at all
At my end of the sky
The moon
Is cold
The stars
Too far to reach
I am, at my end of the sky,
Living
Loving
Hopeful
Is my end of the sky
So very different after all?

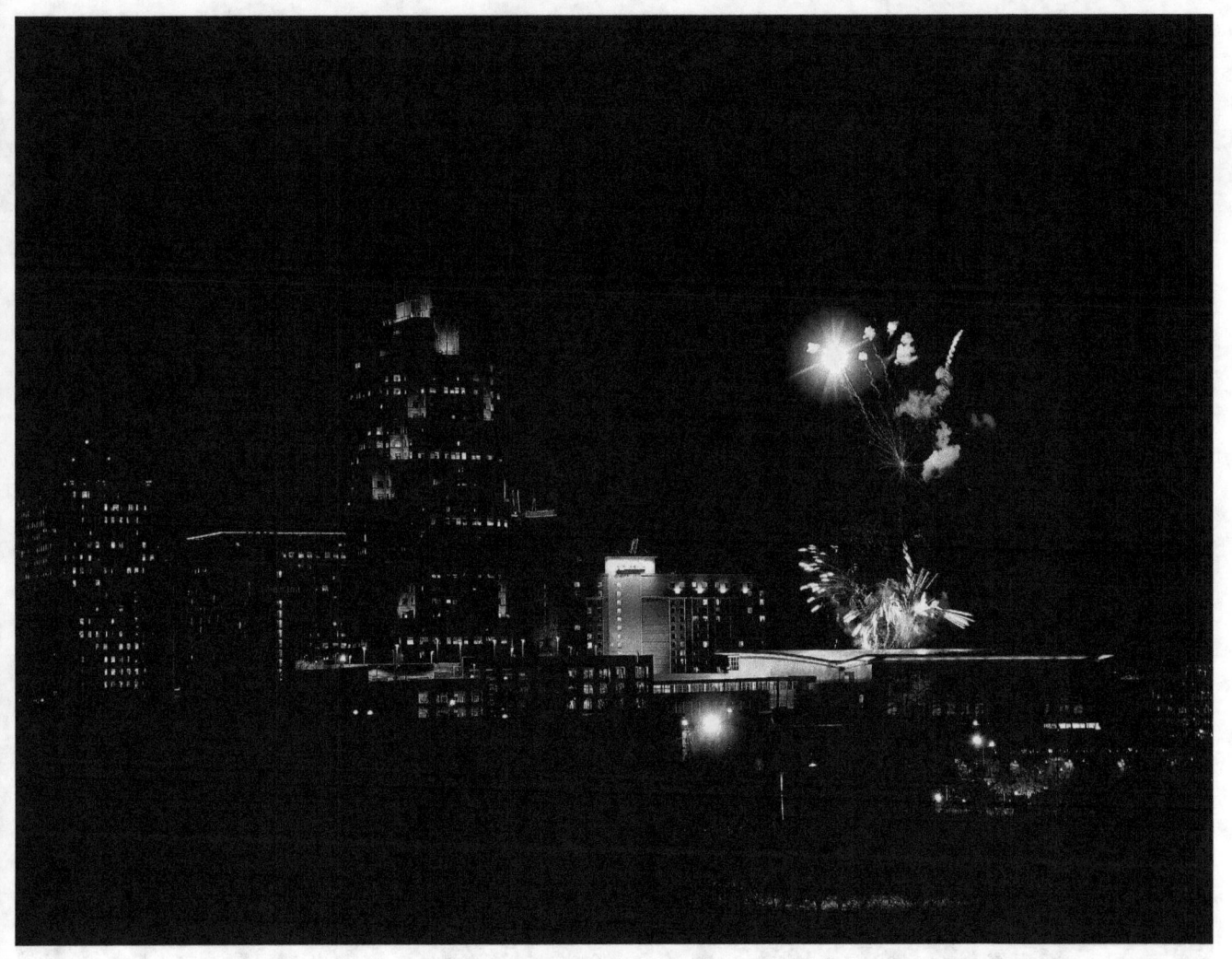

PYRRHIC VICTORY

On a ribbon of fire
The rocket rises
Clawing for the sky
Trying to escape
Its own fiery tail
Knowing
That it cannot outpace
The fire within it
And that in the end
That same fire
That propels it
Will destroy it
Its only redemption
Found in the awe
In the faces
On the ground below
The spectacle
Of dying well.

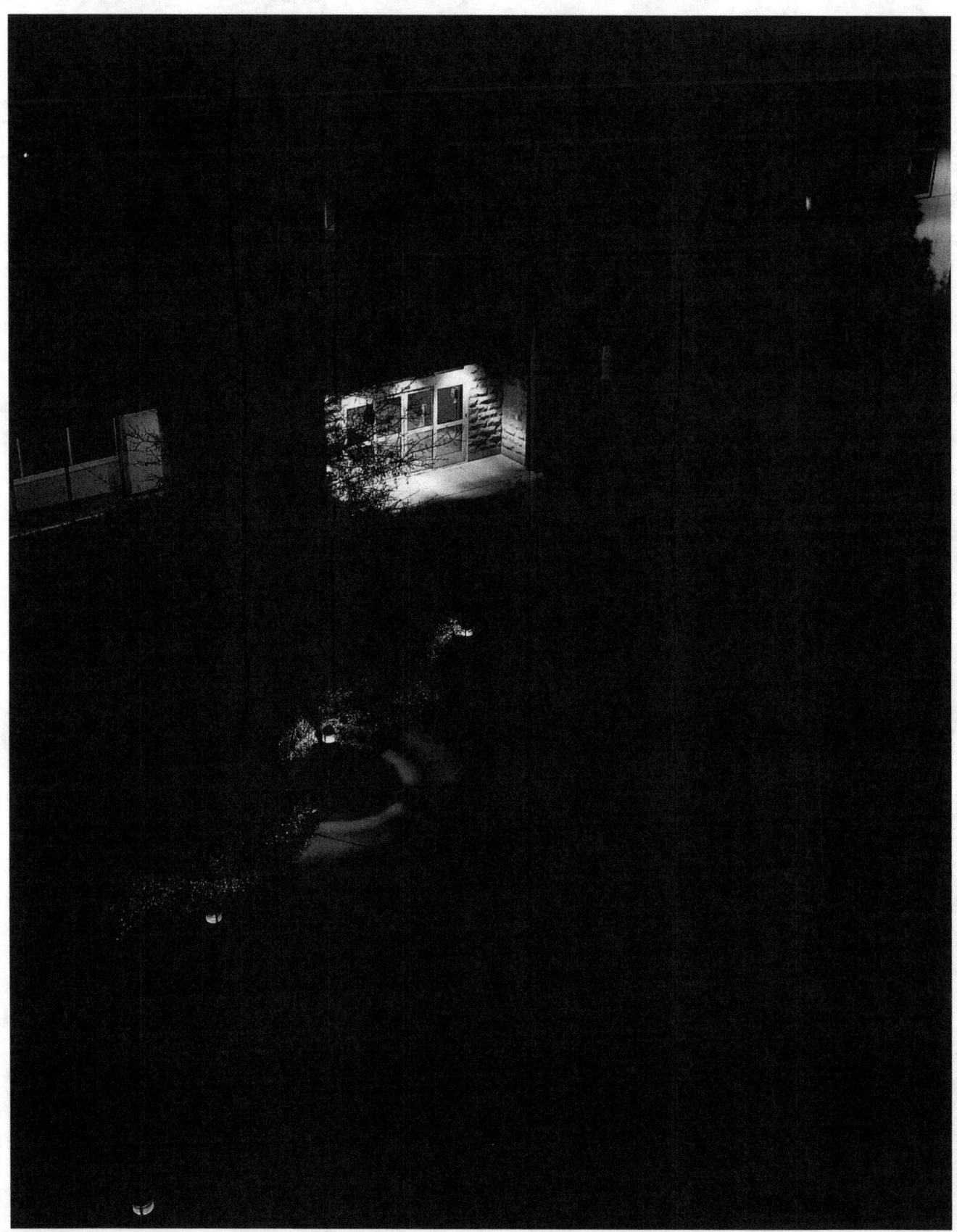

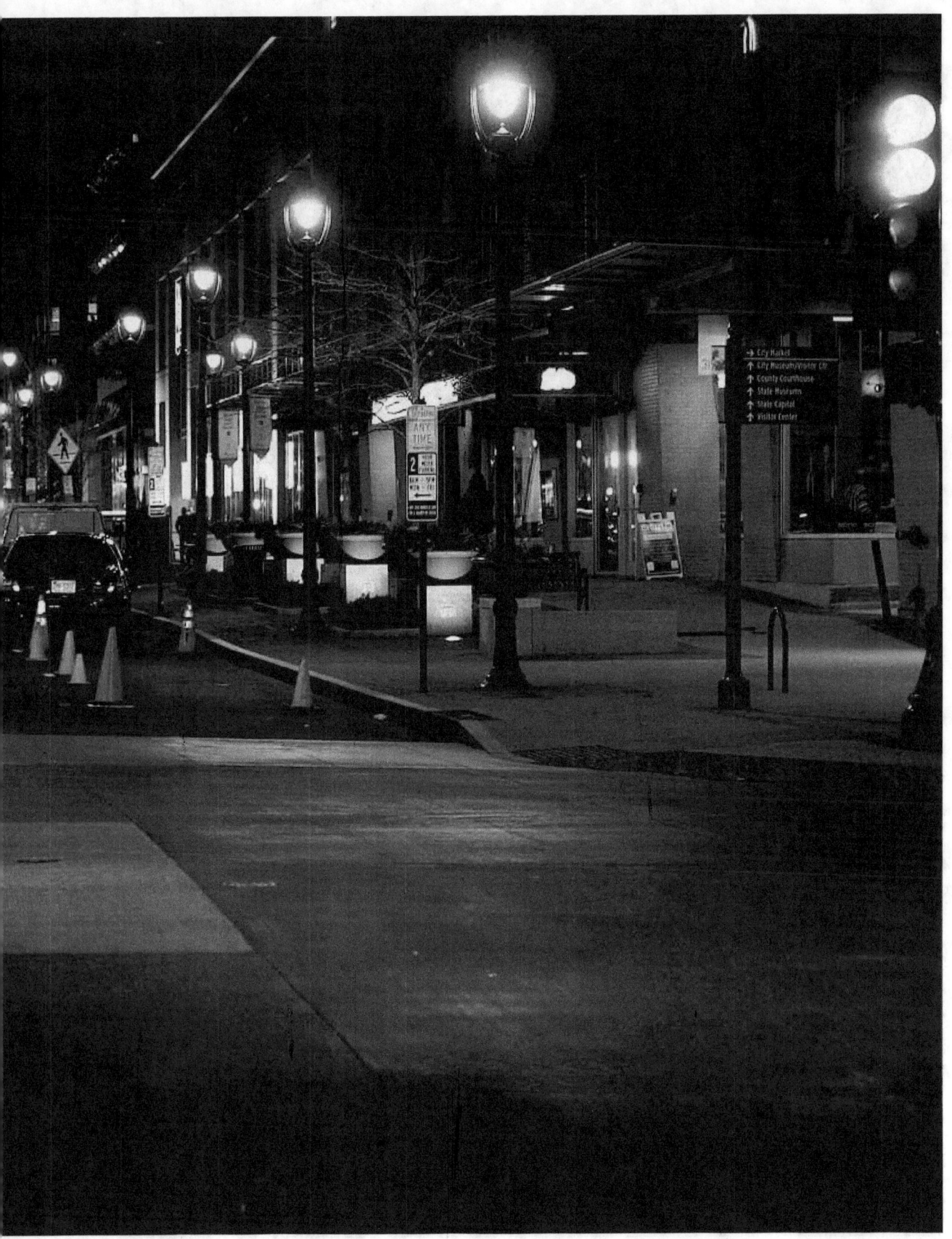

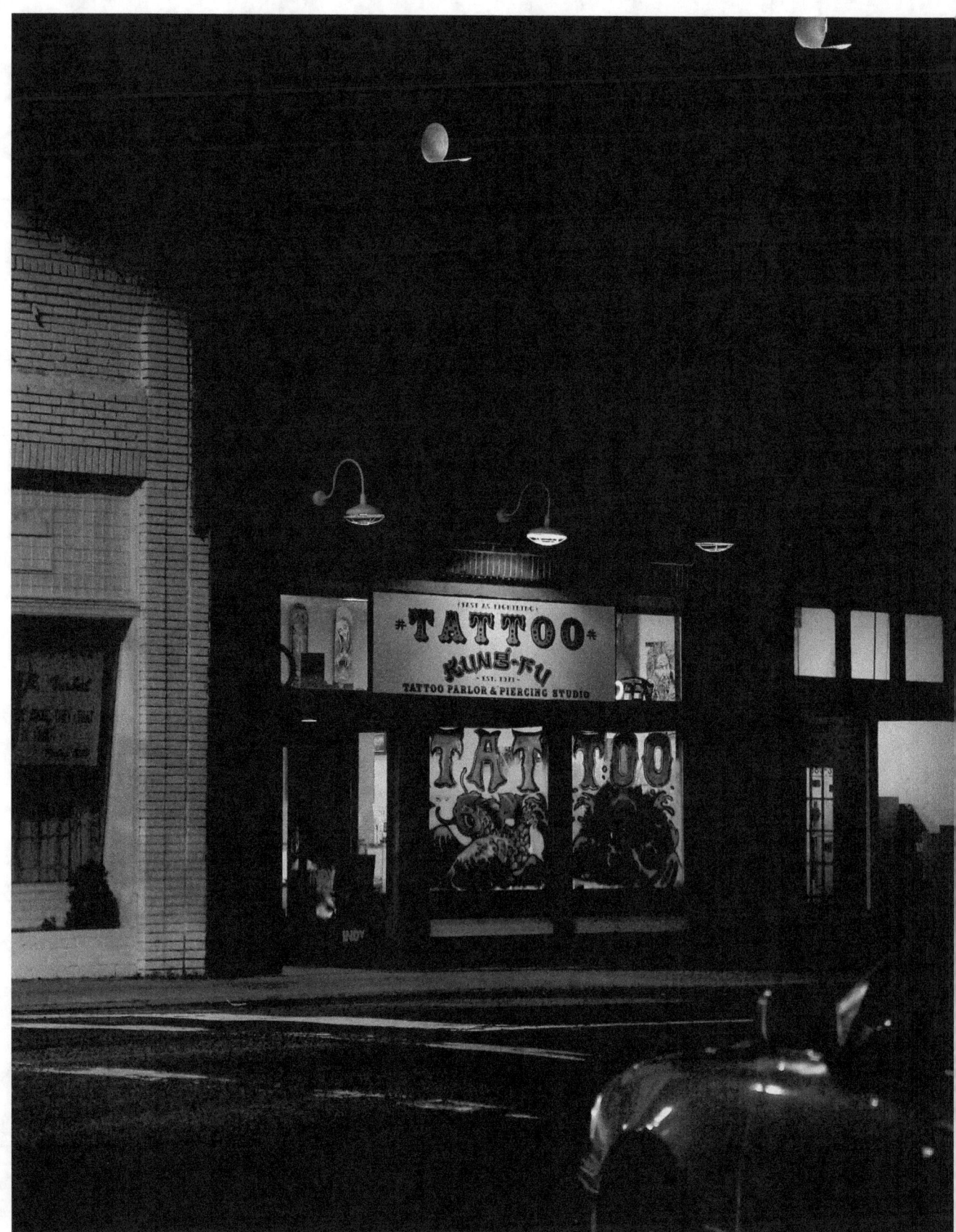

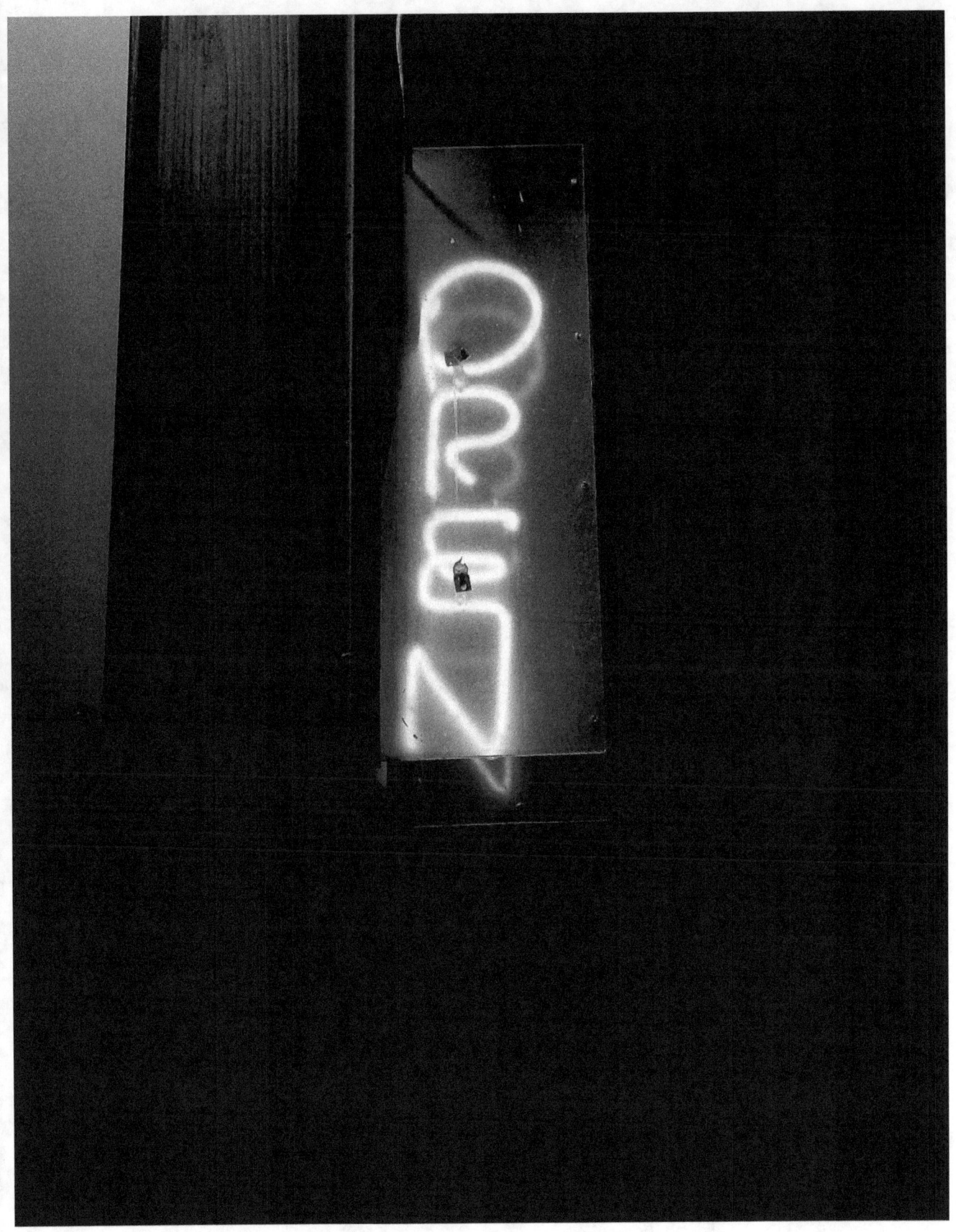

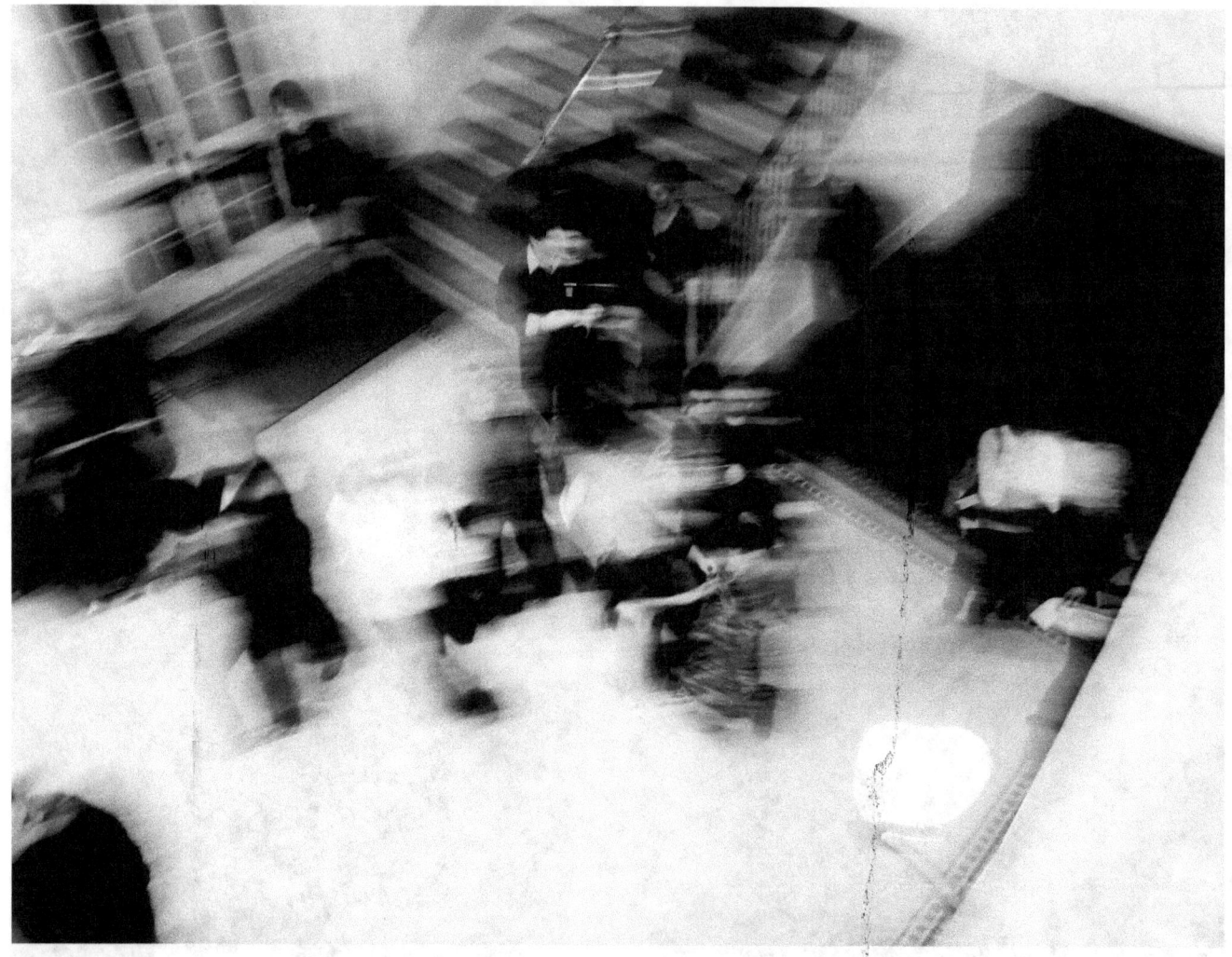

WHEN

When you think no one cares
That no one understands
When you feel the ache of loneliness
Your heart heavy
And your soul too weary for another step

Someone somewhere feels for you
Aches for you.
Someone somewhere echoes your loneliness
And sits waiting
To offer a hand, a shoulder, a heart to lean on.

When the sun is warm
And the wind is at your back
When the road rises to meet you
And your spirit is soaring
And cannot be brought down by any force

Someone somewhere is smiling
In silent celebration

Someone somewhere echoes your joy
And sits waiting
To encourage, to sustain, to validate.

When you are quiet
And still in contemplation
When your mind
Reaches out to the horizon
And your memories stir

Someone somewhere is hoping
To be found in those thoughts
Someone somewhere thinks of you
And sits waiting
Hoping to be remembered fondly.

Someone
Somewhere
Loves You.

THINKING

I read the words you said
And the ones you didn't say
More to the point
The ones you no *longer* say
Reinventing a life
That you never saw coming
Asking me to dance
When you don't dance (you even said so)

Try to catch a butterfly
And you find out how fragile they are

Try to pick one up
As it emerges from the chrysalis
Before the wings are dry
And doom it to a premature end
But wear the right colors
And stand very still
The butterfly will come to you
Land there or there (or even there)
And nobody has to get hurt
Least of all the butterfly.

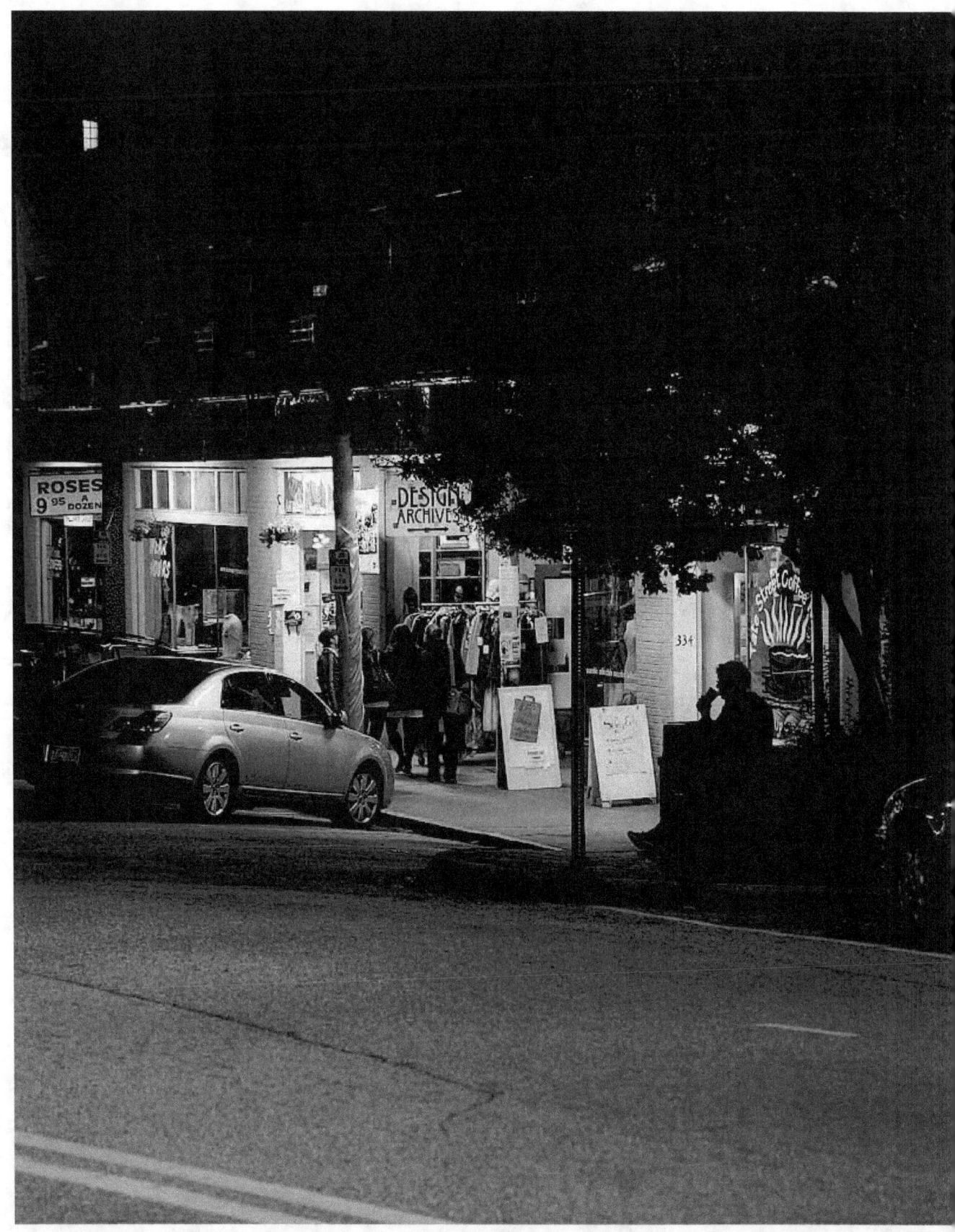

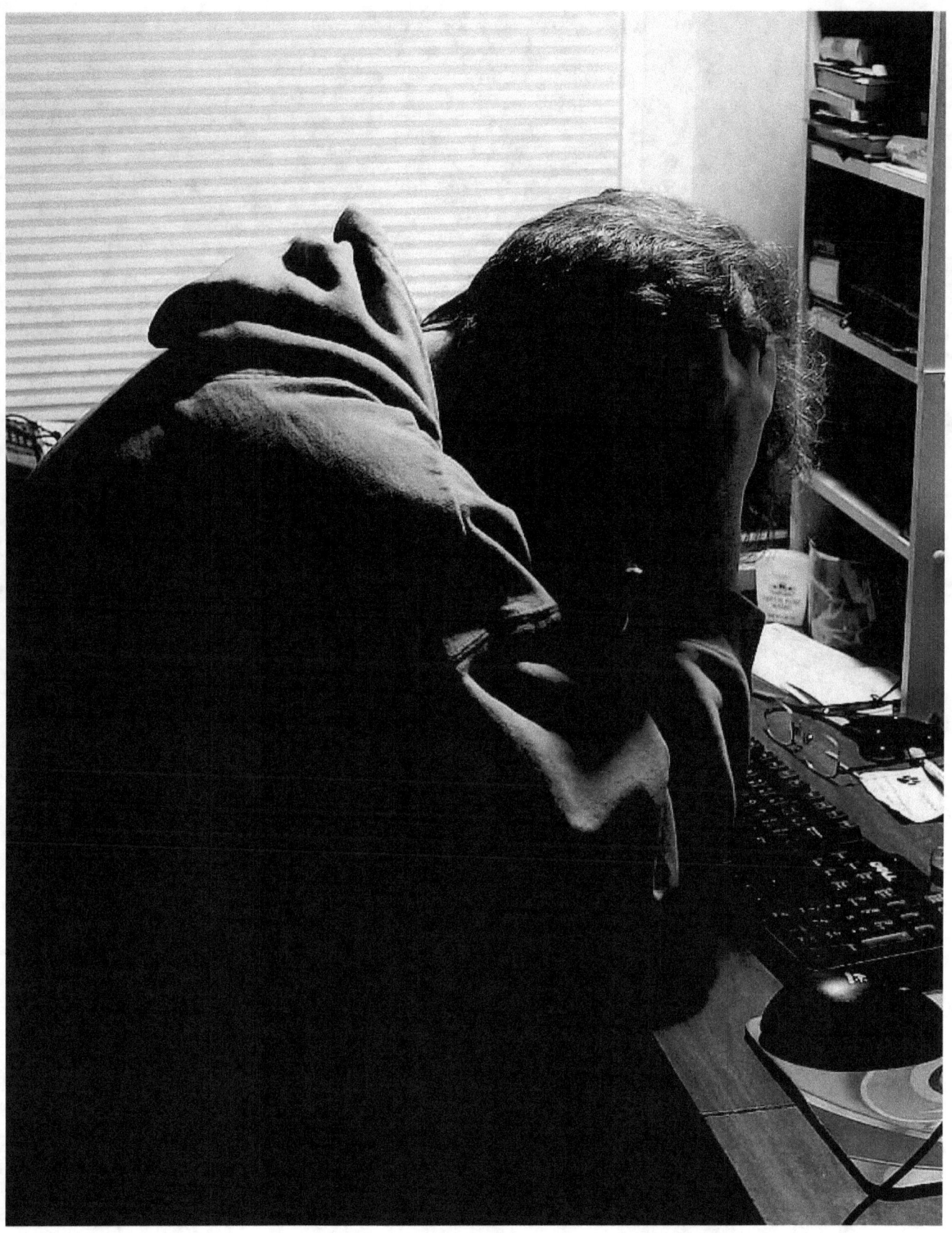

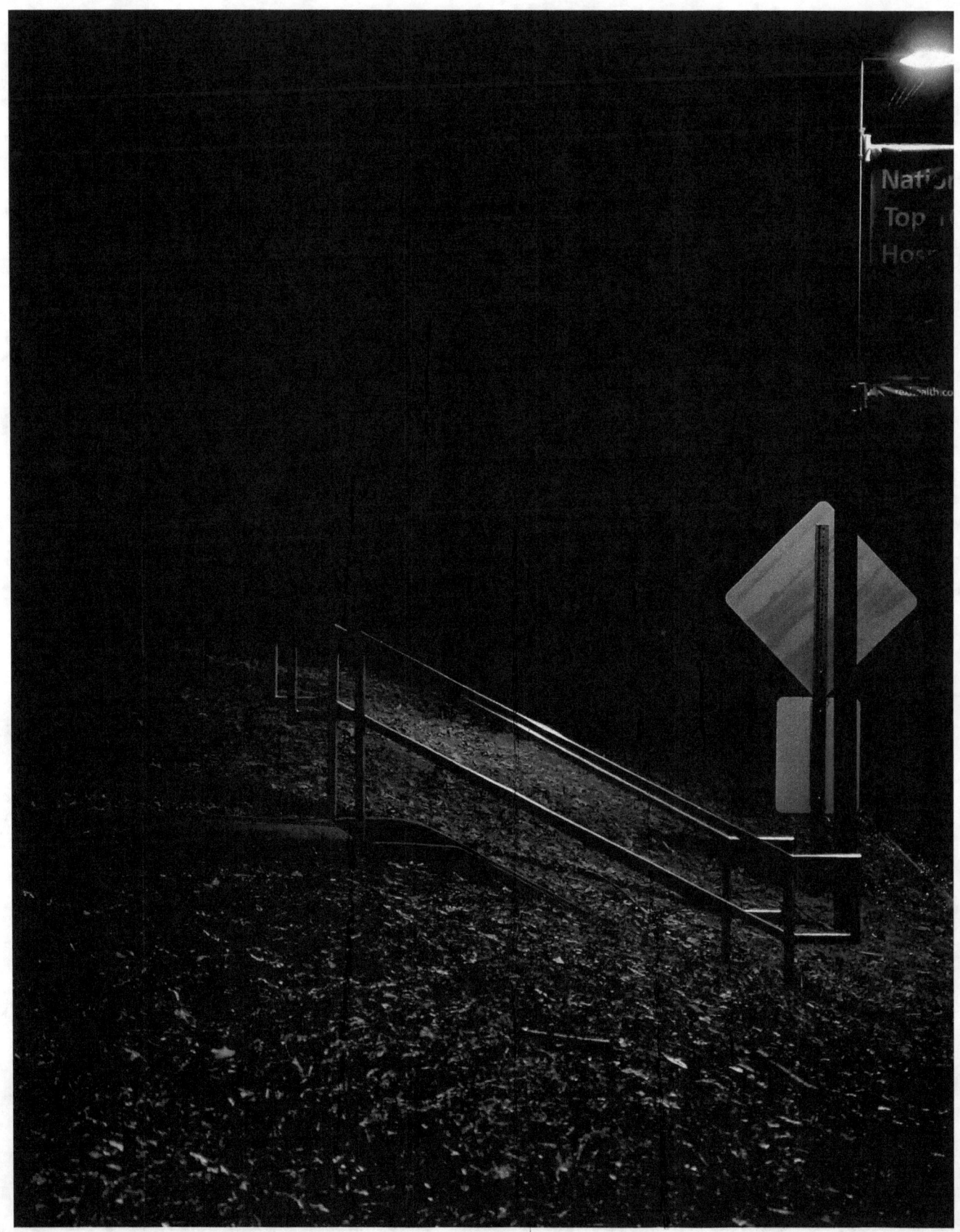

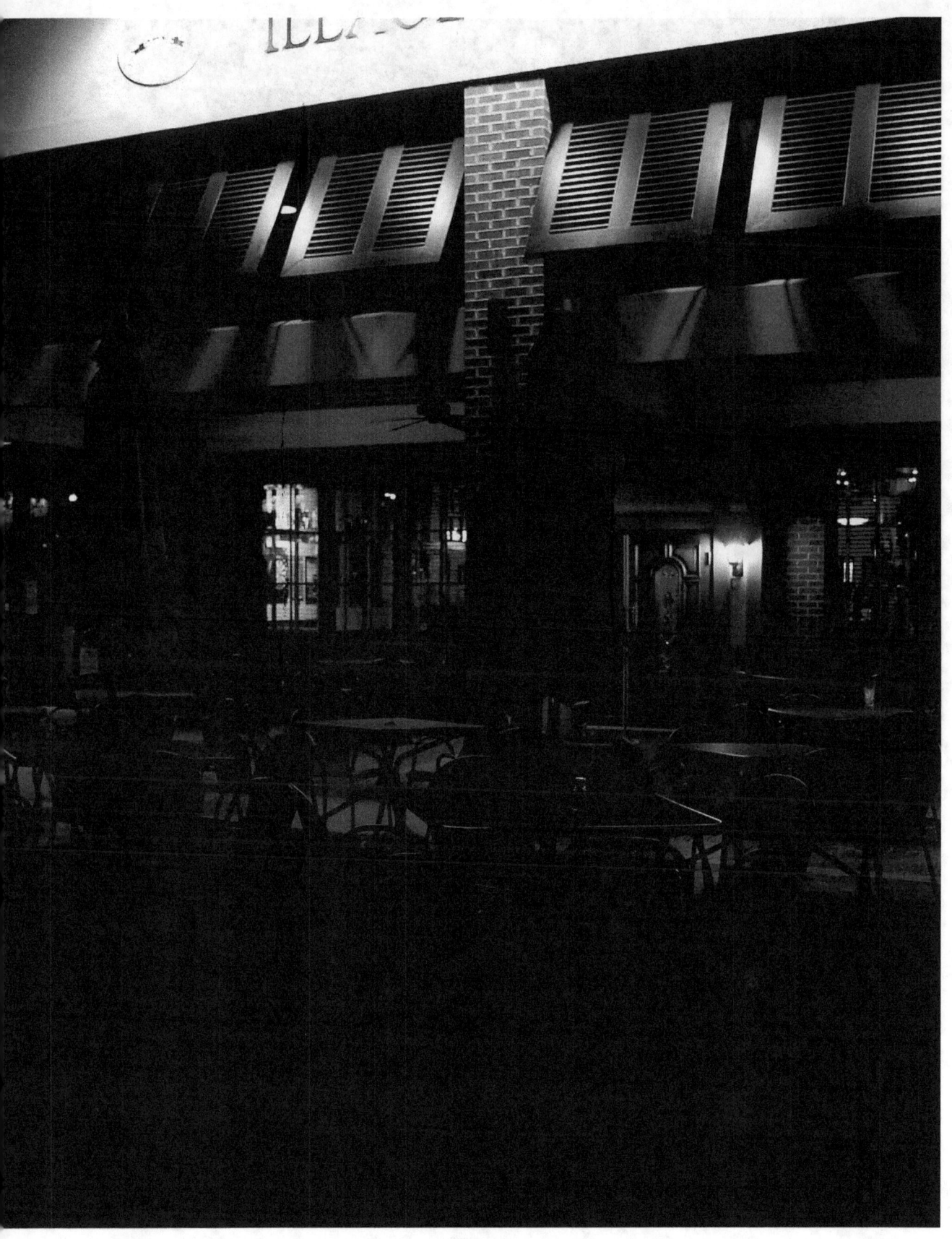

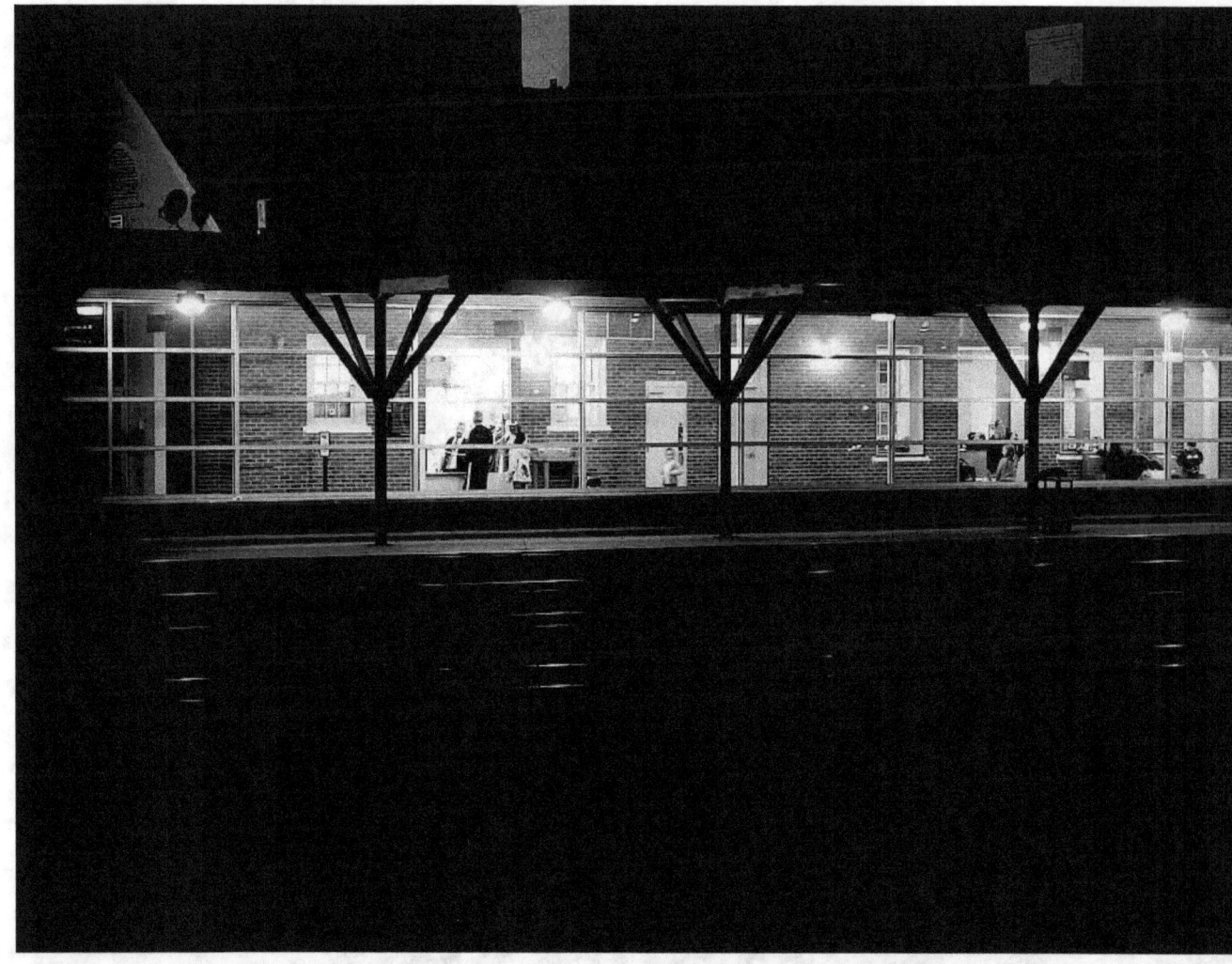

WHAT WOULD THAT BE LIKE?

A ticket in hand
No plan
No schedule
No reservations
No baggage

One-way to that place
Where Hope lives
No hesitation
No backward glances
No regrets

Trade away
Or abandon everything
I can't carry
Exchange comfort
For Joy

What would that be like?

To wake up where you are
To count only the blessings
Of being there
And not the cost
Of getting there

The cost of everything
Is not so high
The cost of nothing
So much higher
Why make those payments?

I pay everything to Nothing
Because Everything
Can't be had in barter
But say the words
And the deal is done.

What would that be like?

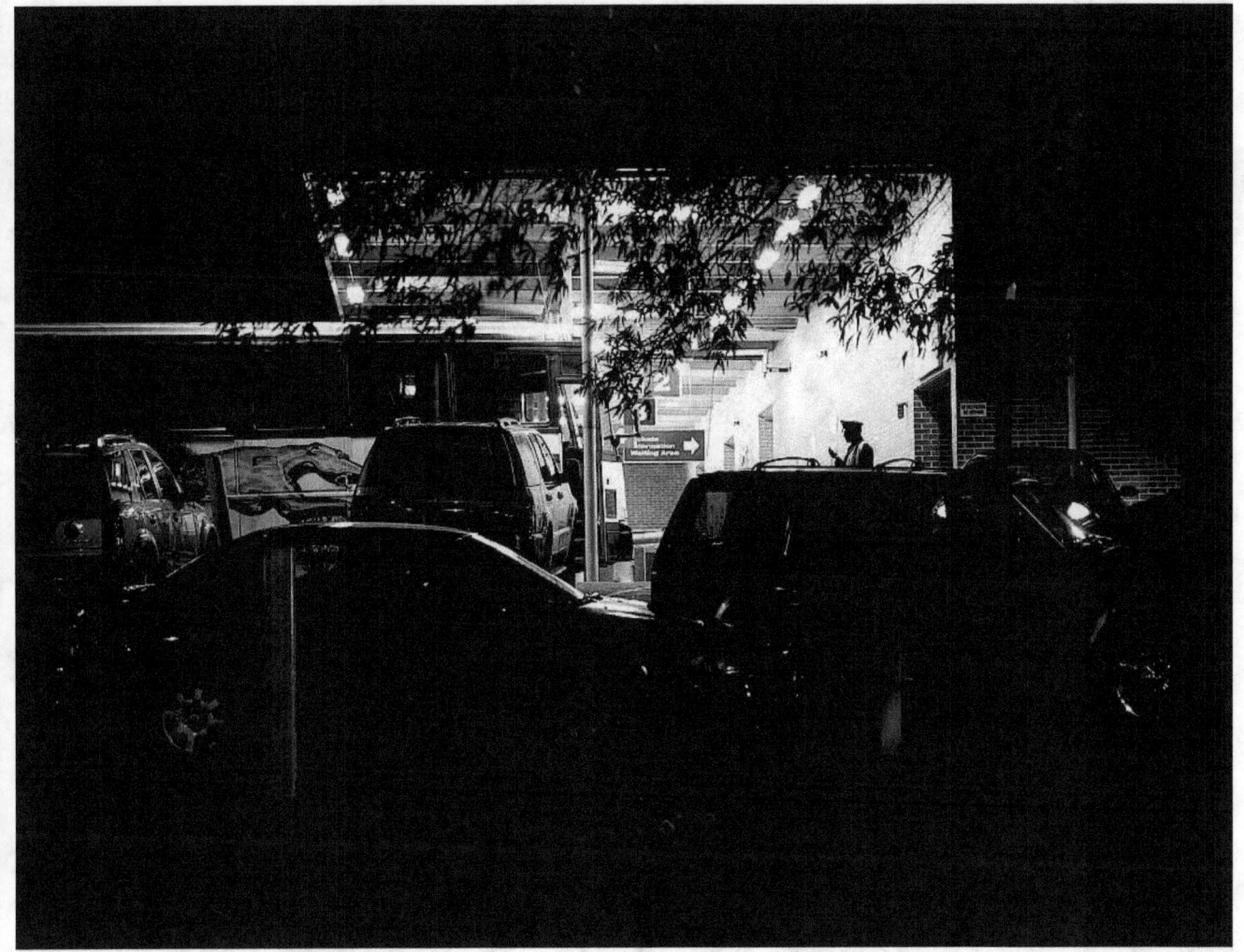

ONCE

Once
There was only
One direction
To go from here
All roads led
To the North
An upward direction
Where snow freshened air
Could fill my lungs
With the clean, sweet
Breath of you

Once
There was only
One place
I ever wanted to be
That mythical place
Where lived
The most beautiful soul
I have ever known
Tir na Nog
Atlantis
And Eden all in one

Once
Upon a time
Isn't how these
Stories always begin?
We melted
Into each other
And I believed
For just the
Briefest of moments
In a thing I'd thought
Put by long ago

Once
There was love
In your eyes
In your voice
In your words
Then
In the space
Between heartbeats
Only cold ash remained
Of the once warm glow
Now any direction will do

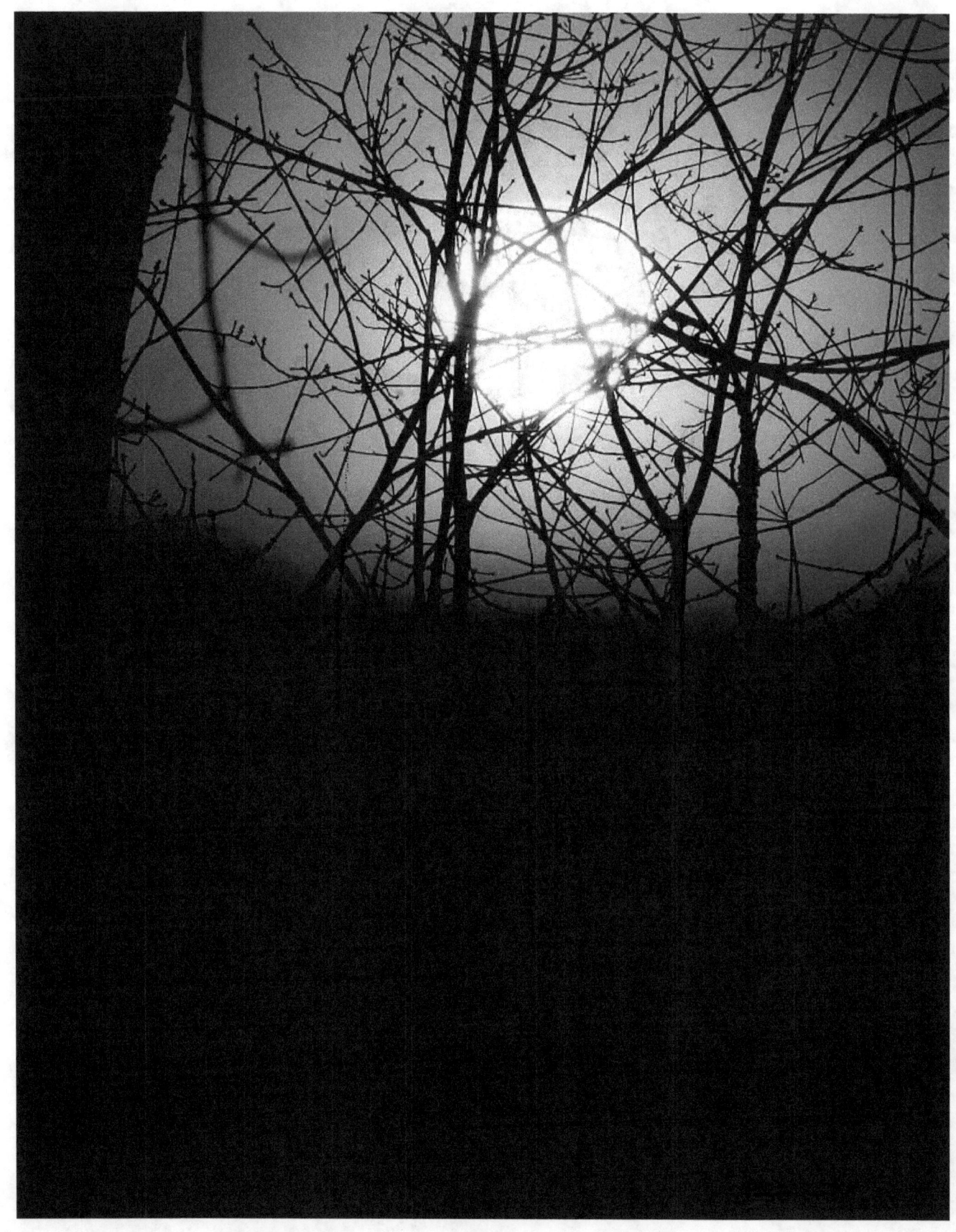

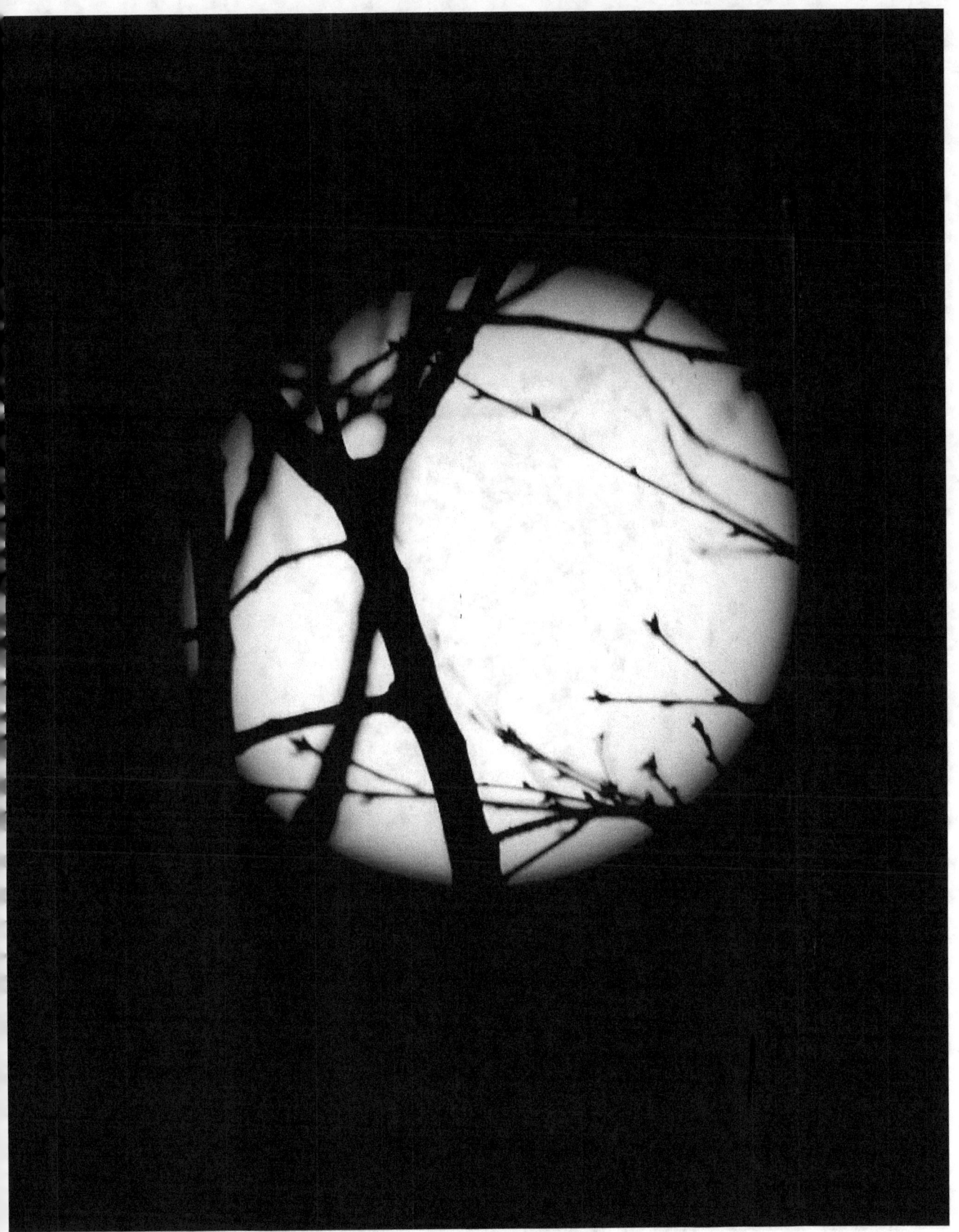

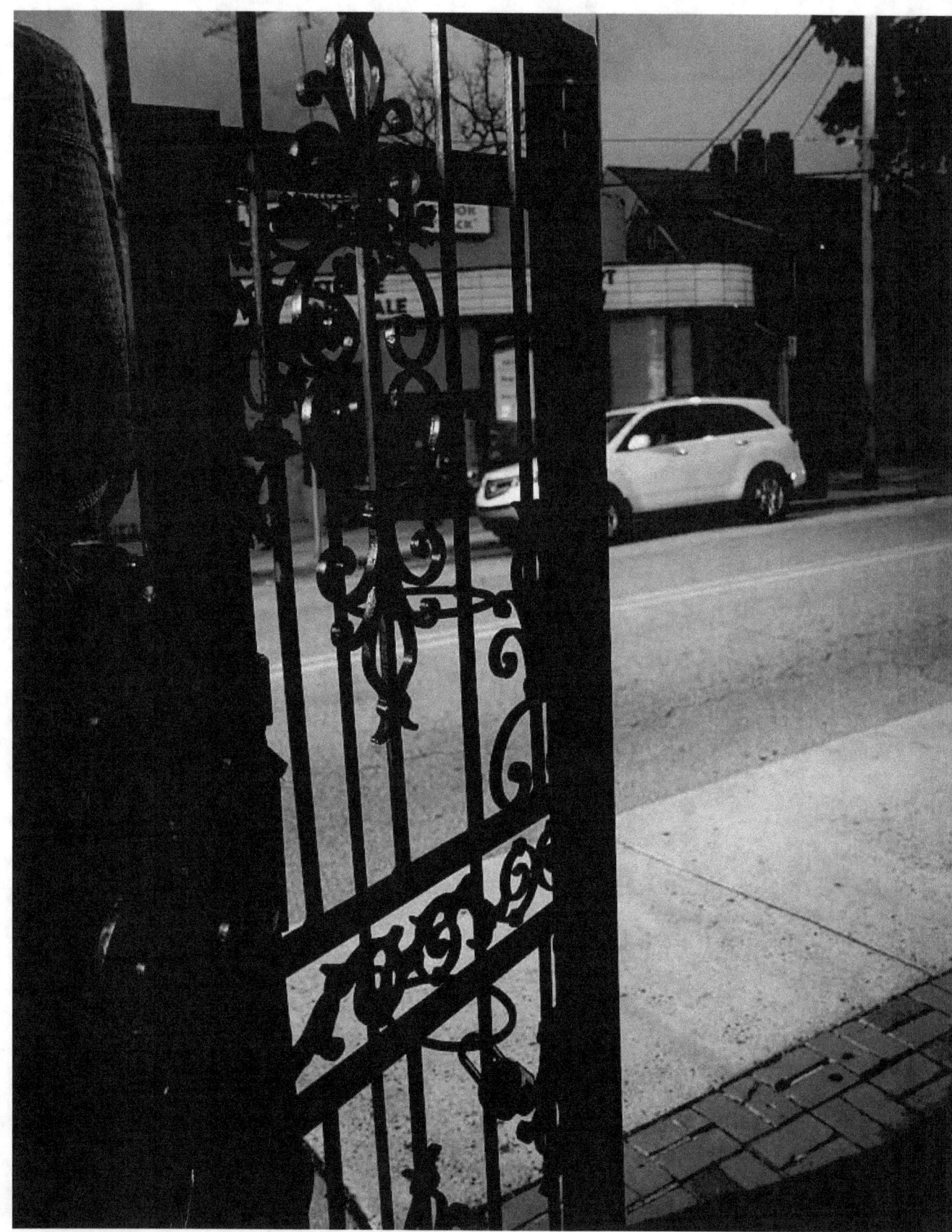

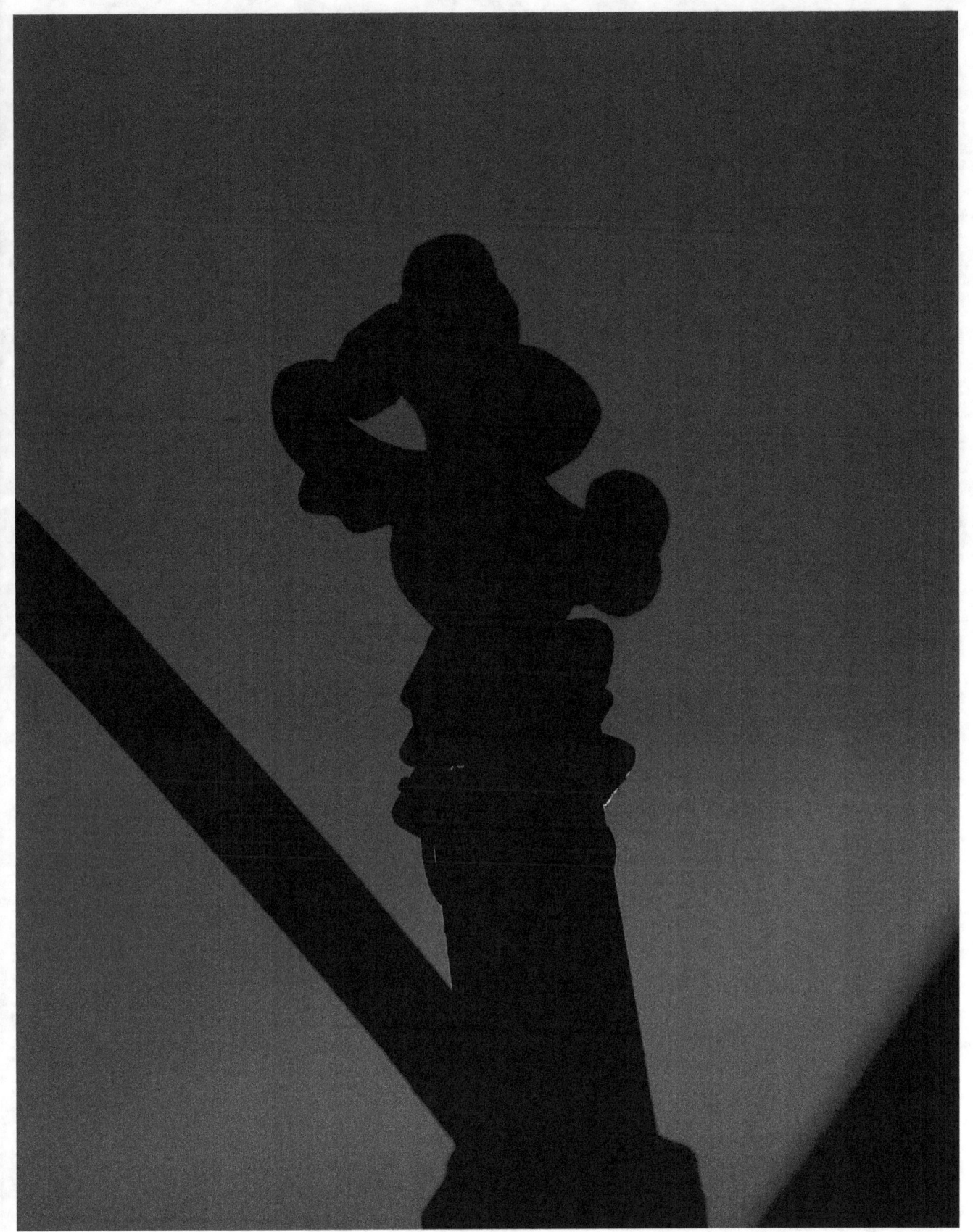

Blurring The Edges

At the edges of the crowd
Are shadows no one looks into
For very long
The eyes that look out
From there are haggard
Red-rimmed orbs of white
Dotted with brown or blue
Or some color
No one has a name for

They gaze not in envy
Not in hunger
Not in predation
But in wonder
In curiosity

They have never known
Life in the Light
Where the crowd lives
Beyond the blurred edges
Of night and shadow

Though they hunger
They do not covet
They know
No other way
They watch and wait
For this gathering
To leave their home

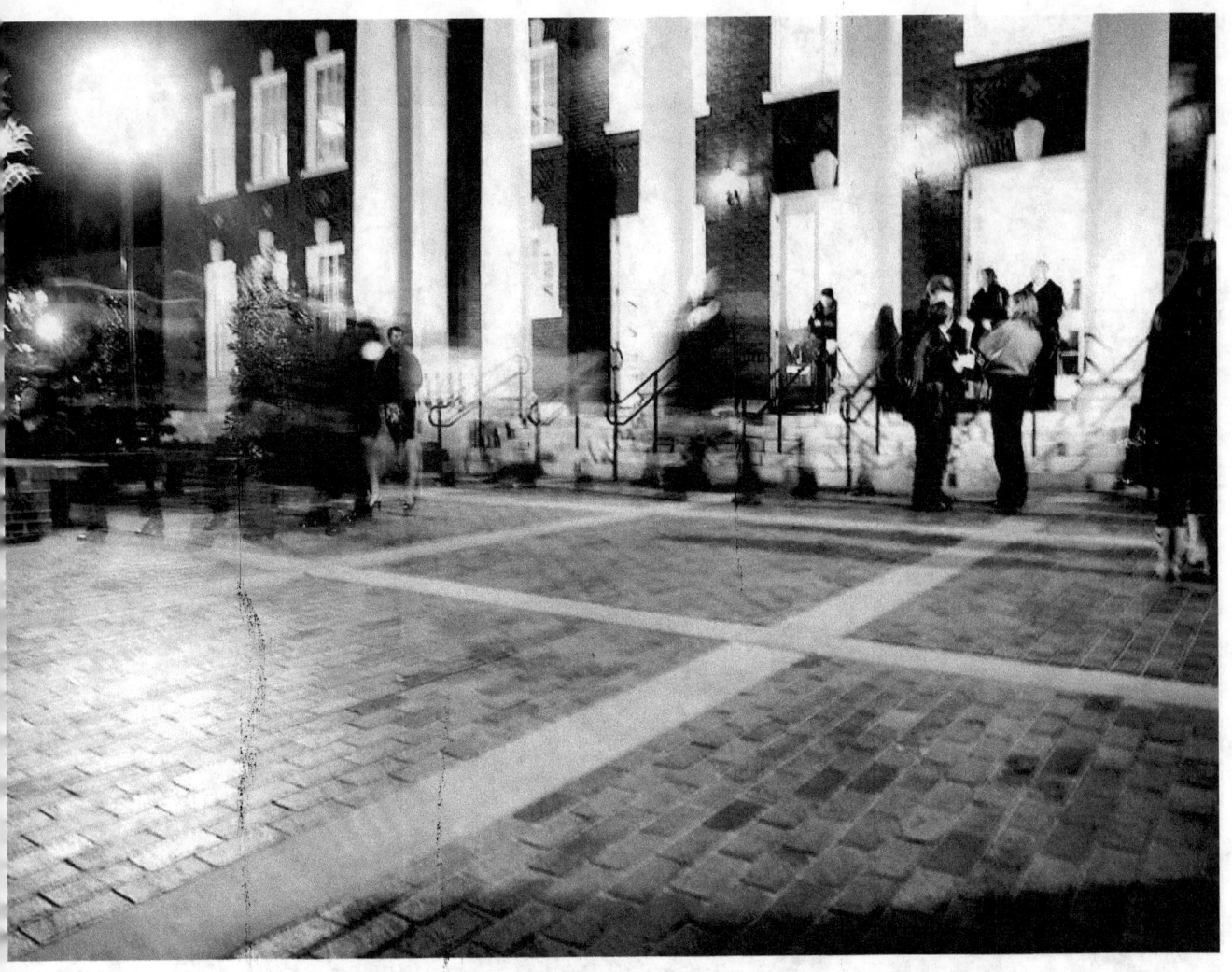

THE HAPPY PEOPLE

The shiny happy people
Glide through the cool
Of evening
Glittering in their glamour
Decked in jeweled gowns
And sleek black jackets.
They float
Seemingly without effort
From light to shadow
And back again
Never lingering long
In the dark places
Never seeing
The dark people.

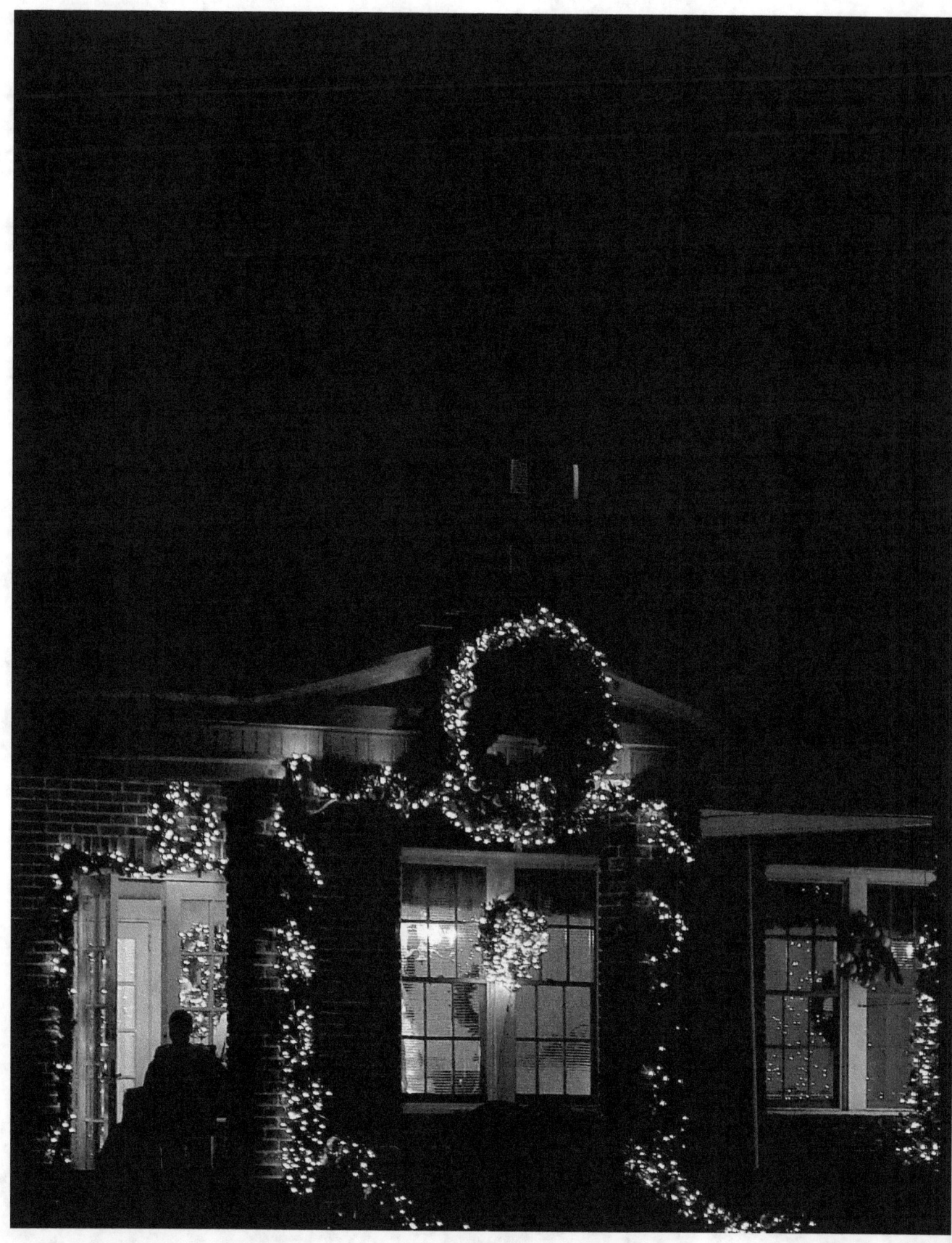

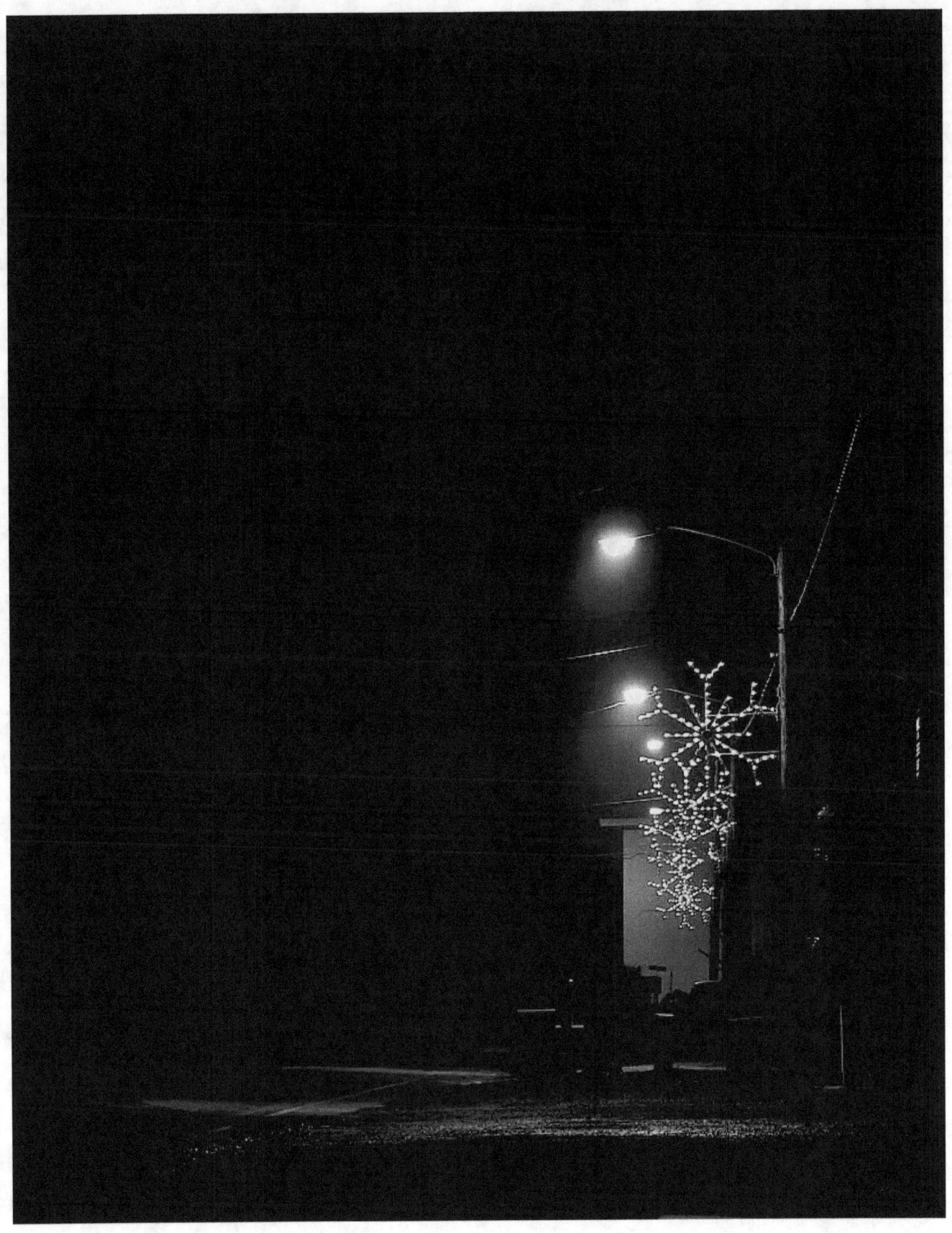

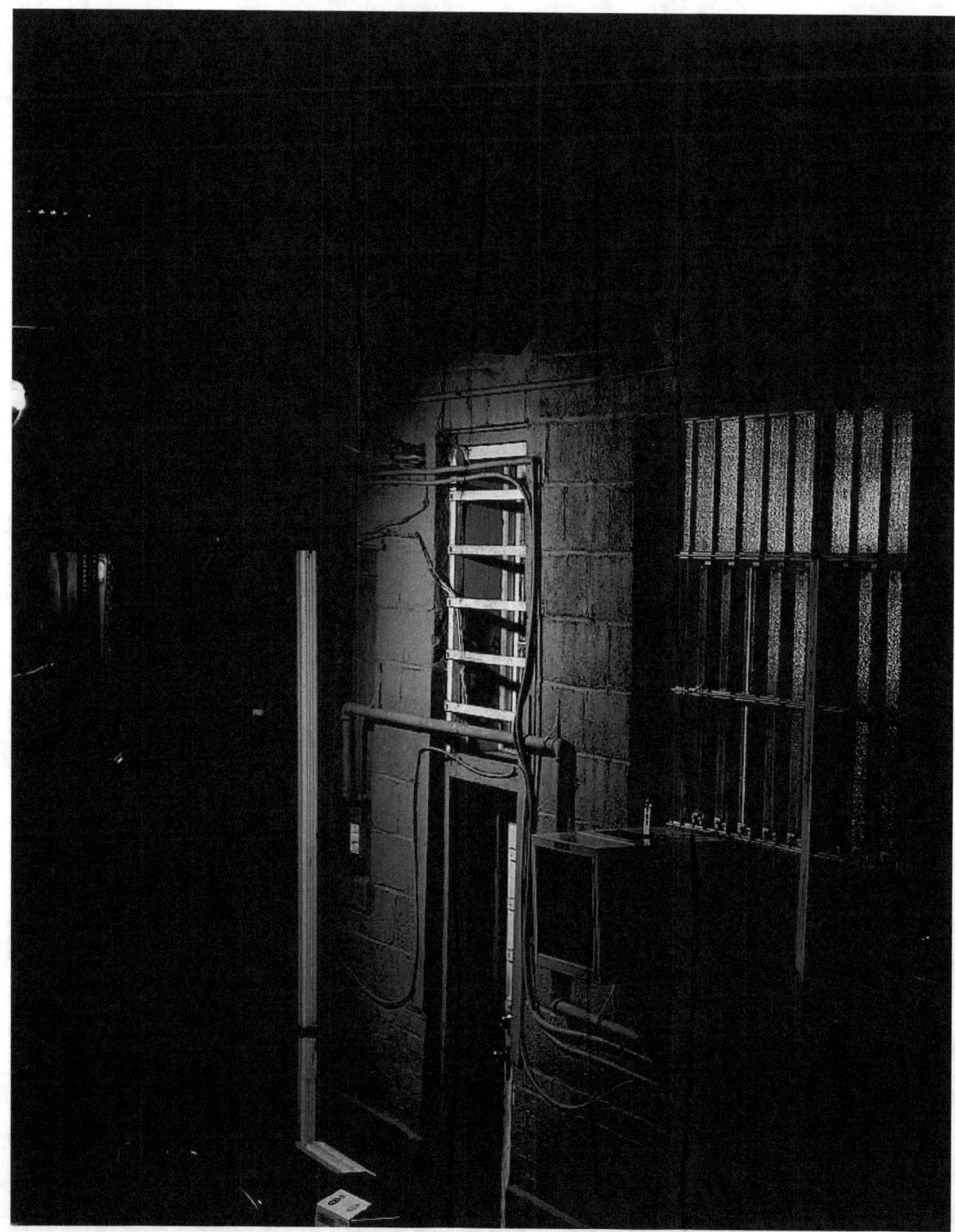

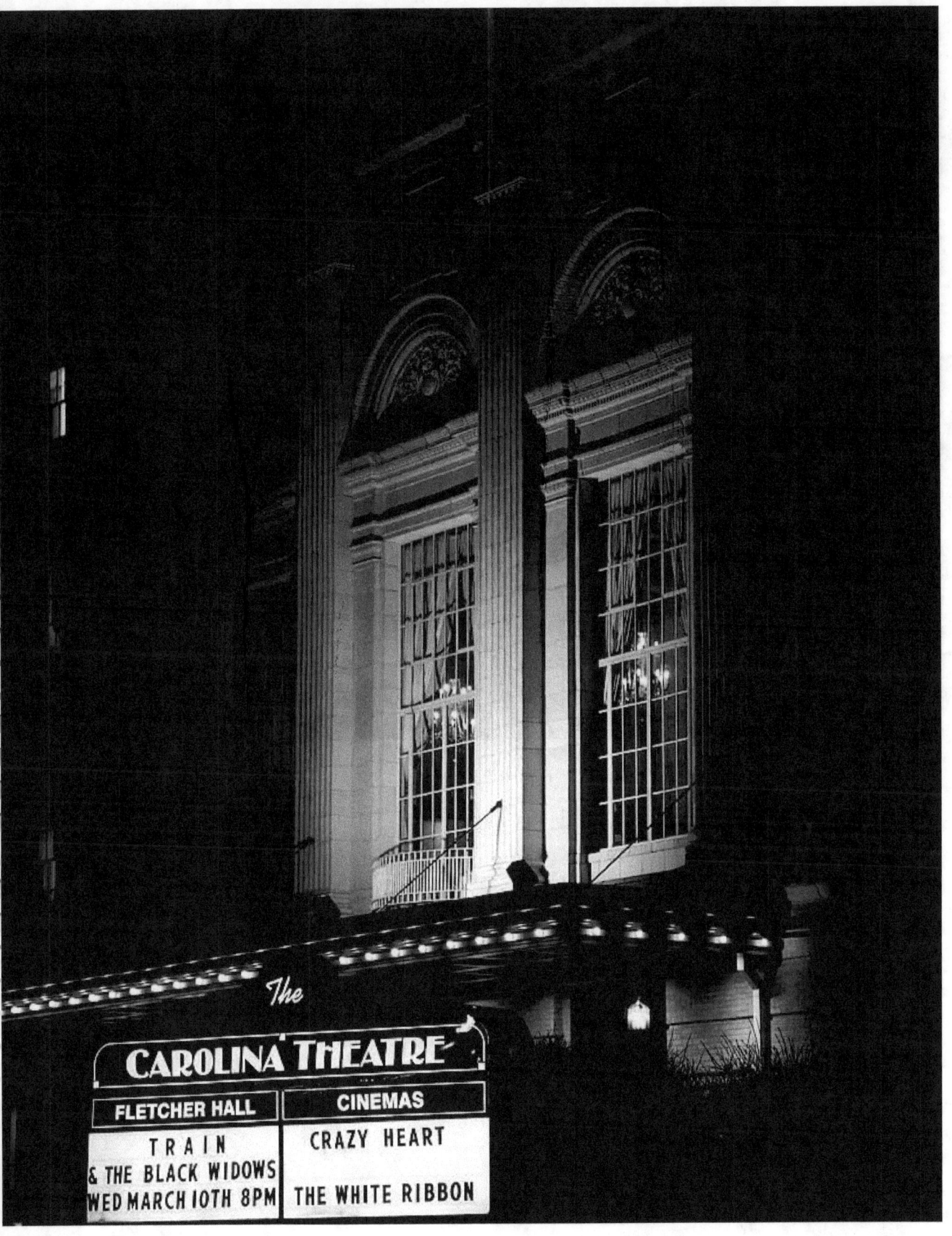

The

CAROLINA THEATRE

FLETCHER HALL	CINEMAS
T R A I N & THE BLACK WIDOWS WED MARCH 10TH 8PM	CRAZY HEART THE WHITE RIBBON

SOMEWHERE, ANYWHERE

Would it be different
If he jumped aboard
The next freight
To rumble across the bridge
Would life be better
In Tulsa or Tuscaloosa

What keeps him here
He wonders to himself
When what he wants
Is somewhere else
It must be there
Somewhere, anywhere
Because here is nothing

It's not as easy, he thinks
To hop aboard
That slow freight
As it was when folks did it
All the time
Not so many open doors now

Maybe tomorrow
He says to himself
After I sleep on it
When I have a plan
When I figure it out
He wonders if
They have beds in Tulsa

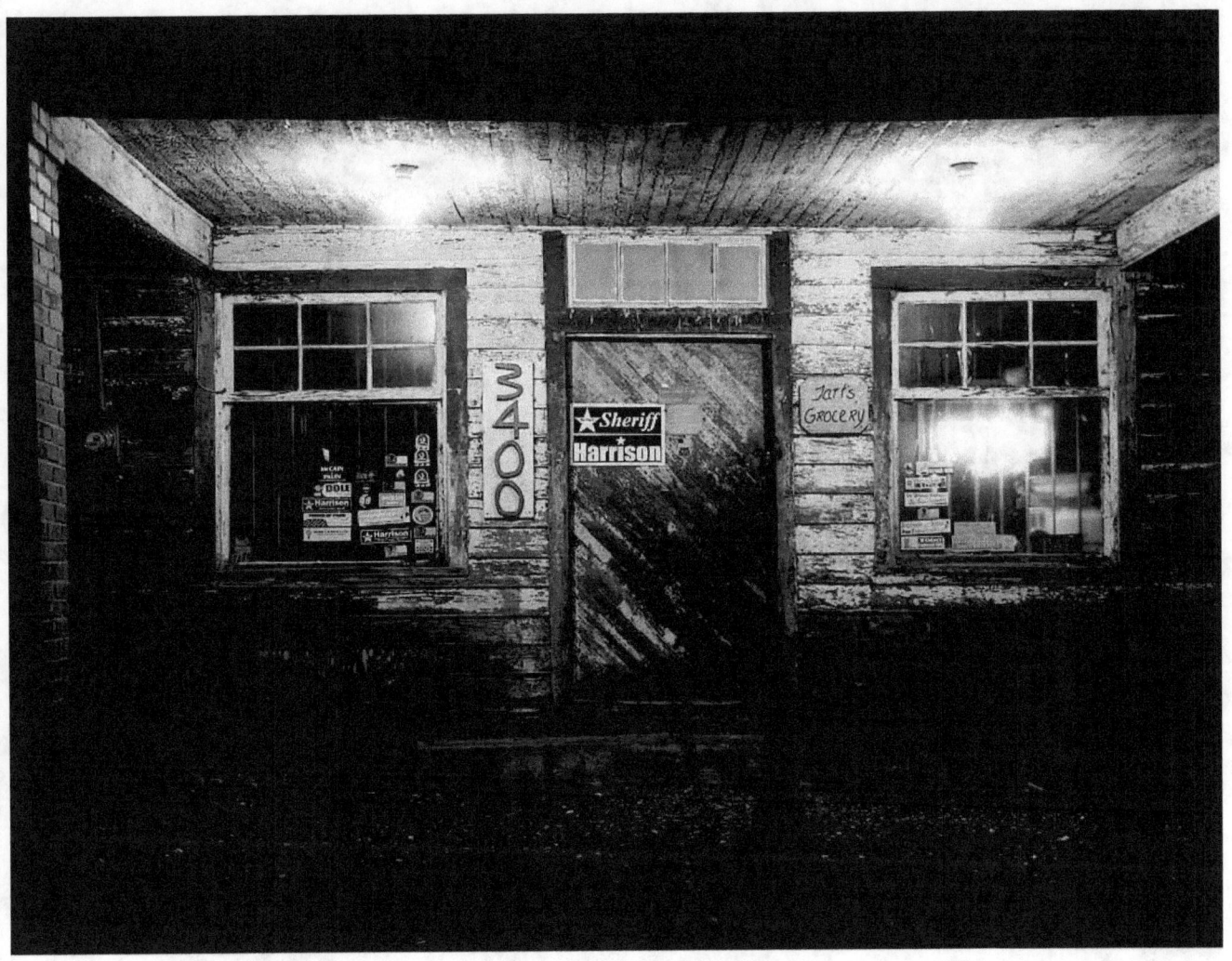

Don't Want To Be Your Jesus

I don't want to be your Jesus
I do not want such power
Such power corrupts
Makes its holder into
Something I never want to be
I do not want
A disciple
A damsel
A kite on a tether
A puppet on a stage
But to be with the soul
Whose passion weaves
Brilliant tapestries
That make me weep
From daffodils and crows
And rain and snow
The mud of the pottery shed
The smoke of the sugar house
And ketchup

The beauty
That cannot be masked
By baggy flannel
And sensible shoes
I am not
A martyr
A patron saint
I do not fancy myself
Your Savior
Your Messiah
Your valiant knight
I am
A mere mortal
Who would be
A friend, or more
Do with that,
Do with me
What you will

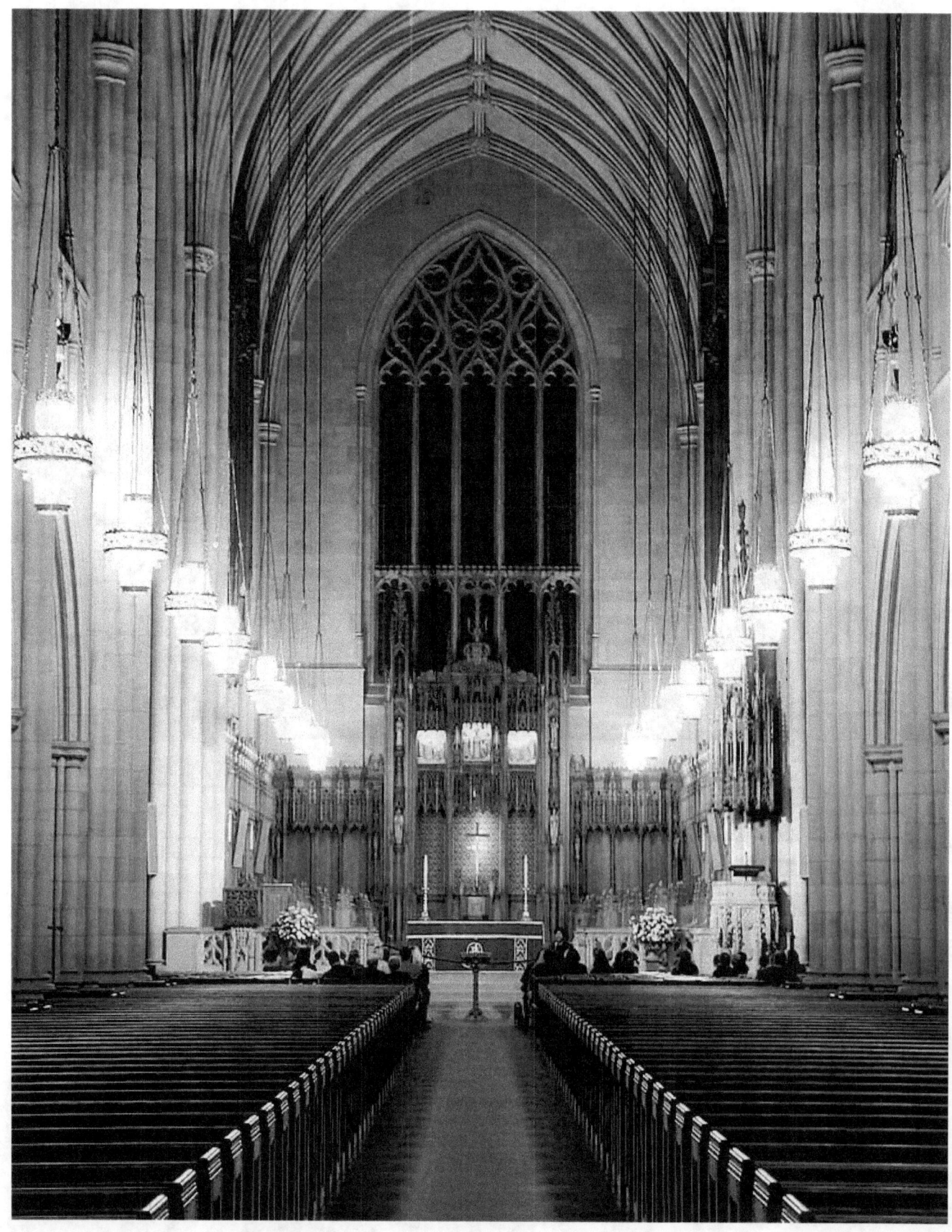

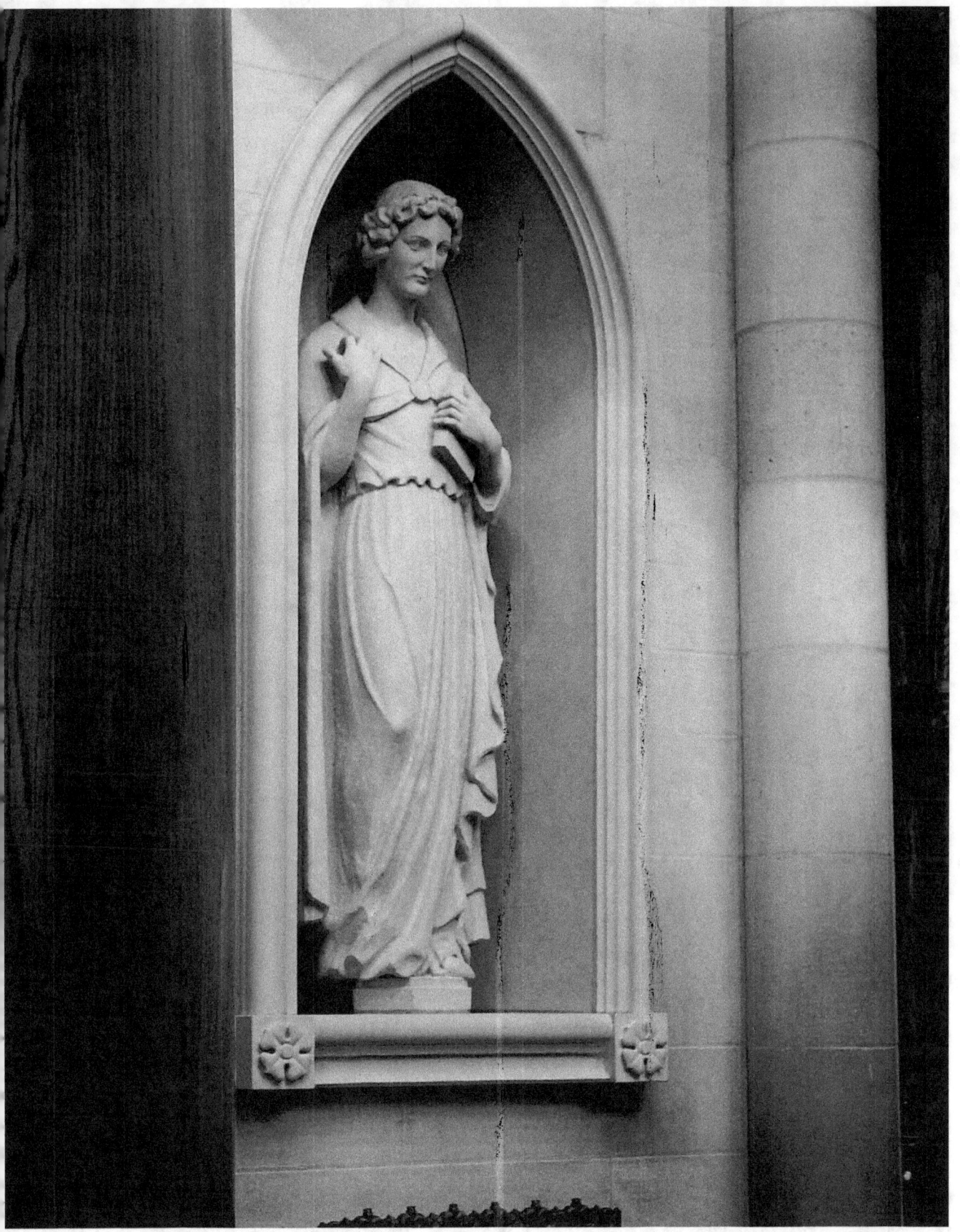

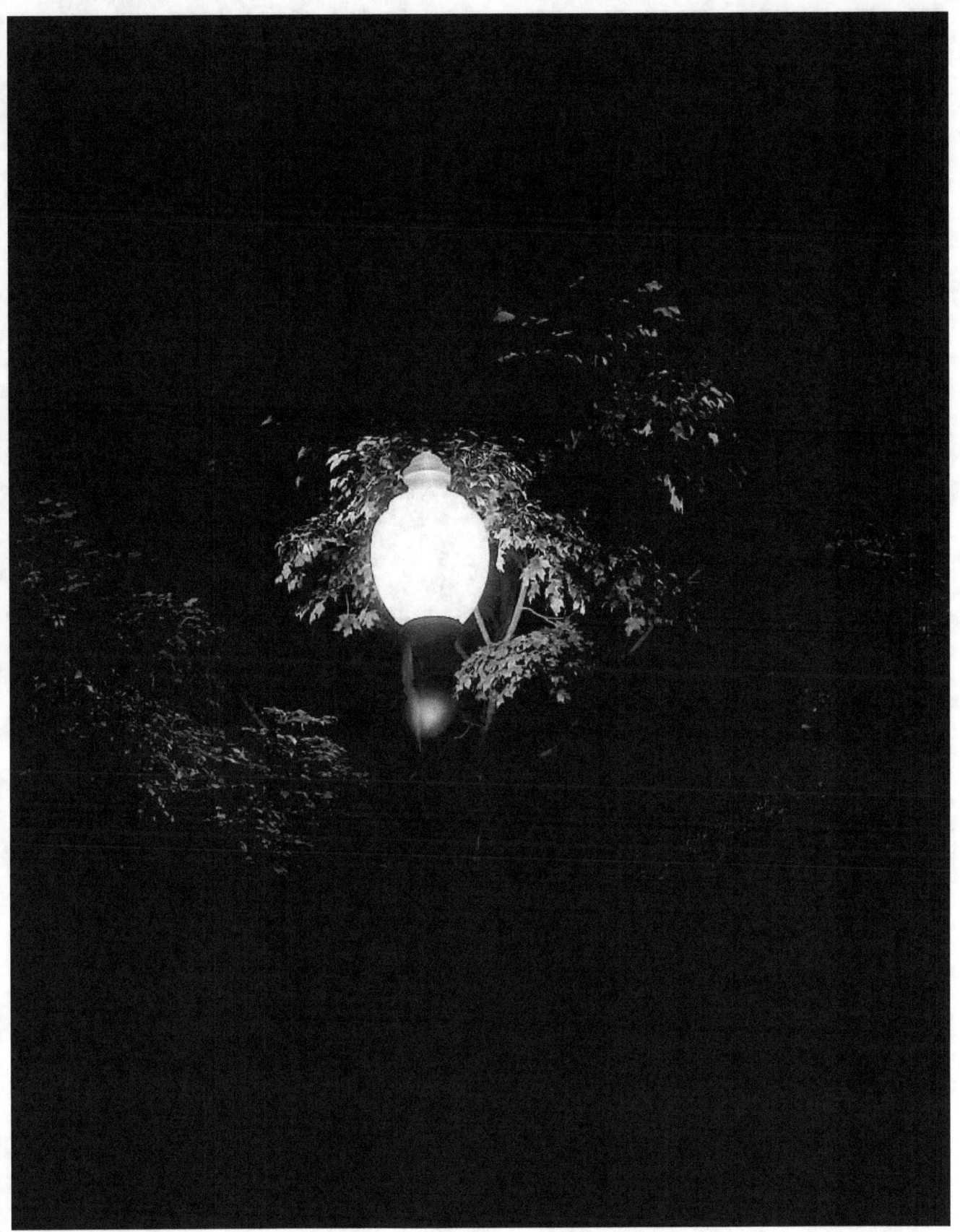

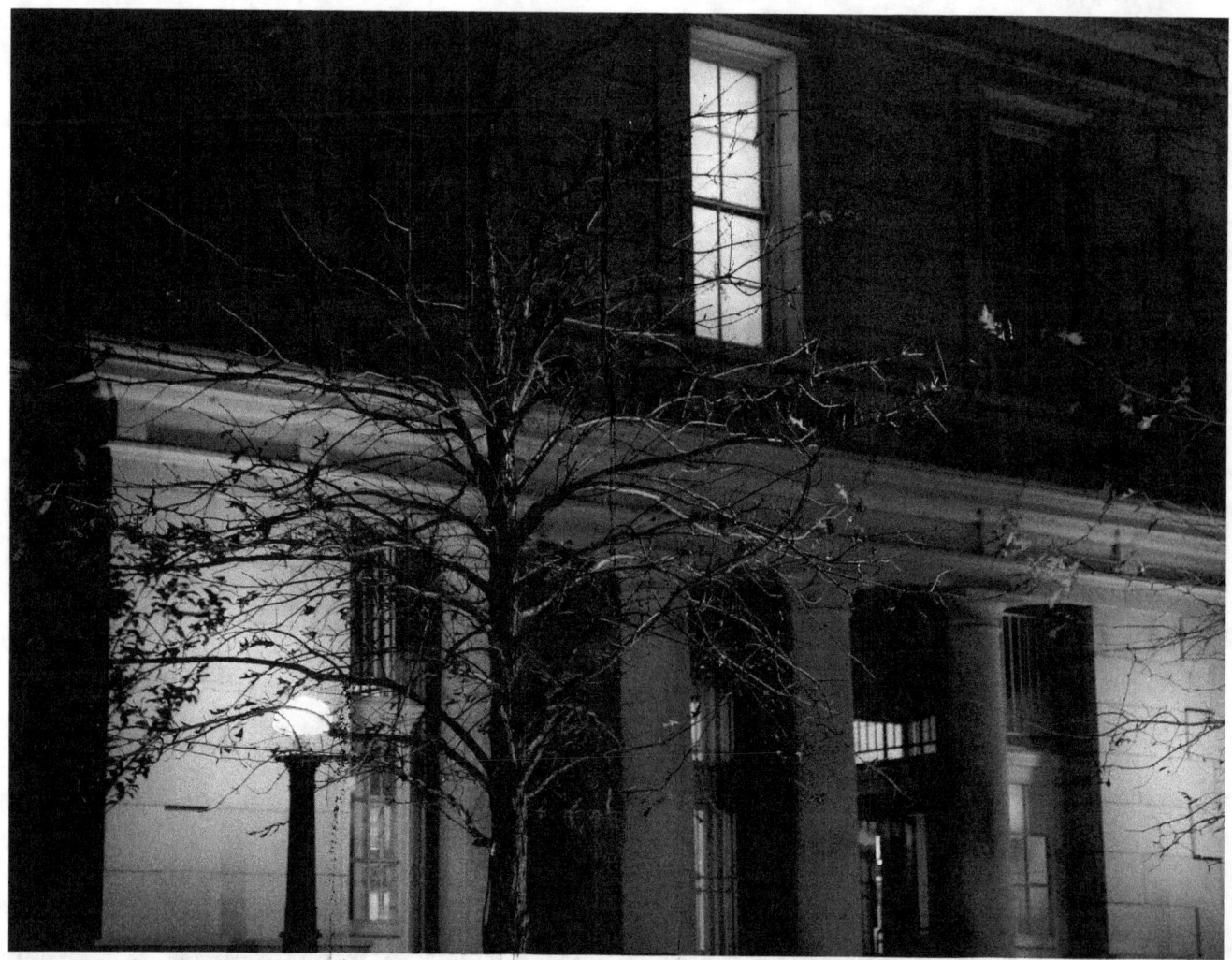

FAITHLESS DAY

What light through yonder window breaks?
What's the story there?
Who is so busy that Day grew tired of waiting
And left him to his work?
Did the Day storm out
Slamming the door in anger?
Or did She slip away quietly
While his back was turned
For some assignation with the dusk?
Does he realize, even
That She has left him here
Alone in his garret?

Ticking another day off the list
Filling another night with
The empty promise of Better Things
If he can only get
This One Last Thing
Complete
Perfect
Finished.
And put out the light
Go home to his empty bed
And wait for faithless Day to return
With the dawn.

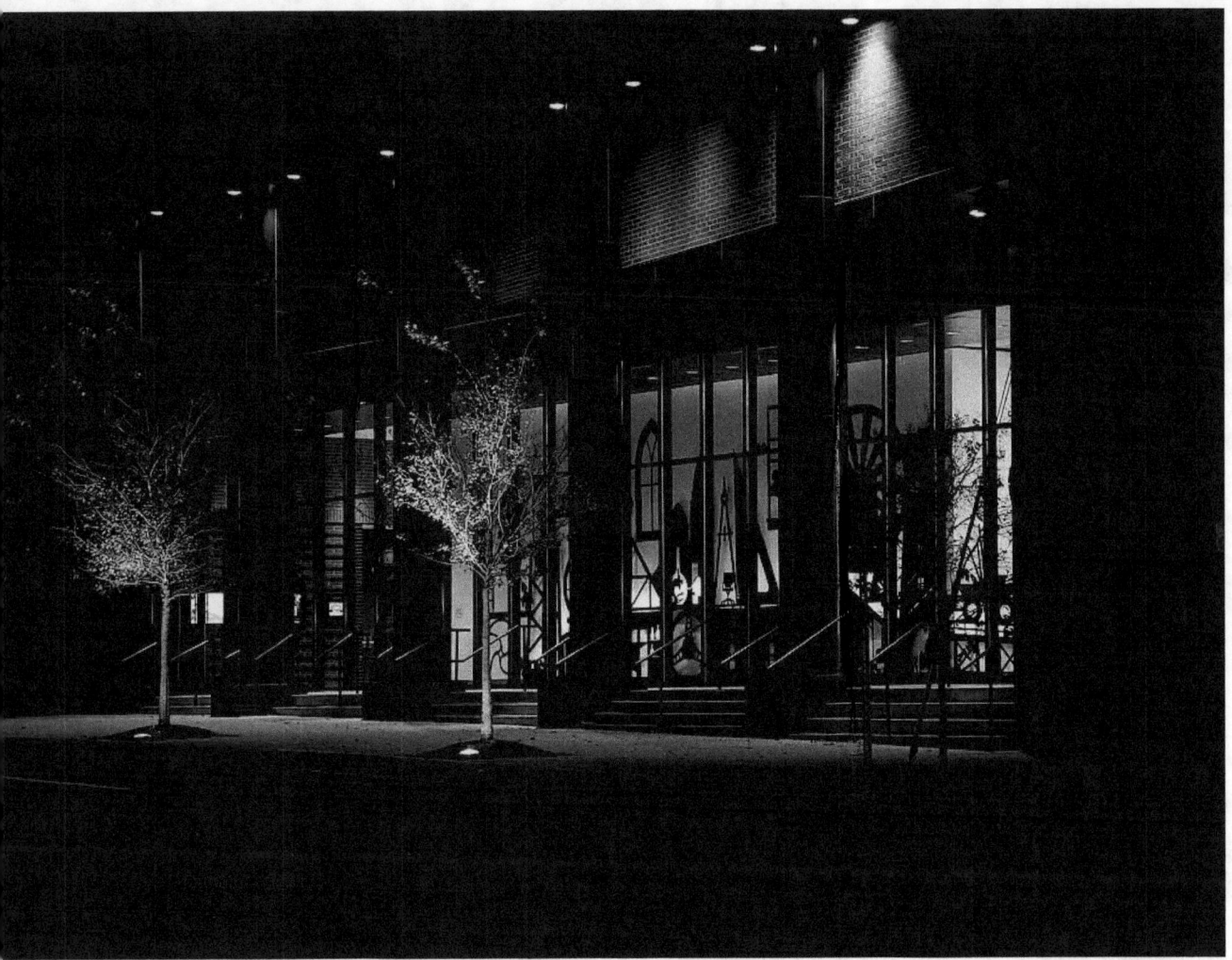

SINGLE

Something happened
In that space between
The time I quit my day
And the time I began my night

Something spoken
In that space between
Turned everything I wished
Into everything I knew

Something heard
In that space between
Turned yesterday's grim and cold
Into today's thousand tiny rainbows

Three simple words
Not even rare ones

Spoken every day by billions
Served up like fast food

But this time
A simple declarative sentence
Subject, verb, object
Became a feast

I didn't realize
How hungry I was
Until it was set before me
Having been that way so long

Something happened
And my hunger is gone
But the table remains full
What to do but share?

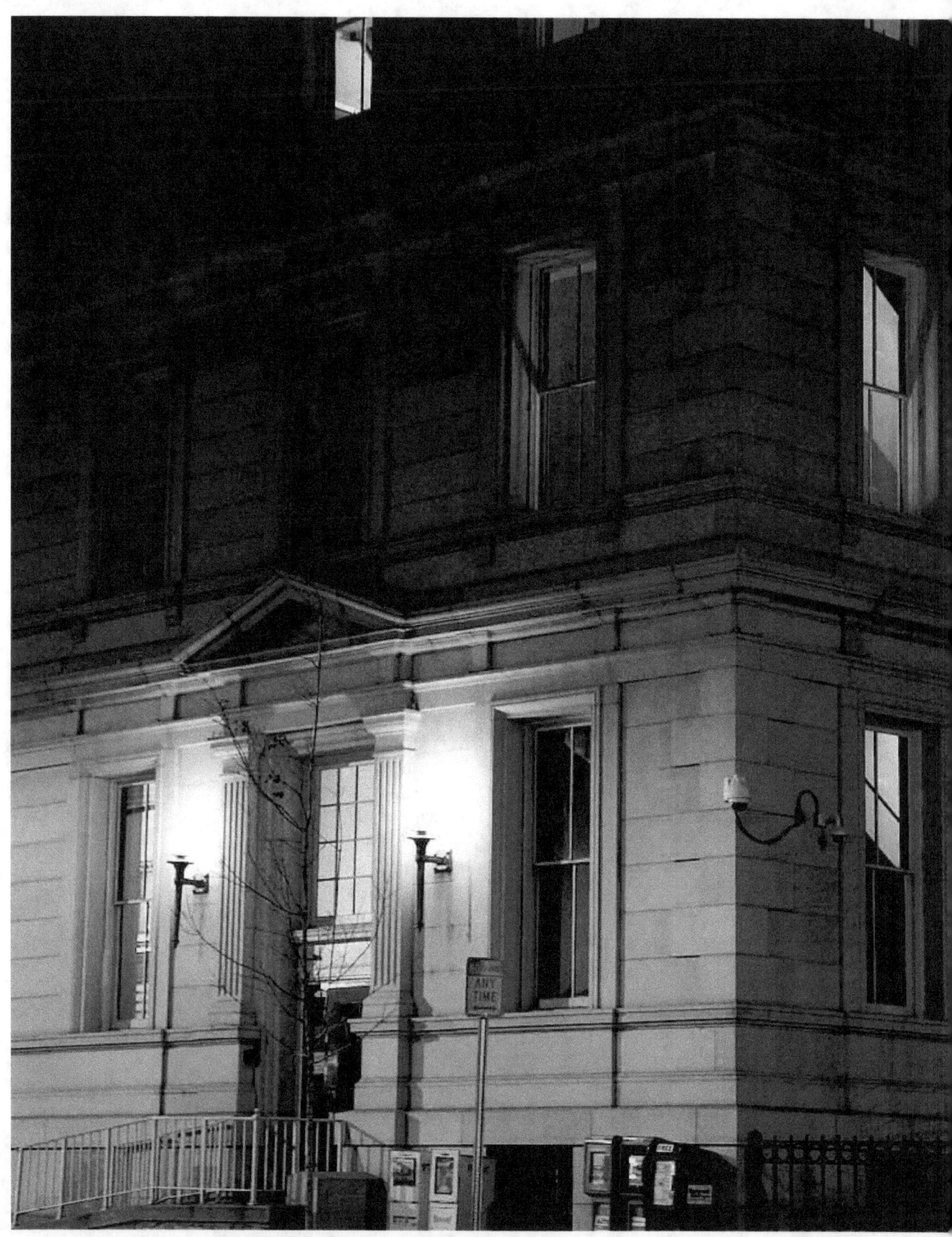

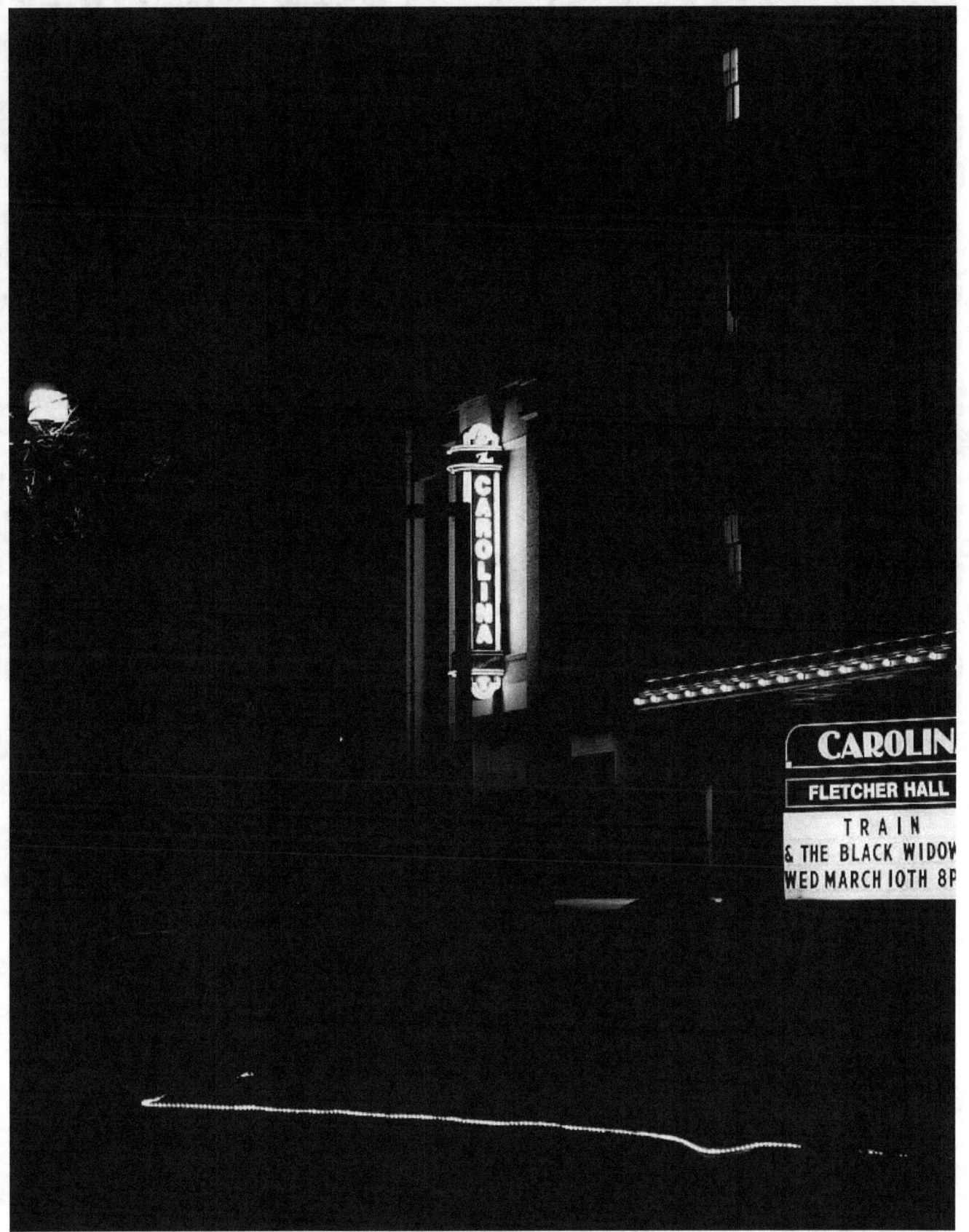

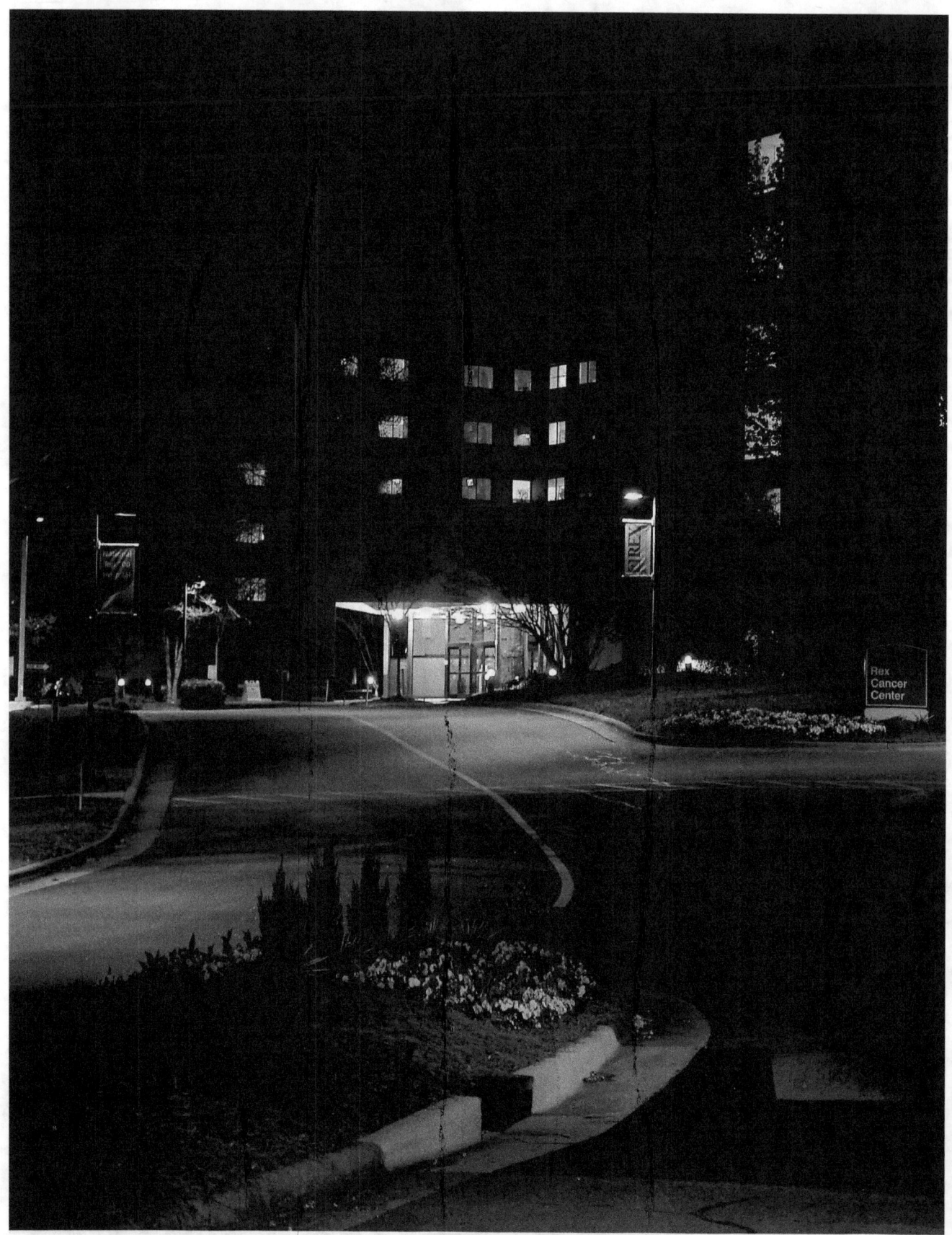

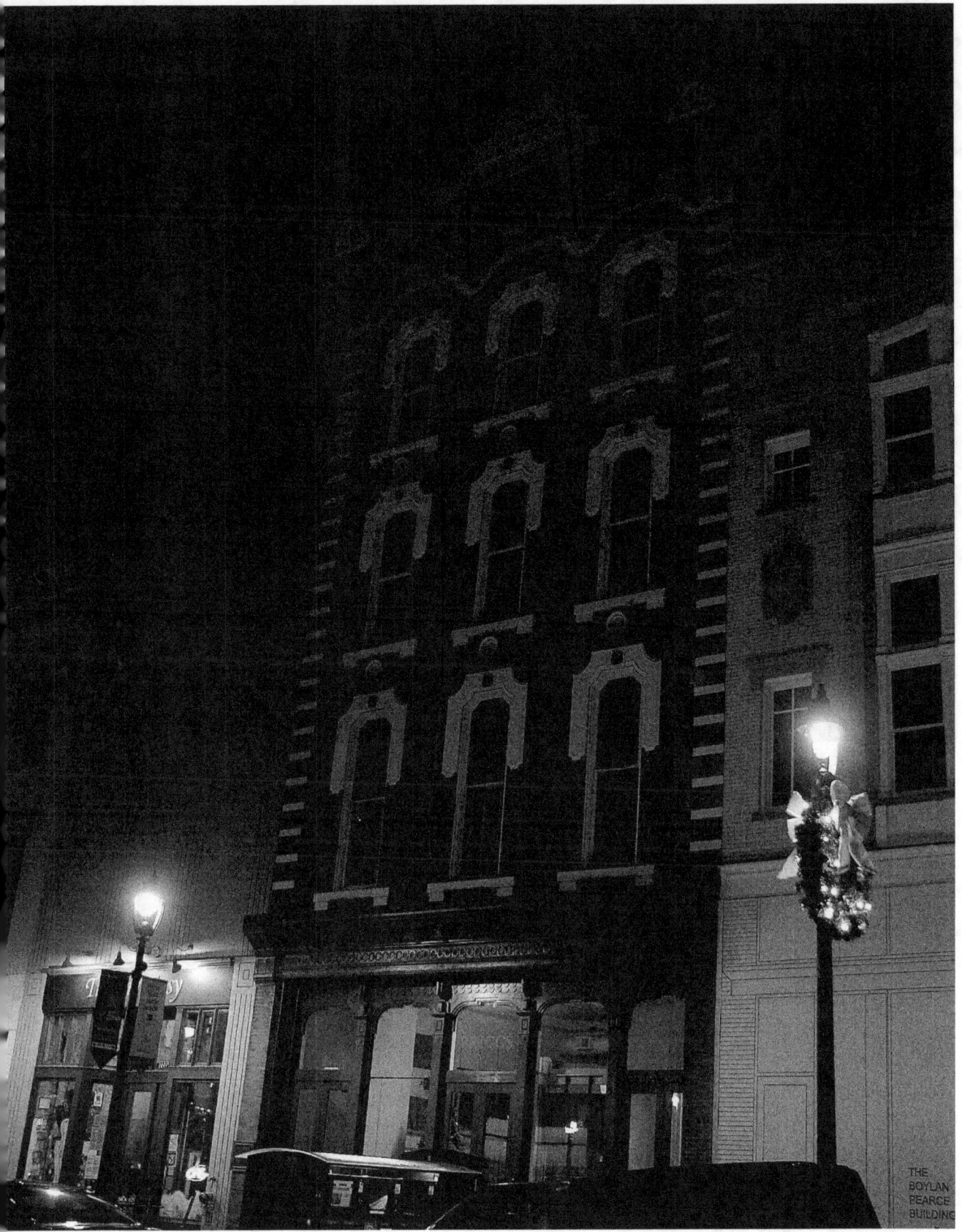

THE
BOYLAN
PEARCE
BUILDING

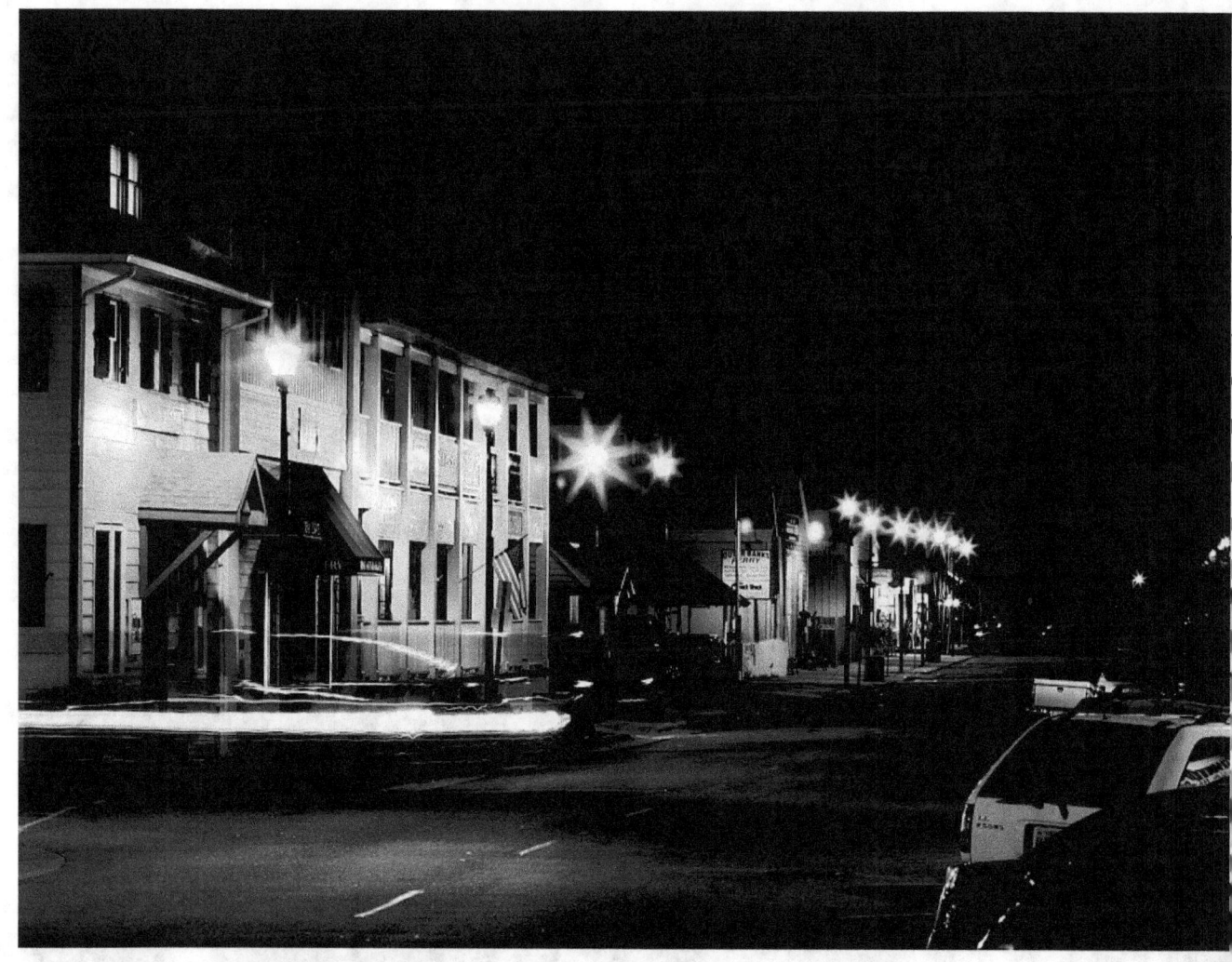

I Am Not Dreaming

I don't remember dreams
But if I did
I would remember the one
Where I stand on the beach
Scanning the ocean
Just beyond the breakers
Where the riptides don't reach
Where the swells are steep
Where you are.

But this is not a dream
This is the reality,
Metaphorical but no less real
That clings to my consciousness

I know you must do this
Must make this journey
I know you're strong
A much stronger swimmer

Than I will ever be
I also know
The mighty, indifferent force
Of the ocean.
So I search for you
Among the swells and the foam
Amid the ocean's vastness
You are not afraid I imagine
Not nearly so terrified as I
Who can only watch and wait
For you to return to shore.

I pray for your safety
Pacing the shoreline
And weeping at the need
For you to be so far out at all.

If I remembered dreams
I would remember this one.

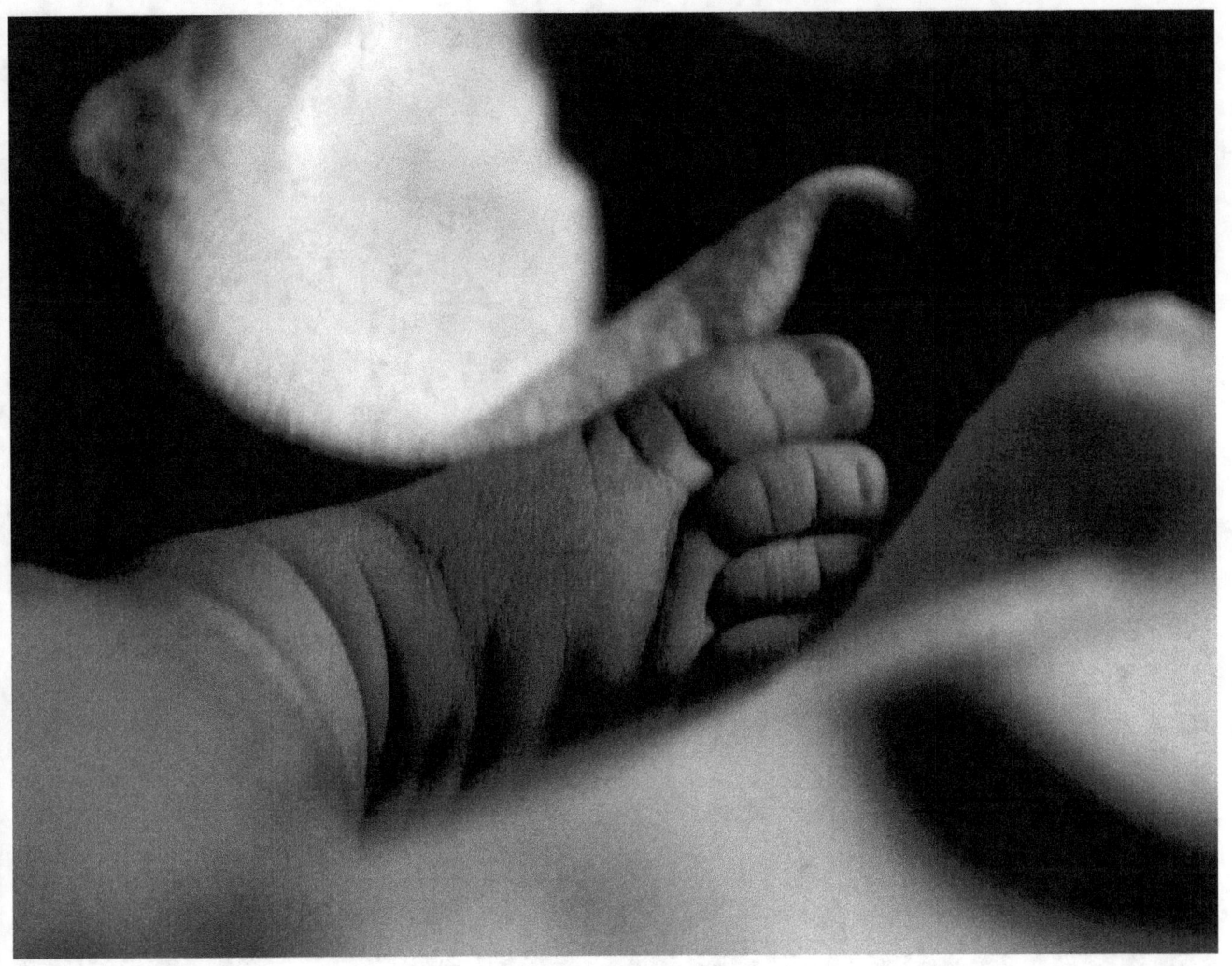

DISCOVERY

Watching my son
Discover his son
This new life
This new person
I think of all the
Fathers that came
Before him
Before me
Before even
My father
Introduced himself to me
In a way I imagine to be
Not very different
From what I am watching
Unfold before me

In that moment
When life is new
And you haven't yet
Had the chance
To do anything wrong
Your child, your bond
Your moment
Is perfect
Unblemished by
Misunderstanding
Or broken curfews
Or missed recitals
Possibility
Is limitless

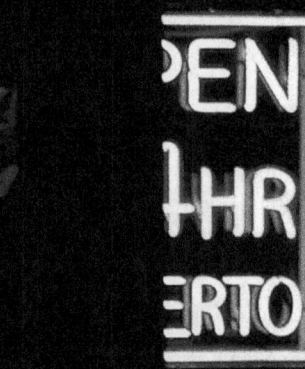

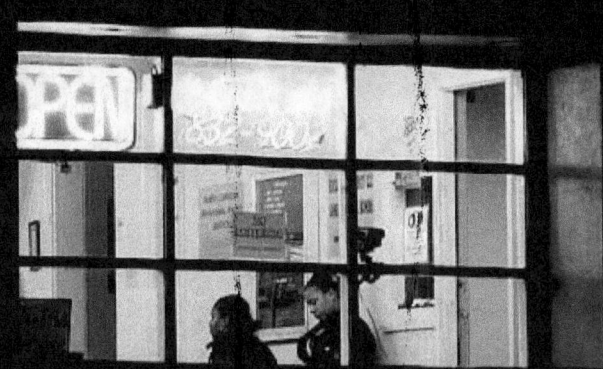

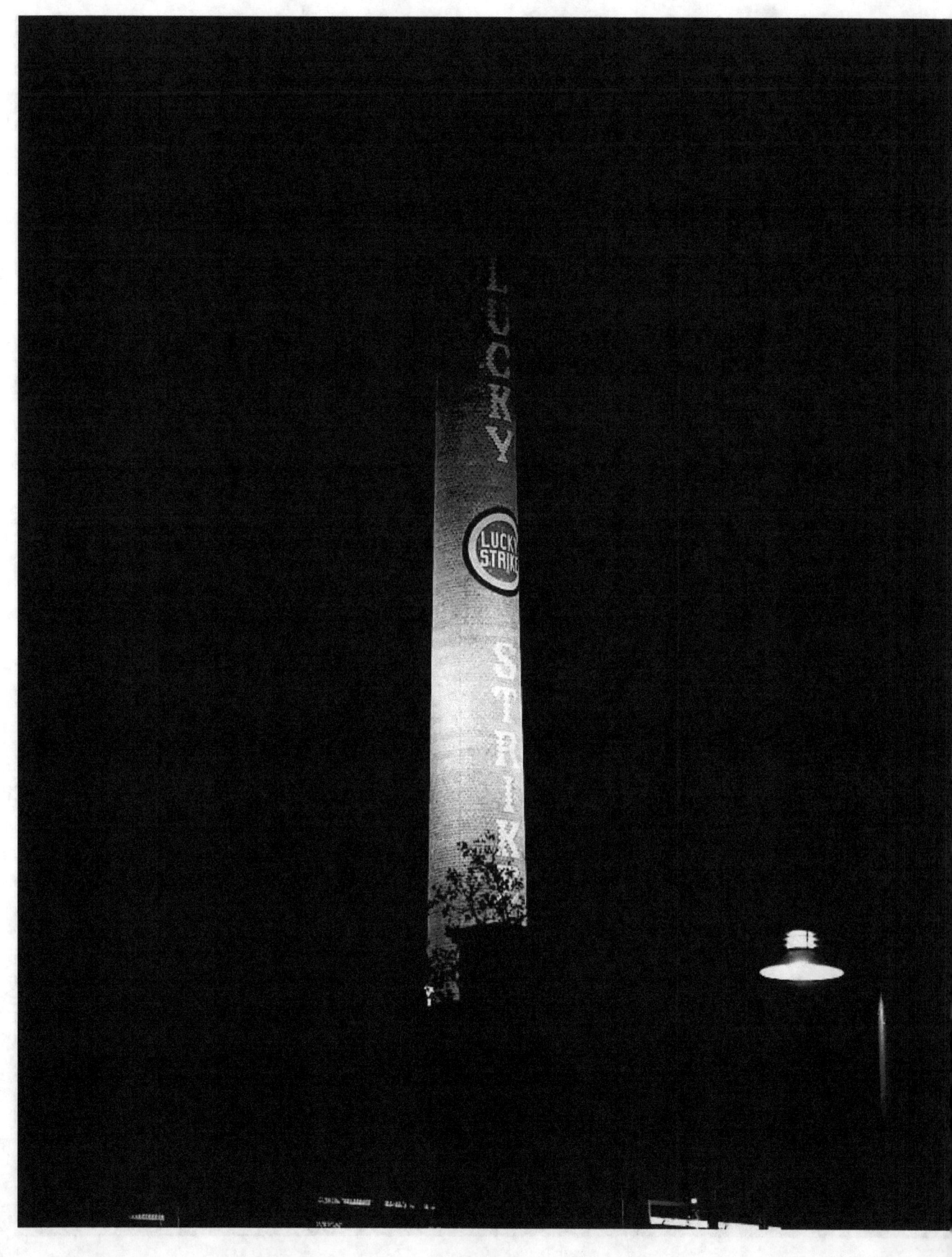

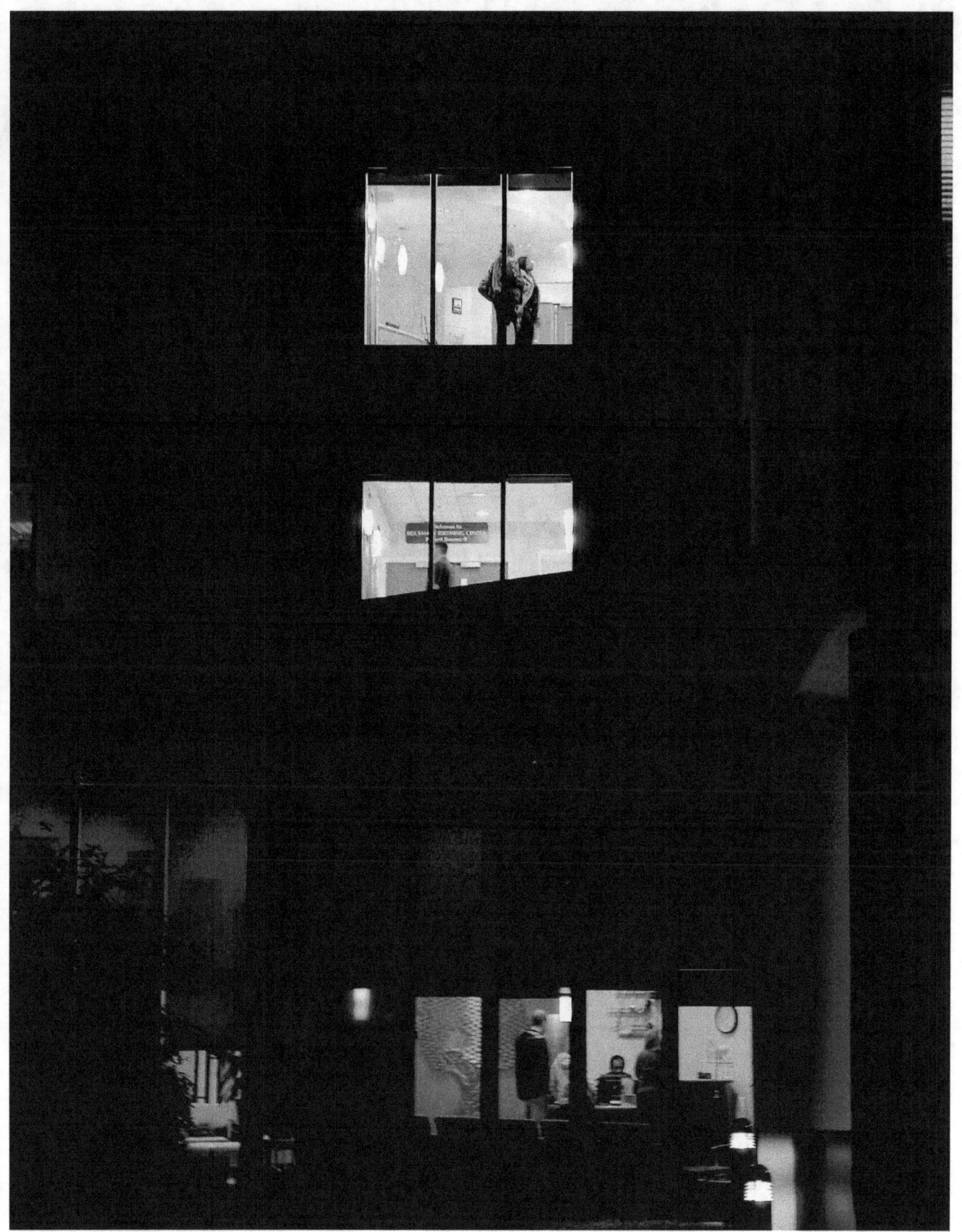

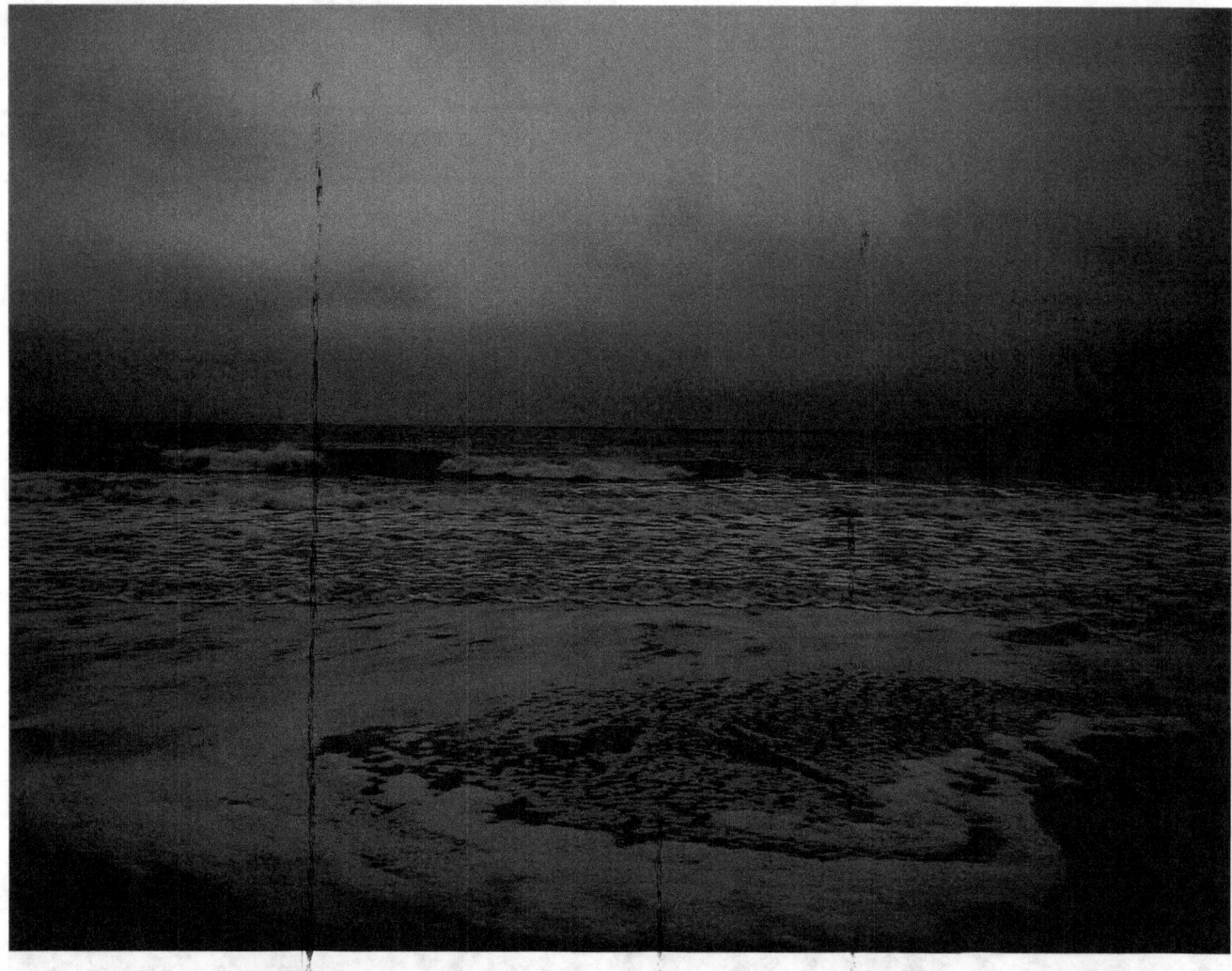

Murmur (I)

A hundred miles away
The ocean murmurs to me
A single word
"Remember"
No others are needed
And in truth
Not even that one
I remember perfectly
I cannot forget
The streaks of frozen crystalline white
Punctuating perfect blue
The sketches the birds drew
On the canvas of the shore
The biting wind, the brilliance
Of the sun unfiltered
How we laughed at the sandpipers
Fleeing the waves that feed them
Marveled at the tide
Pulled up tight like a blanket
Under the shore's chin by a maternal moon

A murmur, *"Remember"*
I remember
A laugh, a touch,
A kiss I'd dared not hope for
In my most unbridled imagination
We planted our flag
Claimed the beachhead as our own
In that pristine moment
Only you and I existed
A day in a life
A life in a day
If I am dreaming, never let me wake, I said
If I am awake, never let me sleep, I said
It seems long ago
Since the searing blue of boundless promise
Deepened to the purple ache of longing
And a restless heart
Alone in the night
First murmured your name
Just to hear it.

Please say you remember.

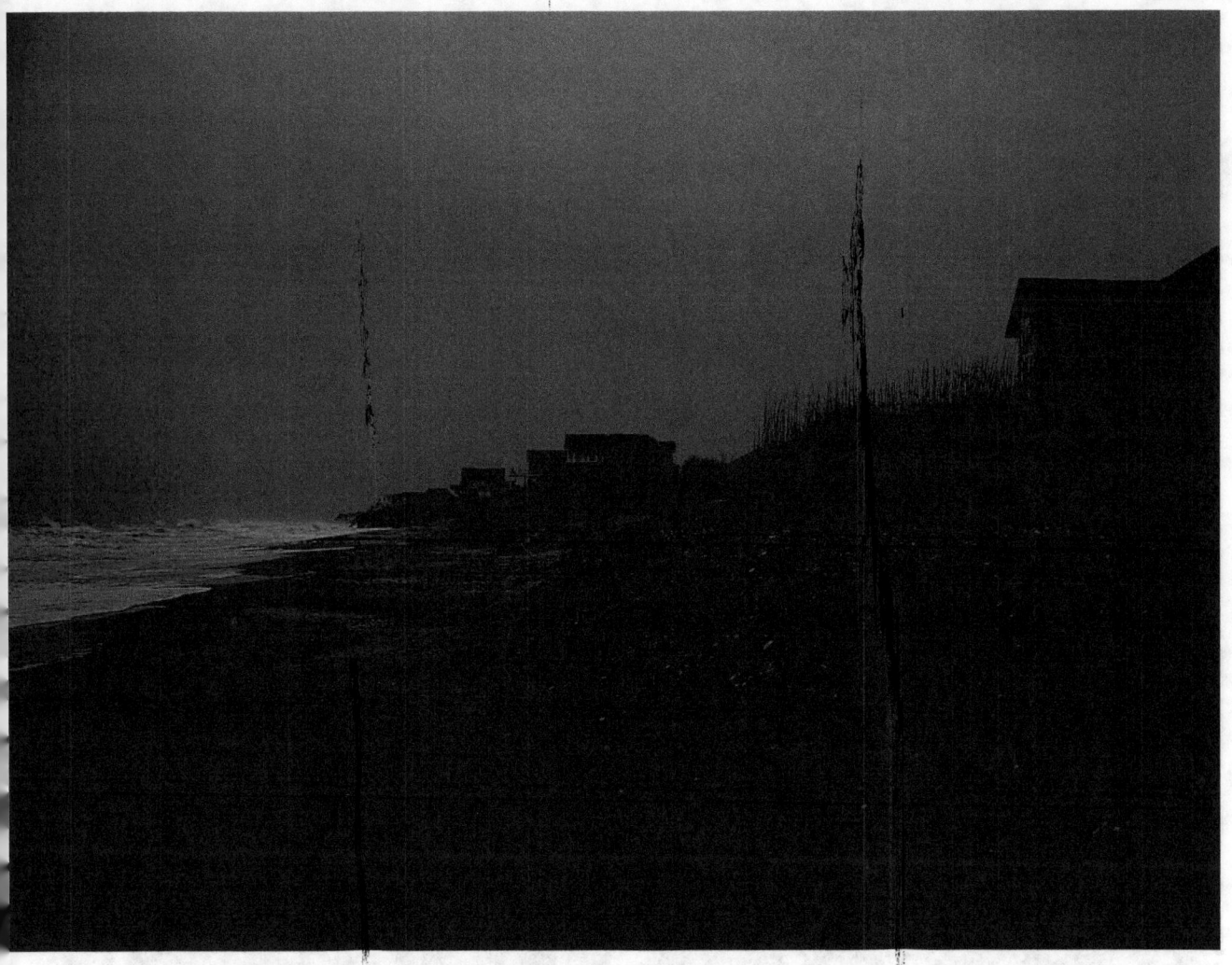

MURMUR (II)

In the twisted dark of sleeplessness
The ceiling fan murmurs
Mocking my attempts at rest.
My dog murmurs
Dreaming whatever dogs dream.
And I rise.

In the cool, damp dark of pre-dawn
The highway murmurs
As truck tires sing a weary work song.
My heart murmurs
As the silence presses in from all sides.
And I listen.

In the jumbled dark of my mind
The ocean murmurs
Its pulse echoing my own.
My lips murmur
"I remember".
And I remember.

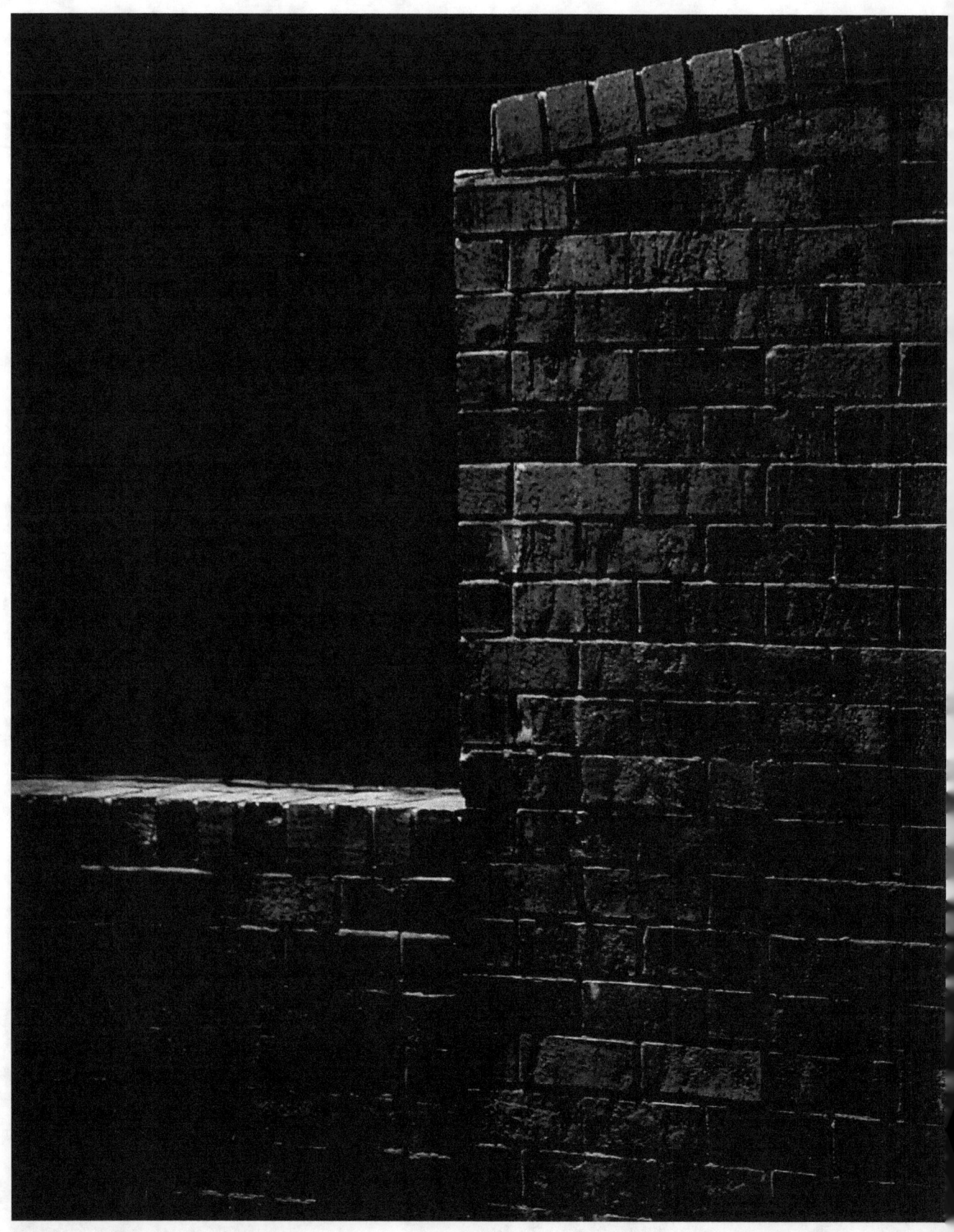

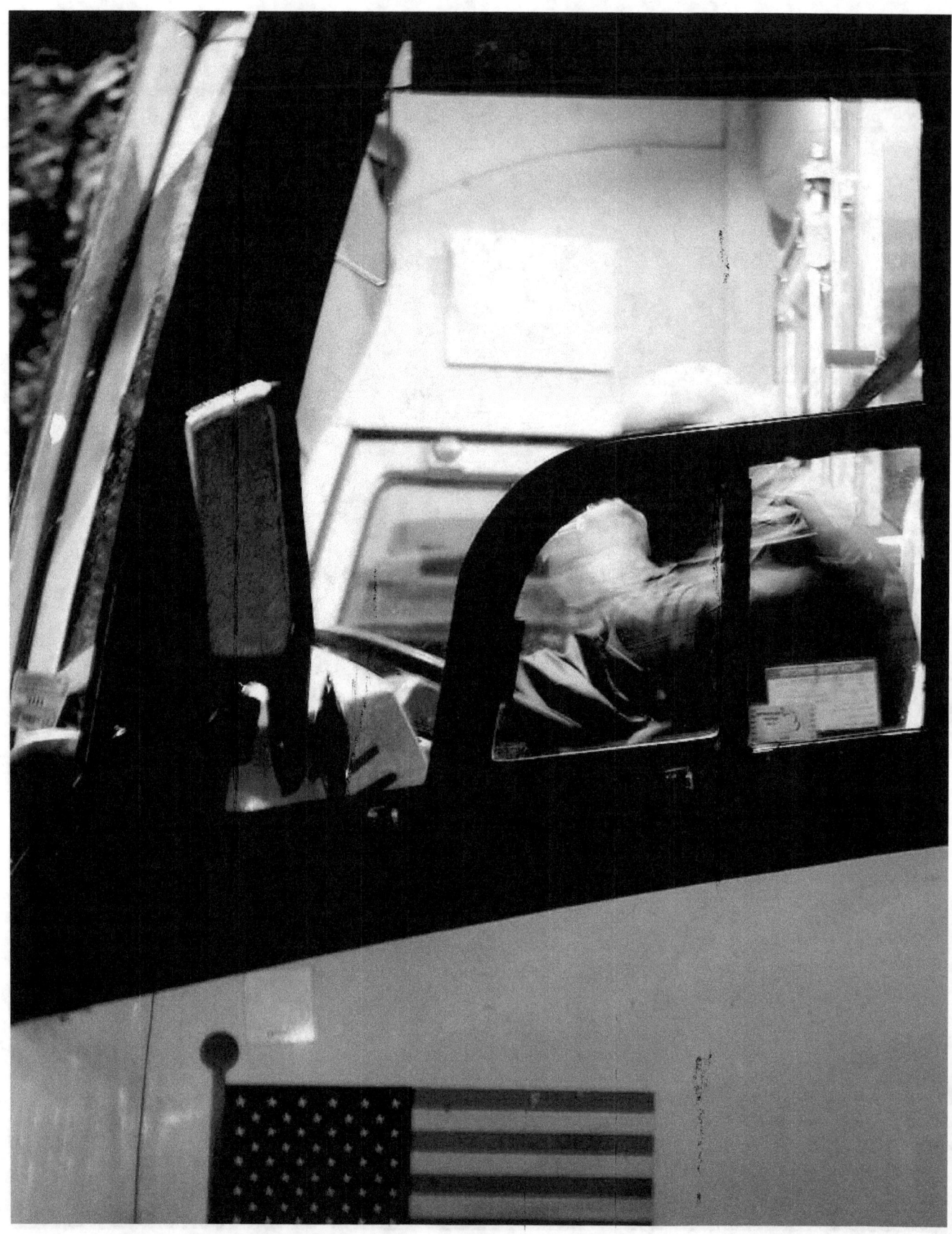

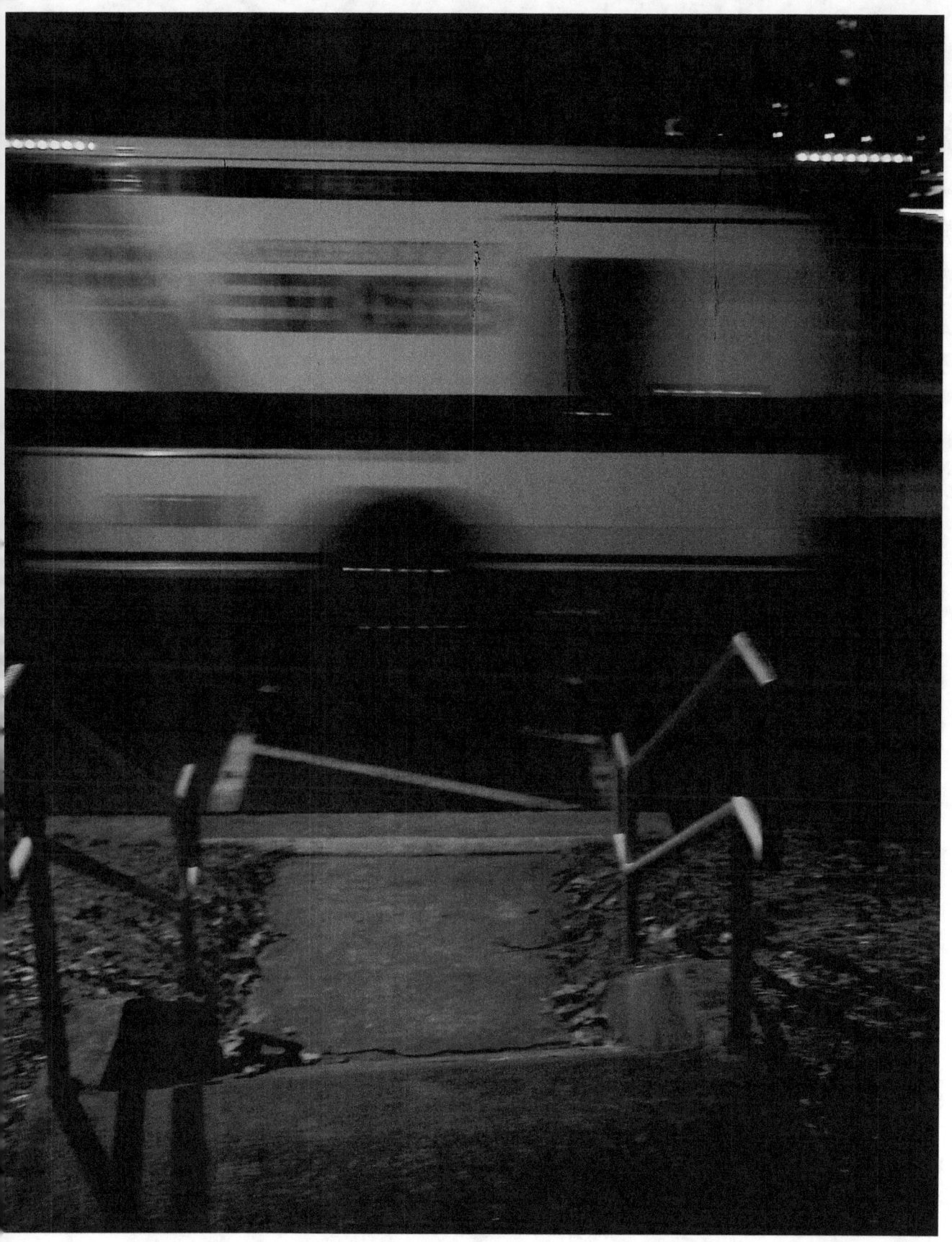

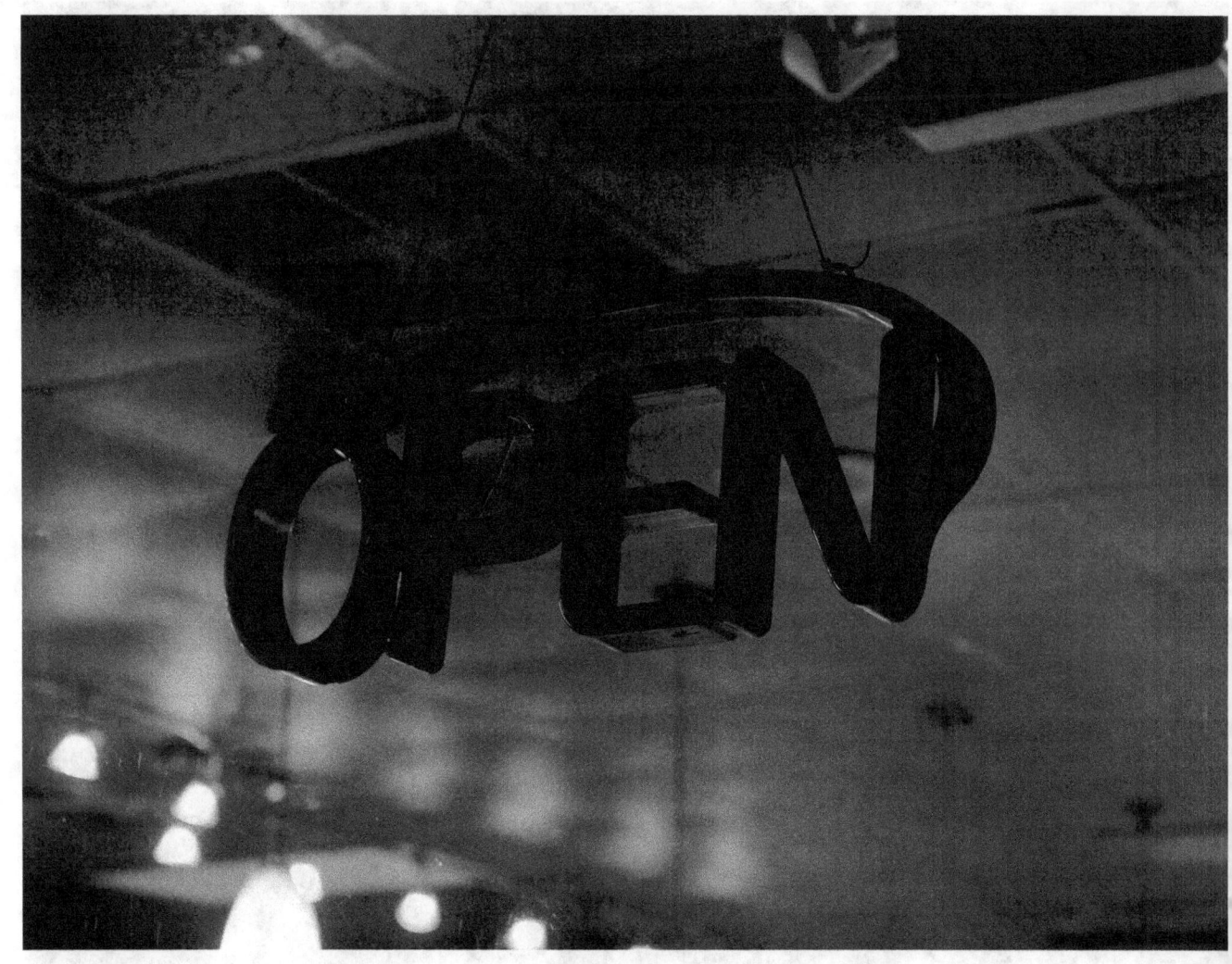

Capitulation

Read the final page
It will tell you everything
You ever need know

———————

You know more ways to
Hide than I know ways to seek
You can come out now

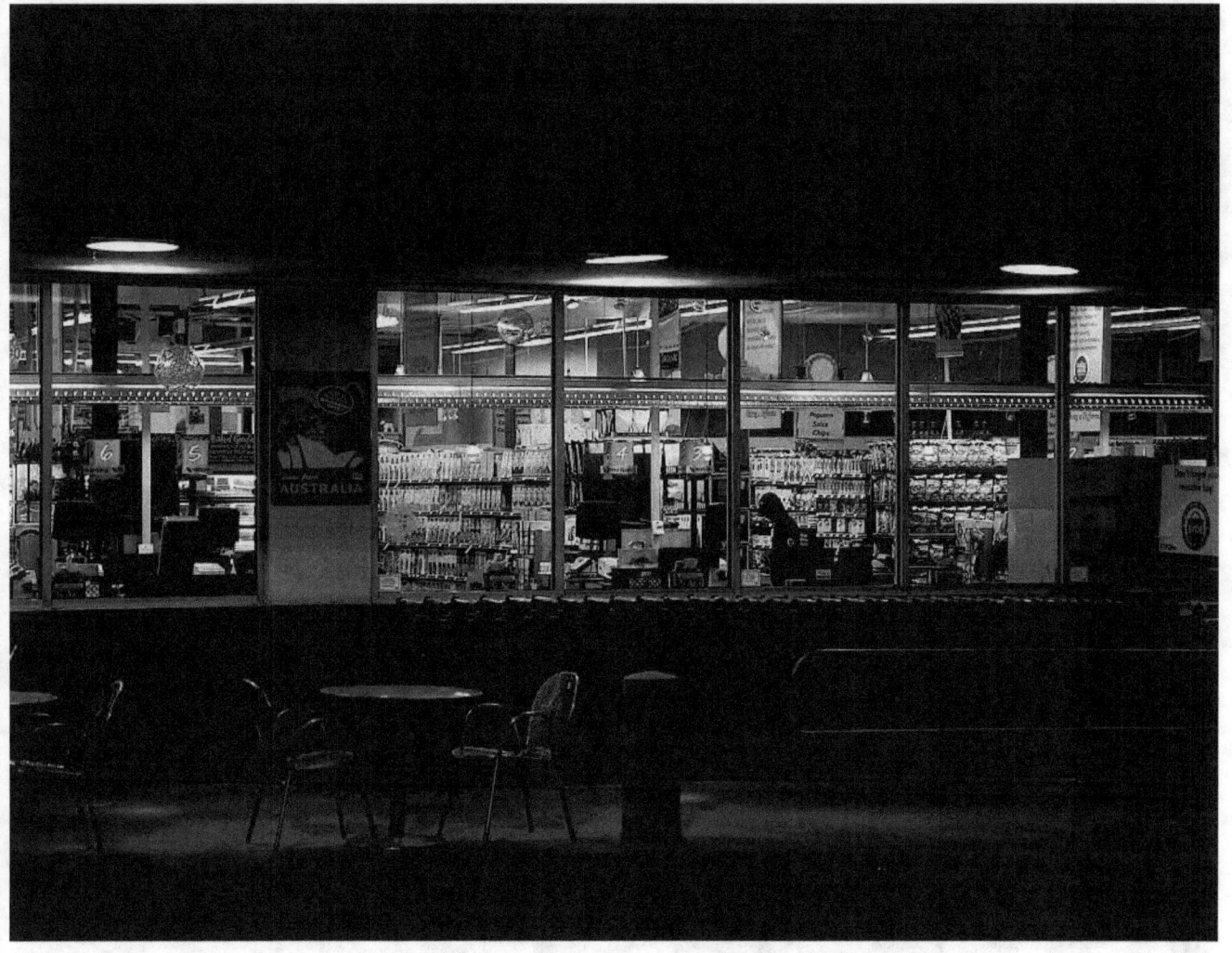

Silence

"Silence is Golden."
Who says so?
Who decided,
And why,
That silence is
Something to be valued,
Prized as gold?

Who was it
That was possessed
Of enough wisdom
That he could know
The nature of something
That by that very nature
Is unknowable?

Is silence gold?
Or is it dross?
Or is it neither of these?
Is it as it appears,

Simply formless, shapeless
An absence of anything, really.
A void.

The airless vacuum
Of the space that
Surrounds me
Engulfs me
The highwayman that
Steals my breath
My sleep.

If only
I could bring
The silence without
Inside where it might
Serve some purpose
Quiet the chorus within
I might feel differently.

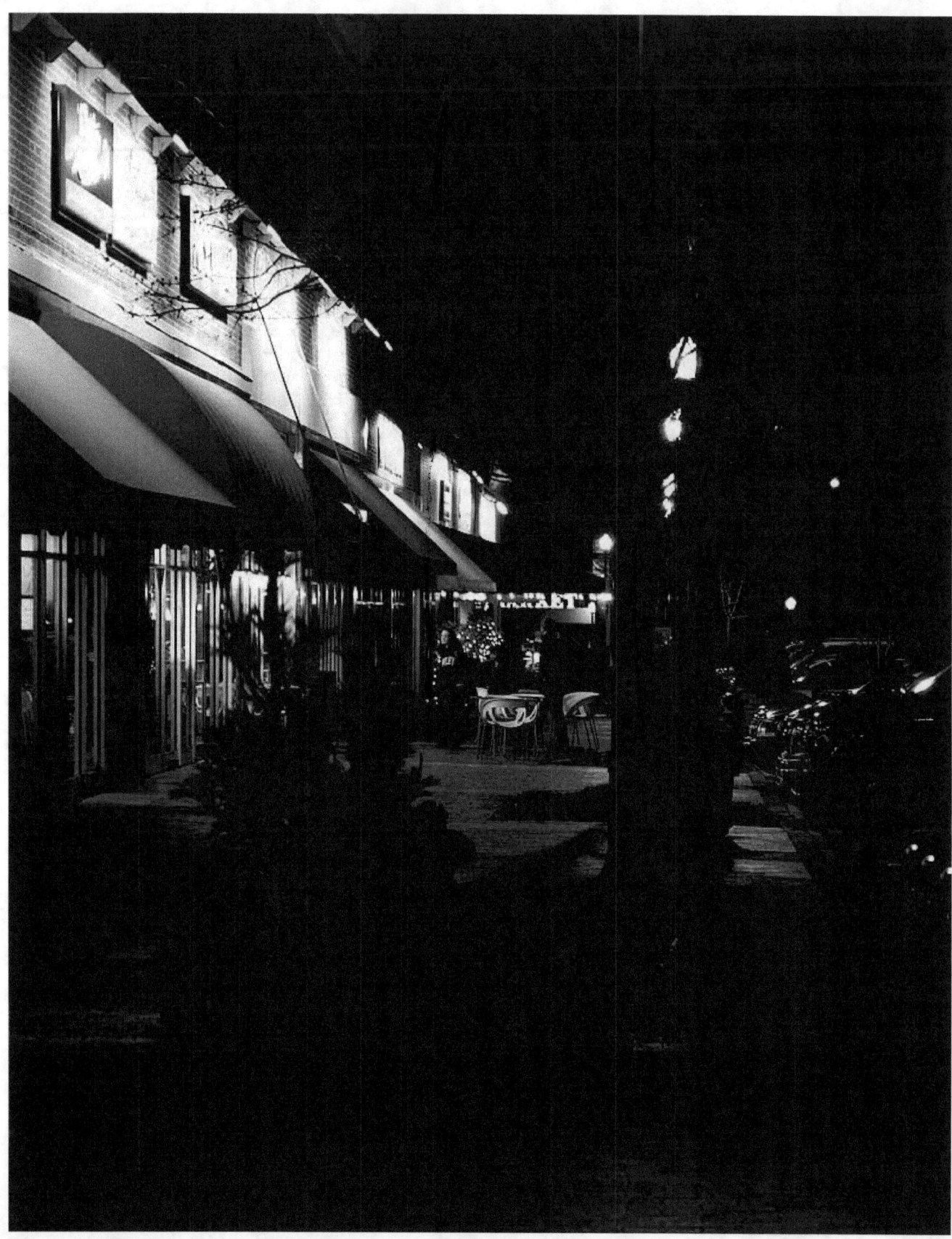

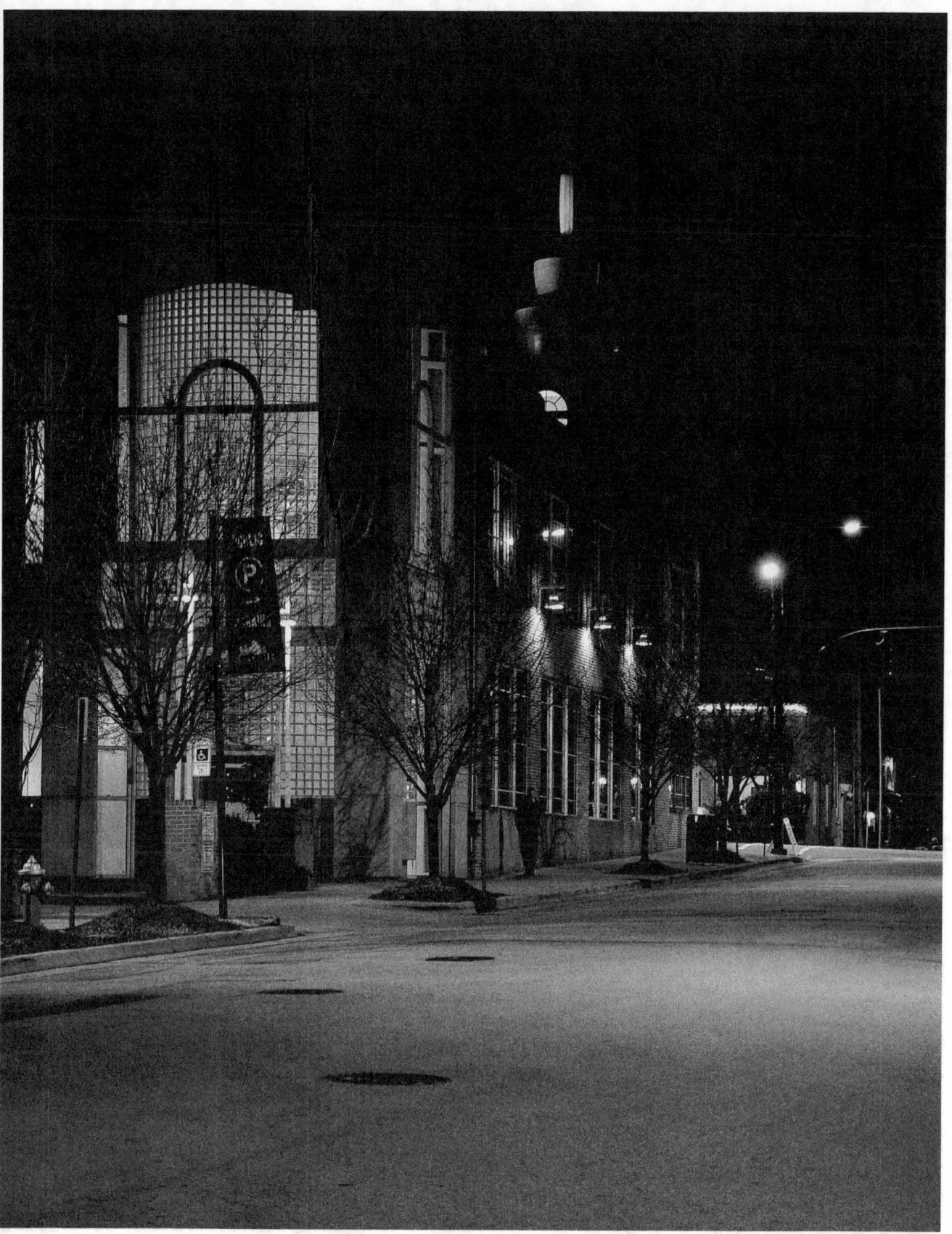

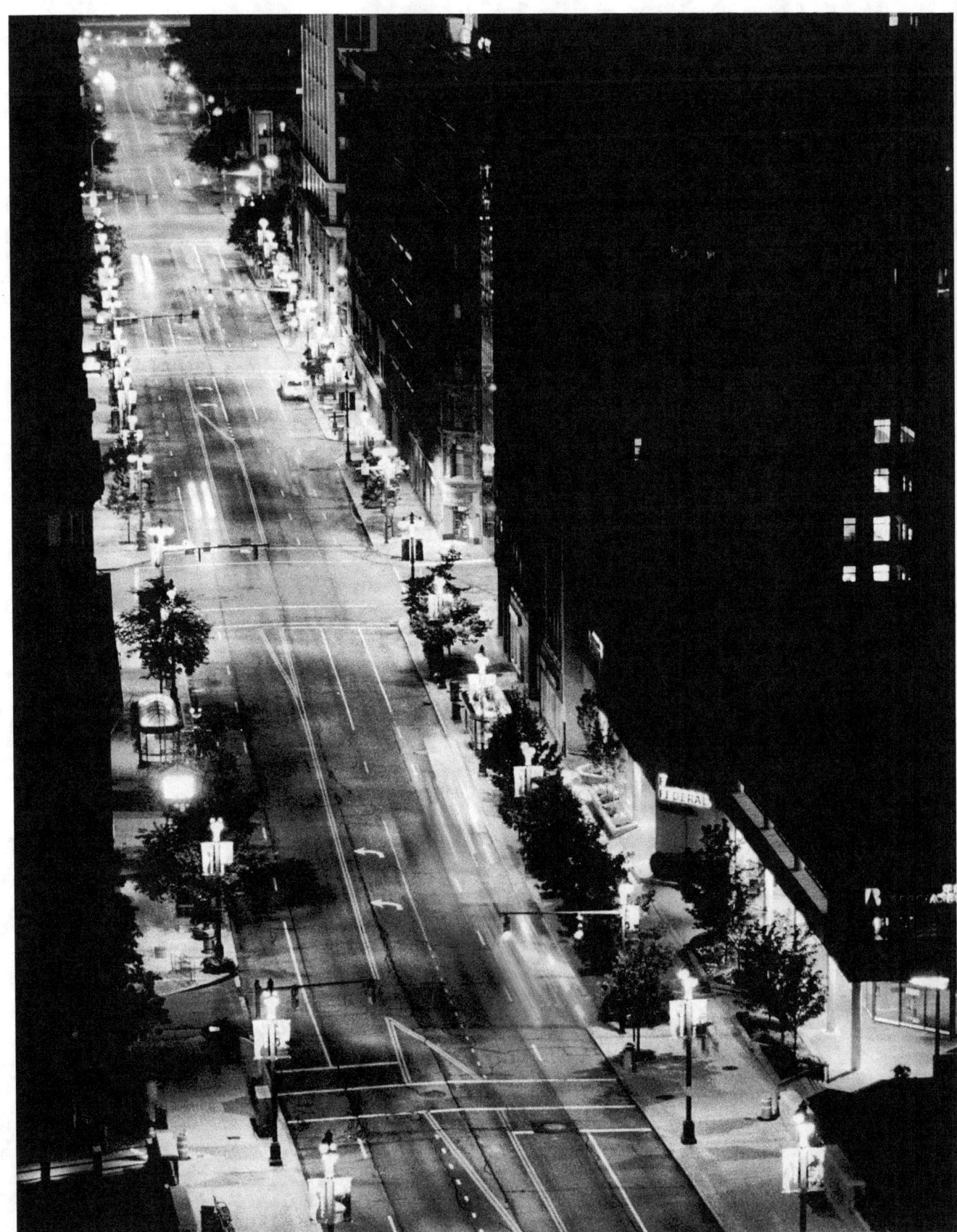

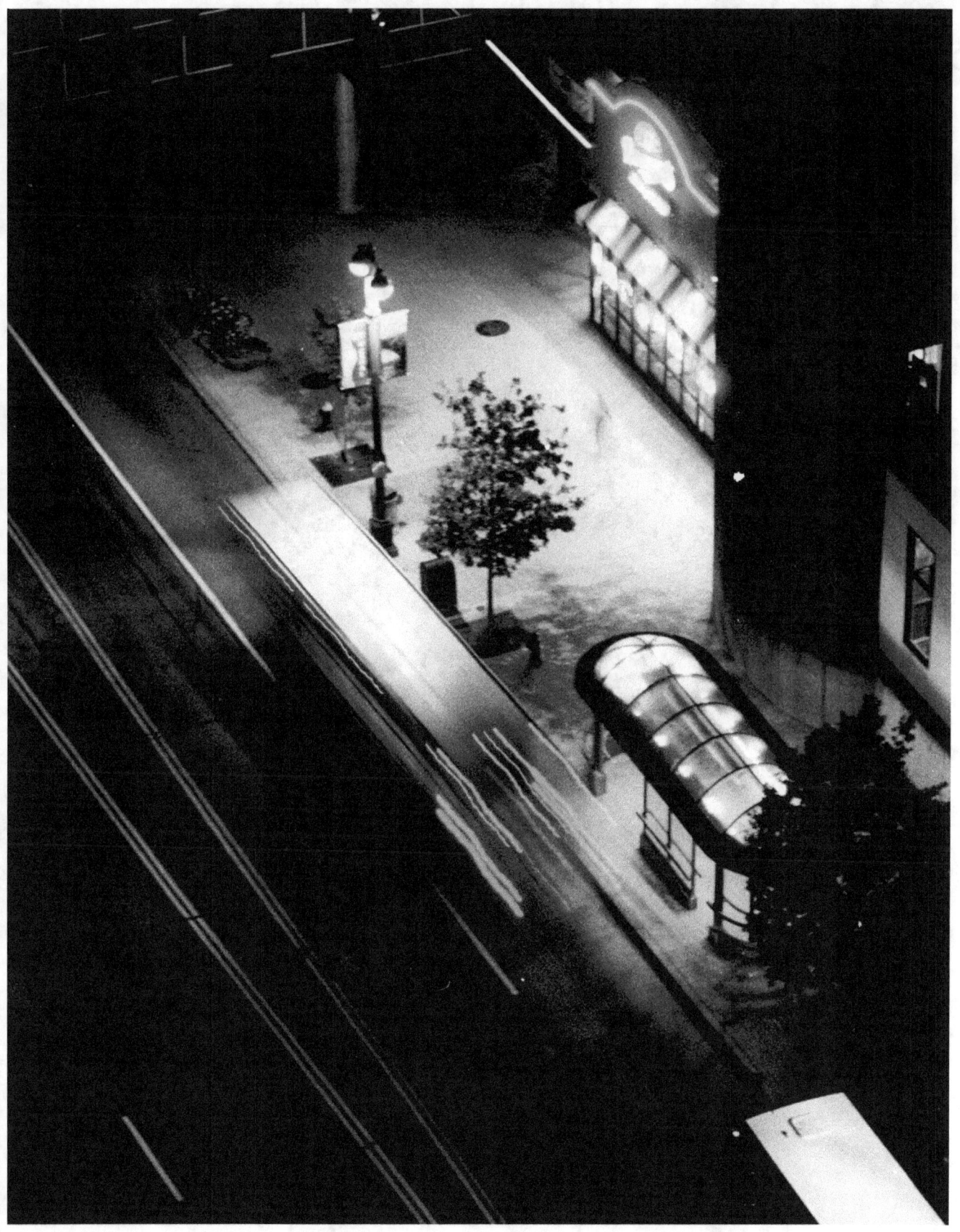

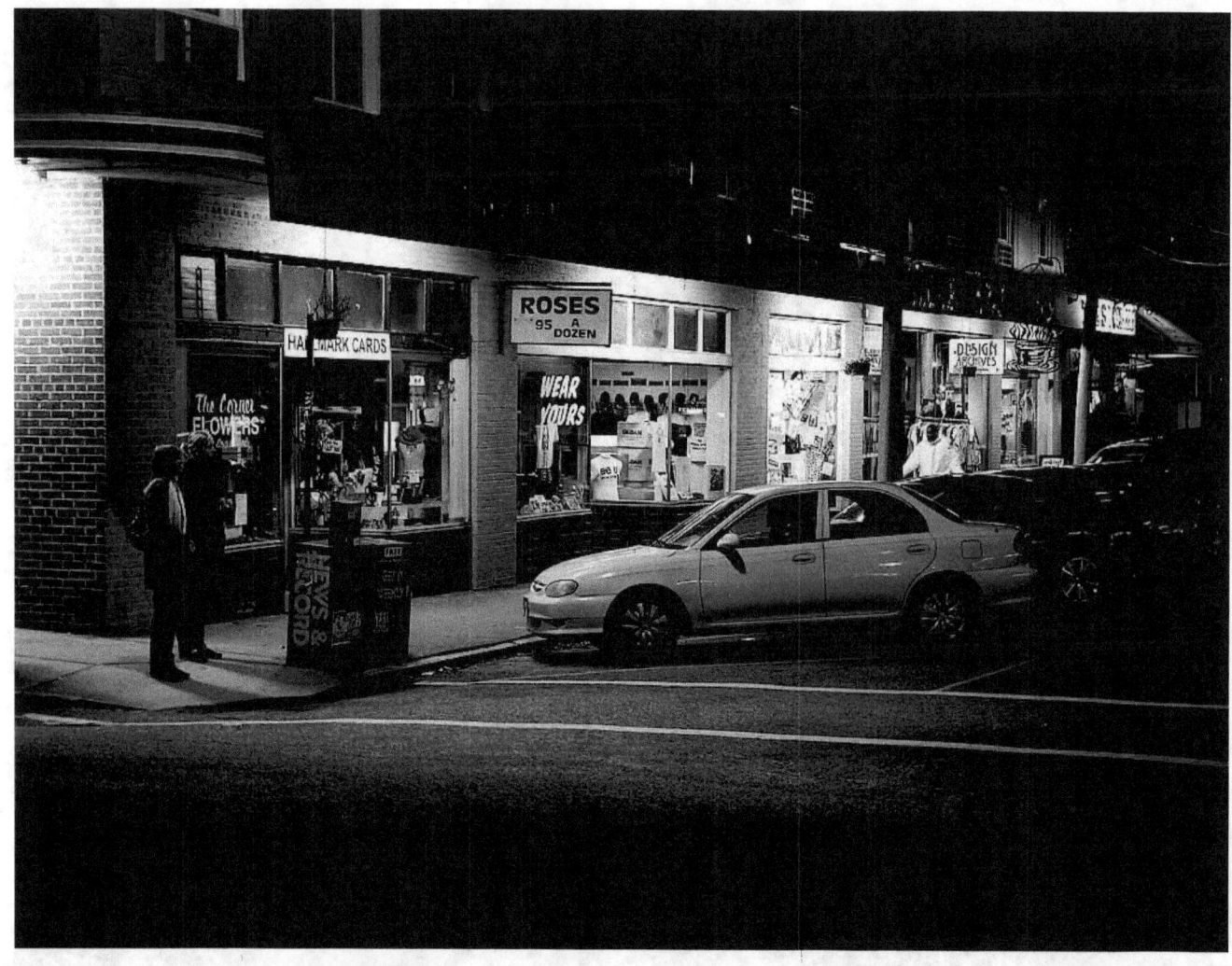

DON'T SAY ANYTHING

Yellow fringe
Edges the purple blossom
A remnant
Of what passes for love
Don't say
Anything
It will only make it worse
It will
Get better if I can only
Be better
If I can only
Do better
If I can only

Make it better
He doesn't
Mean to do it
It just happens
A loss of control
A few too many
It's my fault really
I should have known
Better
Don't say
Anything
I know

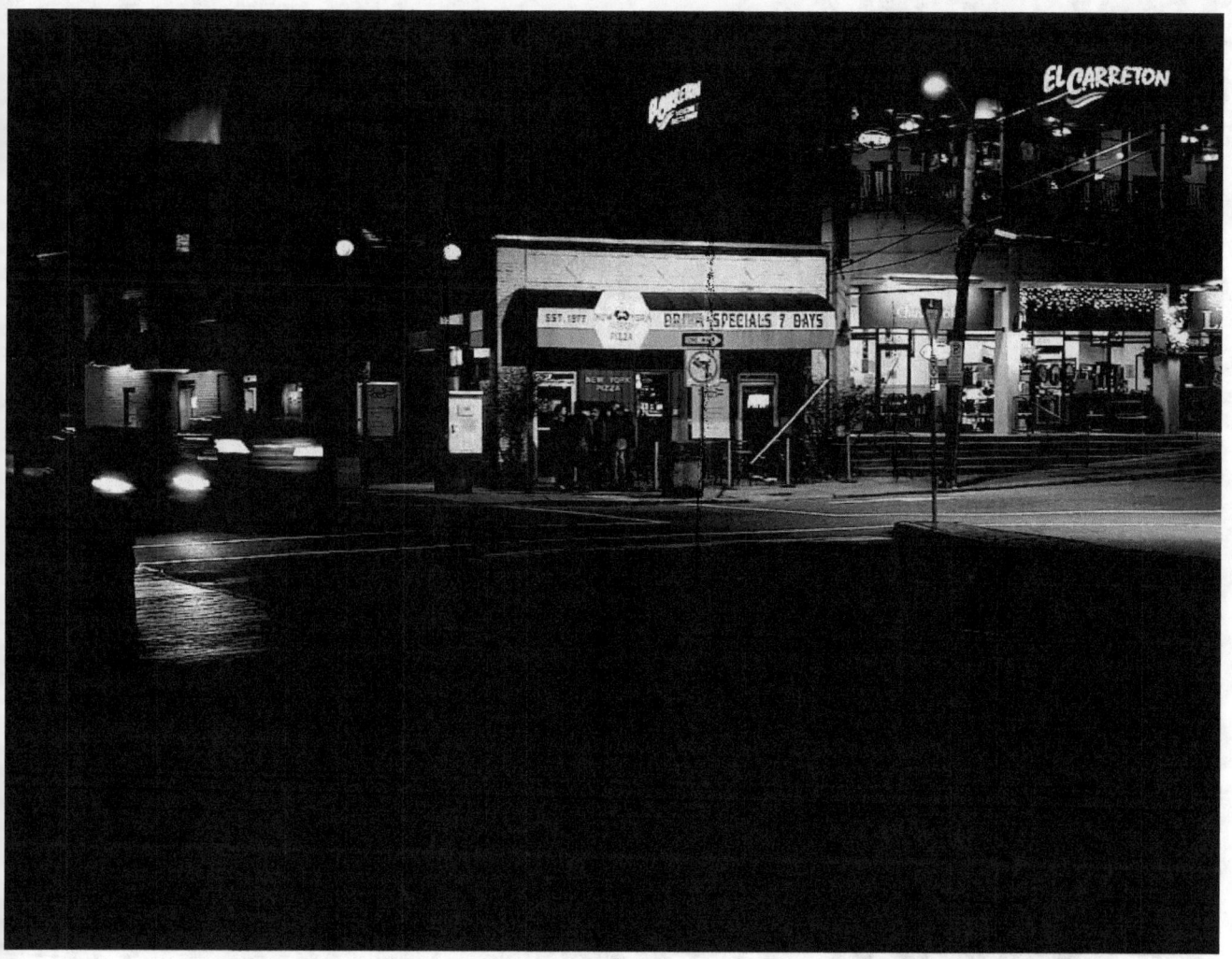

HIDE AND SEEK

We're strange, you and I
Such similar creatures
Both wanting what we fear
Both fearing what we want
Both longing to be able to
Embrace
This feeling
Satisfy
This hunger
Soothe
This ache.

And so we dance
This dance of friends
Now and then
Dancing closer
Then quickly returning
To the classical form

Breathlessly aware
How close we came
To crossing the line
Between what we desire
And what we have.

We're strange, you and I
We wish, we hope, we dream
We know the risk
We can't know the reward
And so we play
This game of
Hiding in plain sight
Only from ourselves
It seems
We were
The last to know.

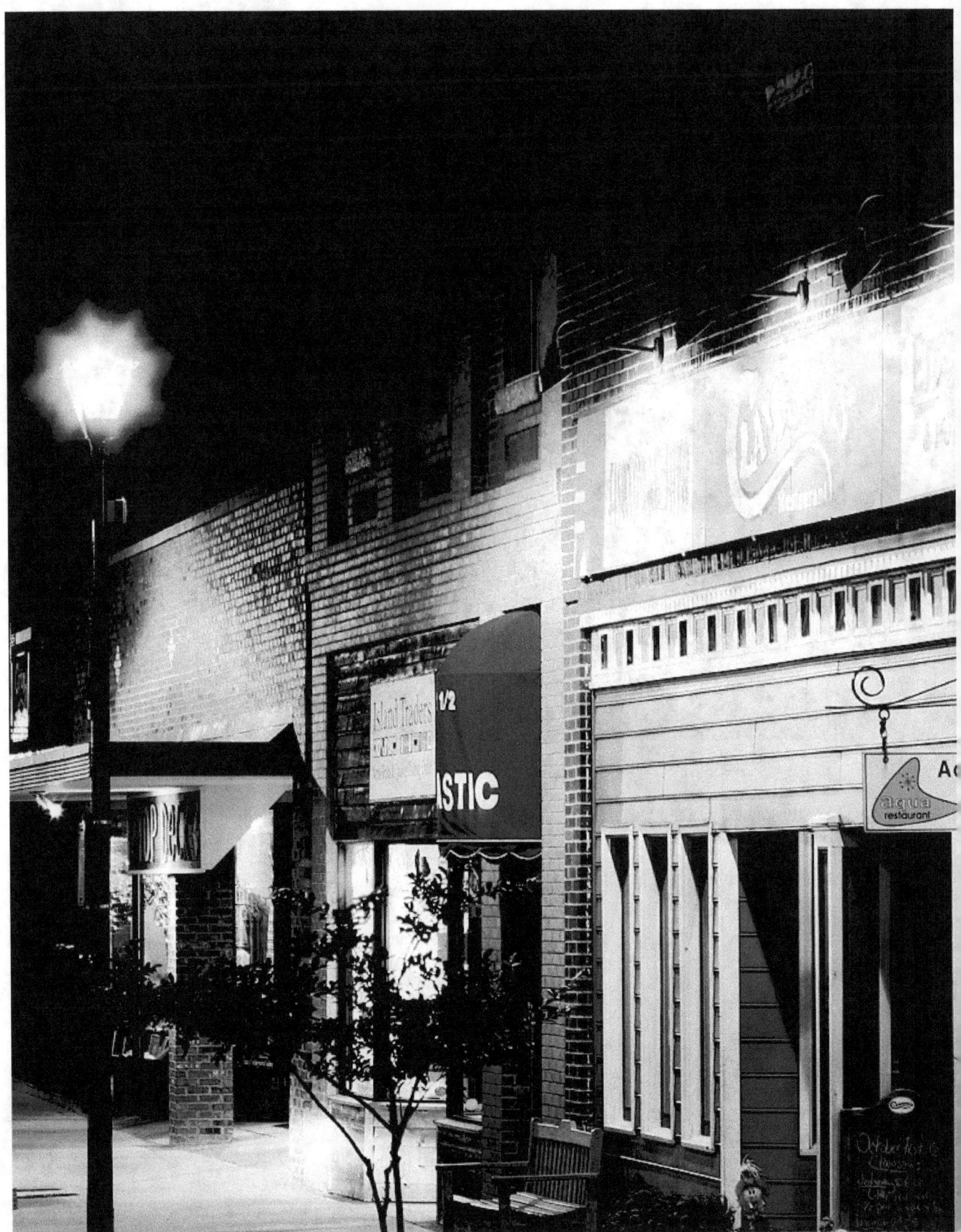

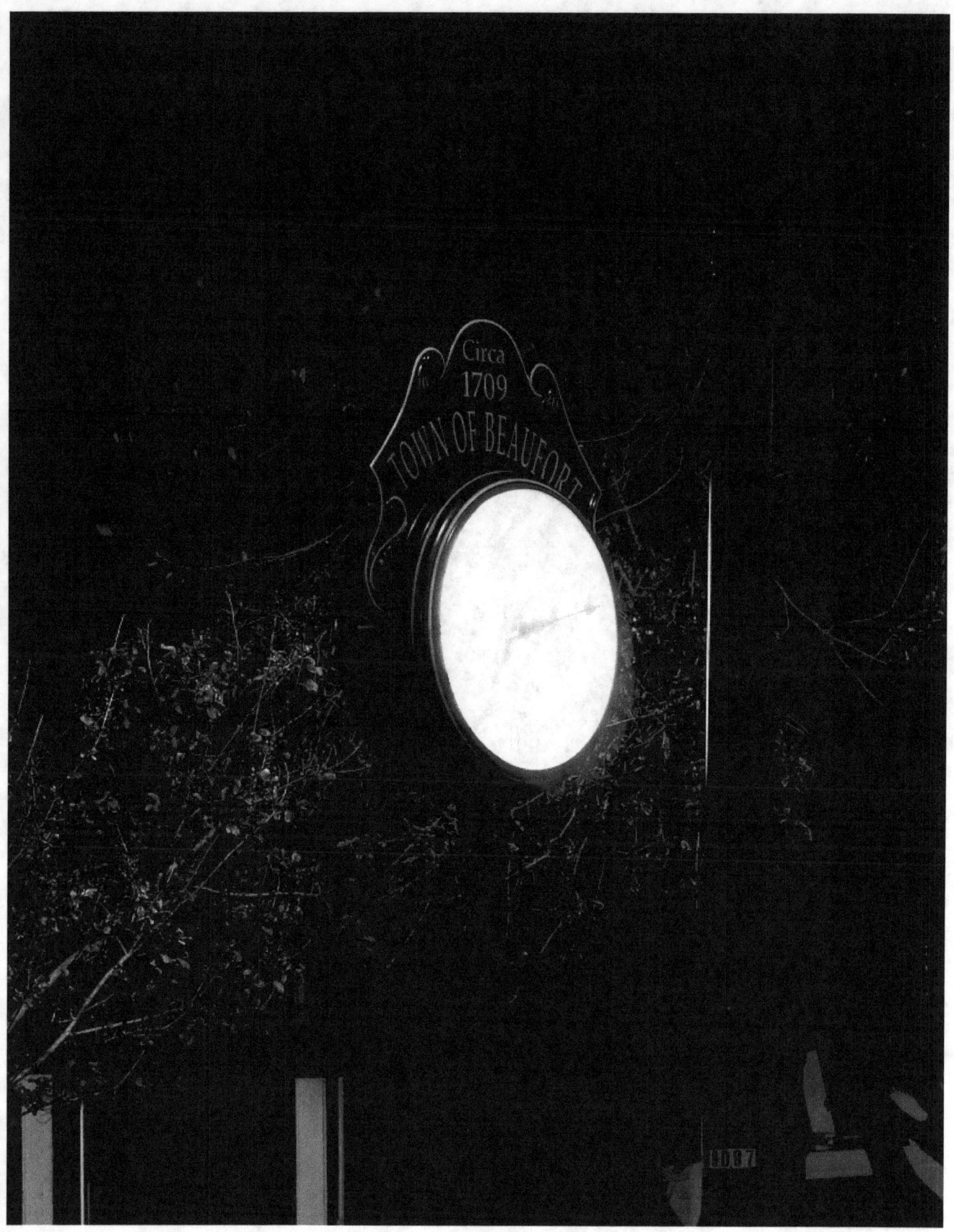

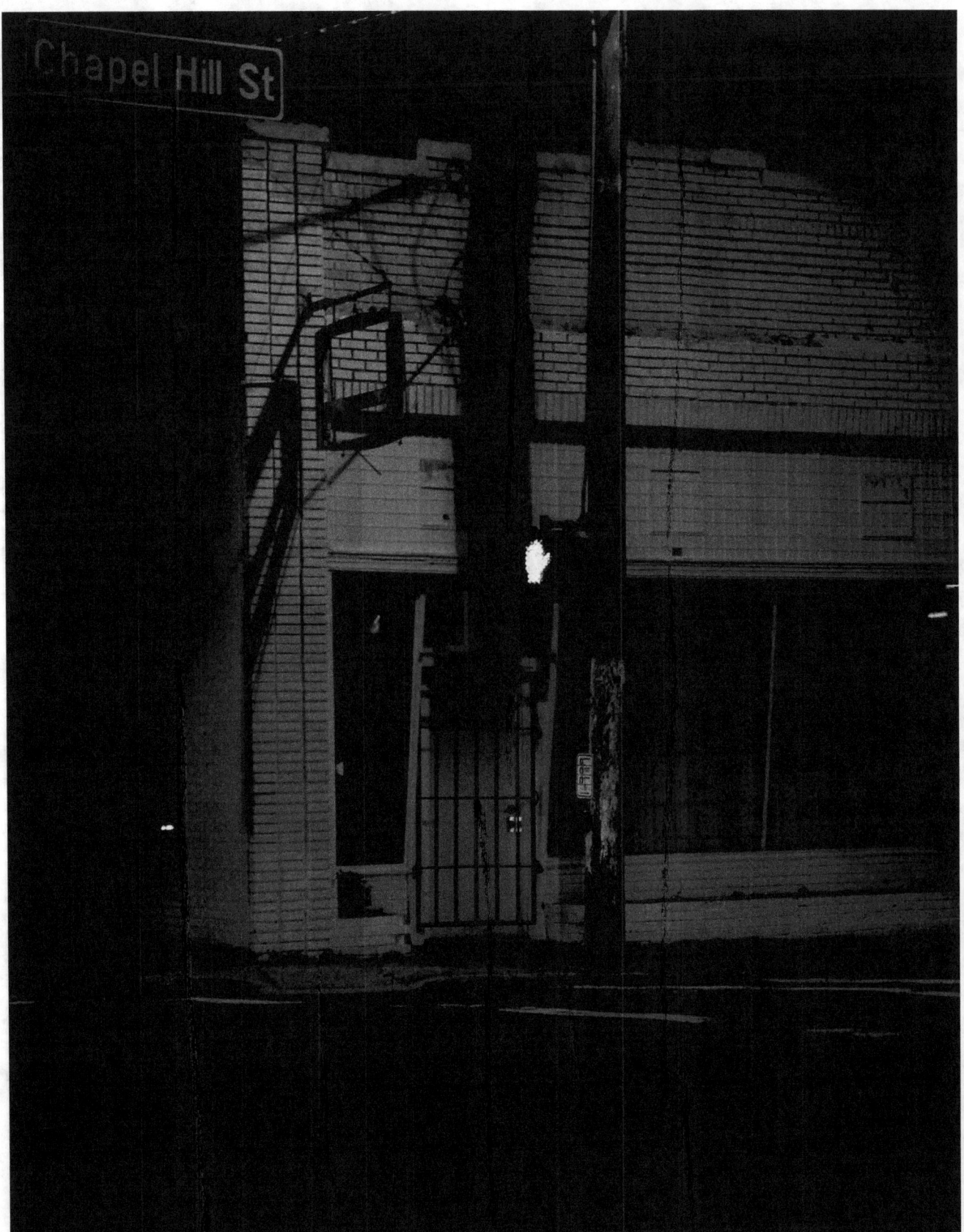

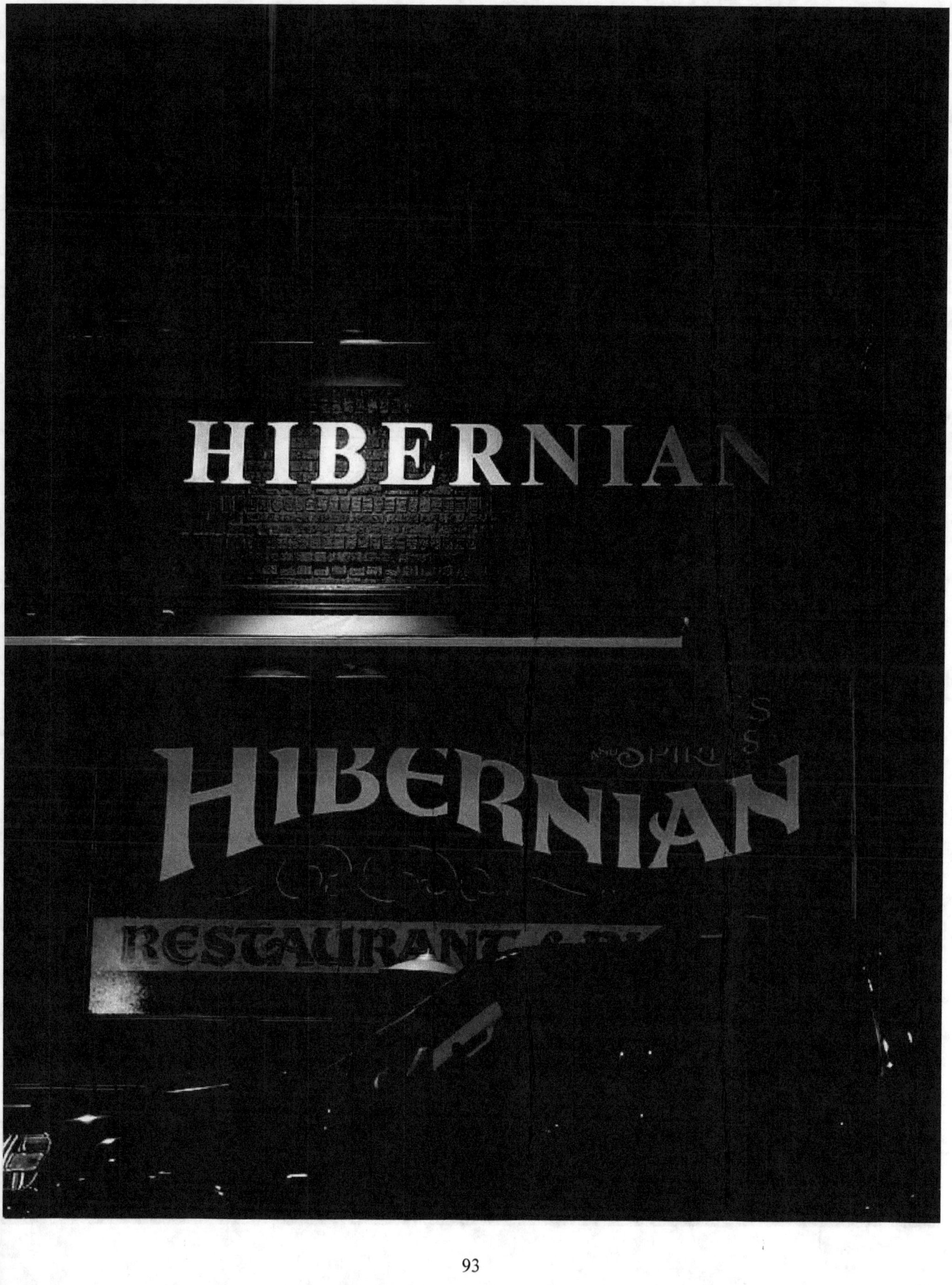
HIBERNIAN
HIBERNIAN
RESTAURANT

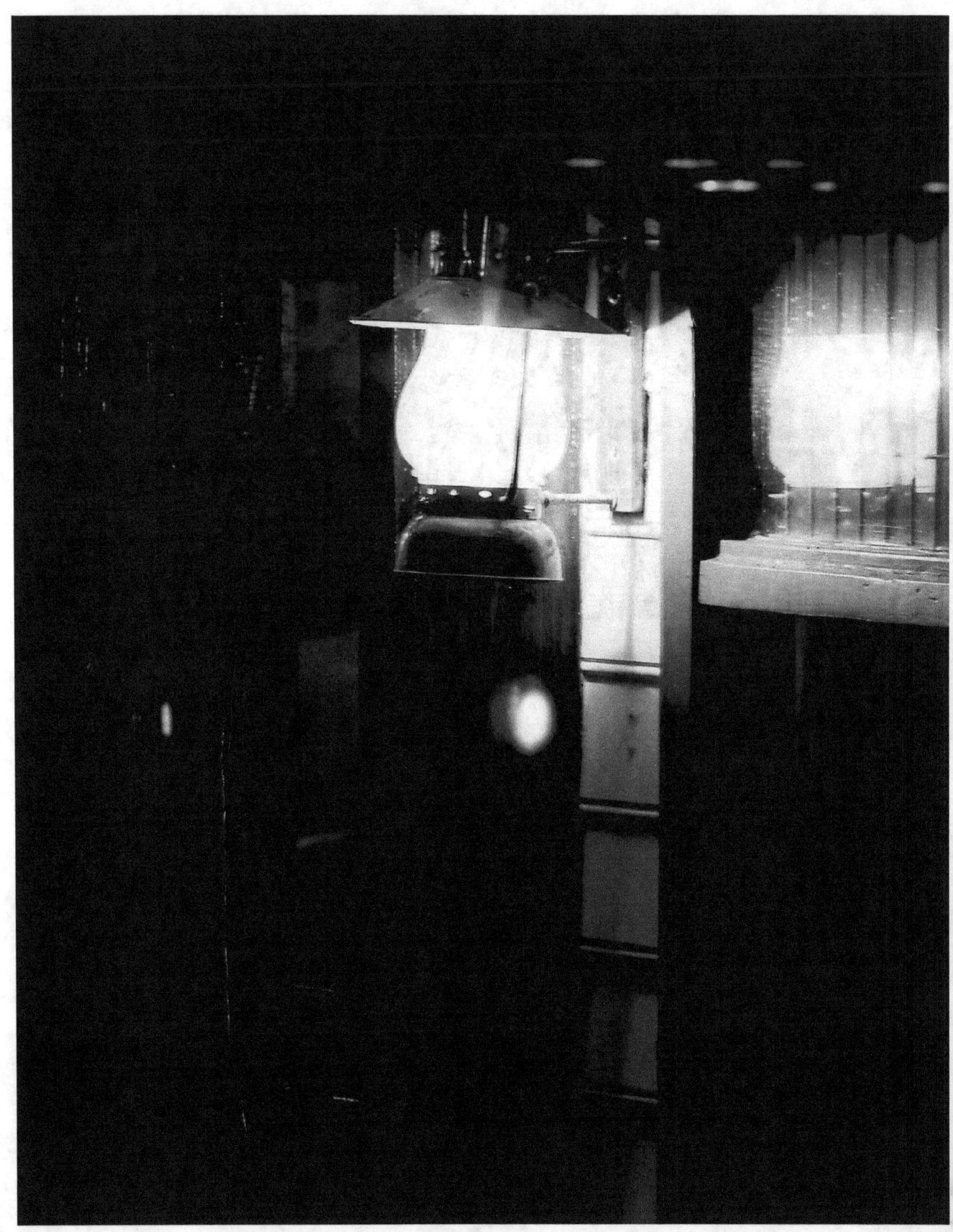

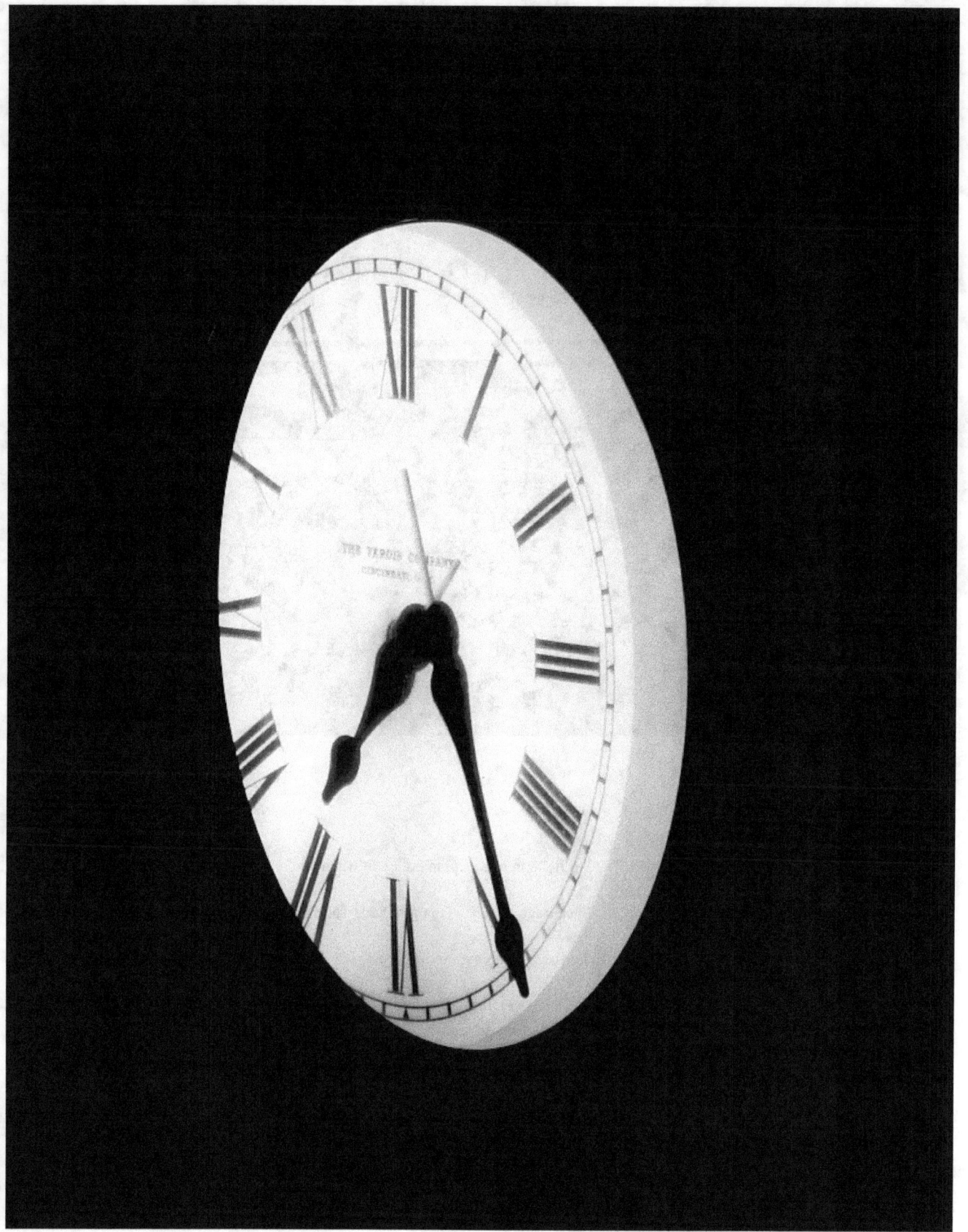

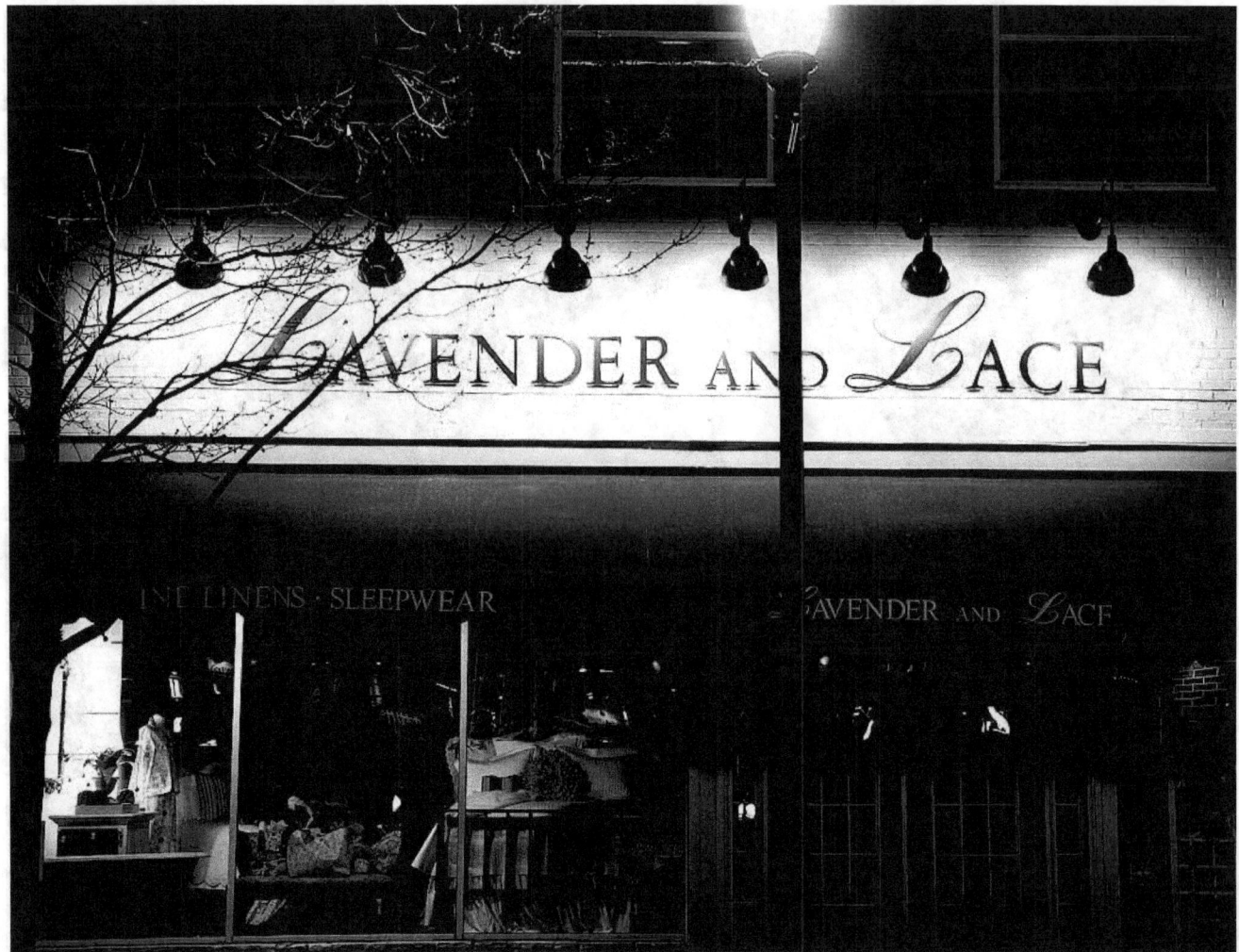

THE CONVERSATION

"What do you want from me?"

"Not *from* you. *With* you.

I want to laugh with you, to cry with you , to fight, to make up, to hold you when you're sad, to apologize when I've hurt you.

To talk, to listen, to ponder, to marvel, to encourage, to renew, to uplift and, when you forget, remind you just how damned special you are.

To bring you Damn-It-All Nacho Eggs in bed on a Saturday morning, complete with daffodils or asters I cut myself because I know they're your favorites.

To discover, to walk, to create, to stop traffic while you move that box turtle out of the road.

To sing - badly and loud, to dance - badly and clumsily, to read, to write and sit on the same stupid sofa watching the same stupid shows on TV.

To make you soup when you're sick, to rub you're shoulders when you're tired and tense after a long day.

To sit on the porch on a cool autumn evening without a word and feel like I've just had the best conversation of my life.

To wash the dishes because, dammit, you worked all day too and then fixed dinner.

To let the random strangers we meet know just by looking that this man loves this woman more than life.

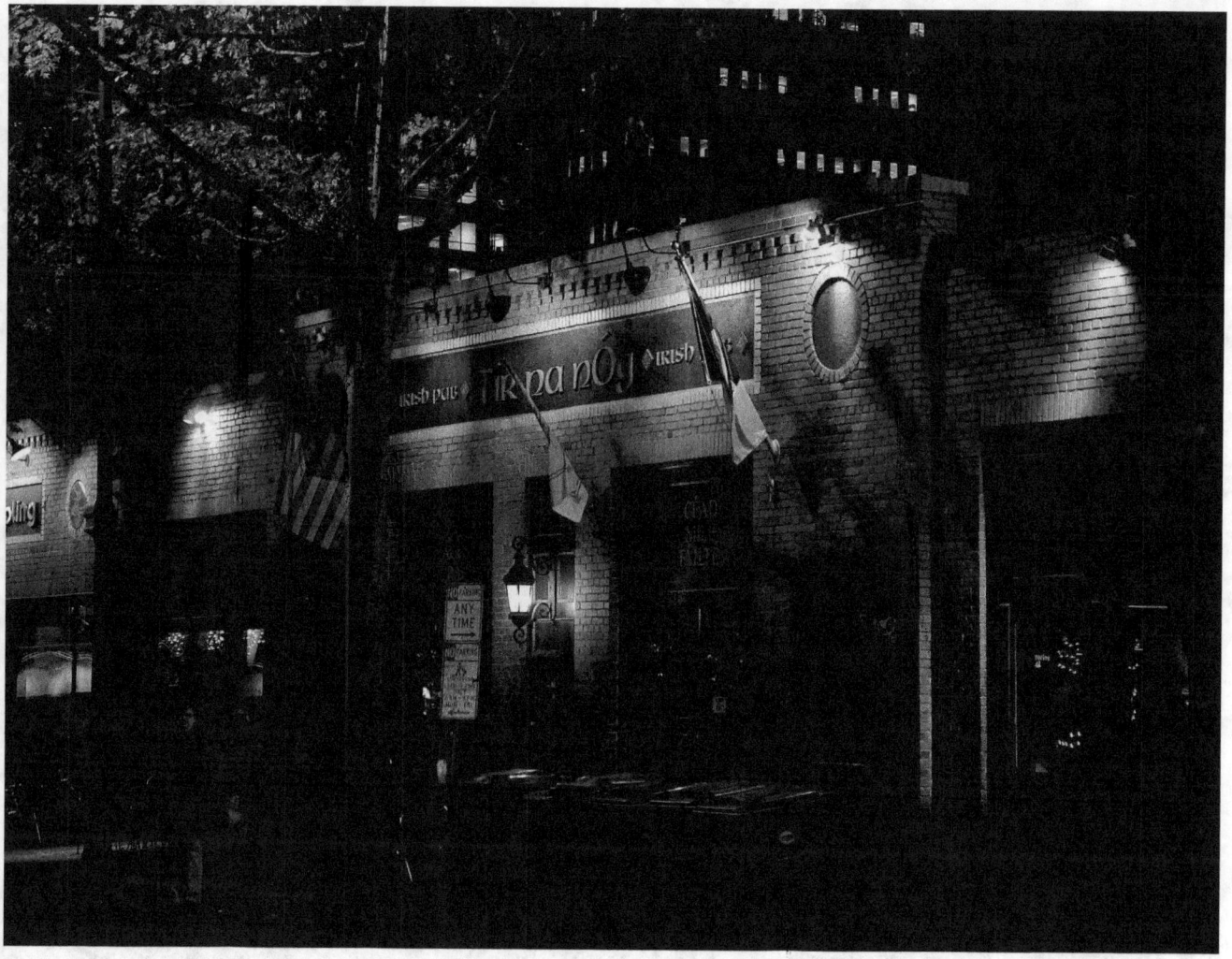

To let *you* know without doubt, without question, without asking, that the heart that beats underneath this cheap, tacky shirt beats only for you.

To do laundry with you, to always put the seat down, to send you flowers just because it's Tuesday and I was thinking of you.

I want to lay my head down at night regretting only that this day has been deducted from my balance of Days With You.

Most of all I want to repeat this same day tomorrow and all the tomorrows that follow it.

Until I lay my head down for the last time regretting only that I didn't know you sooner.

I want to know you, to love you, to be good to you always.

I want all of this.

Not with a mythical, theoretical, fill-in-the-blank Somebody.

With you.

And I'm not too old or feeble or proud to dig ditches to make it possible.

All that's missing is for you to want it too."

"So actually, you *do* want something from me."

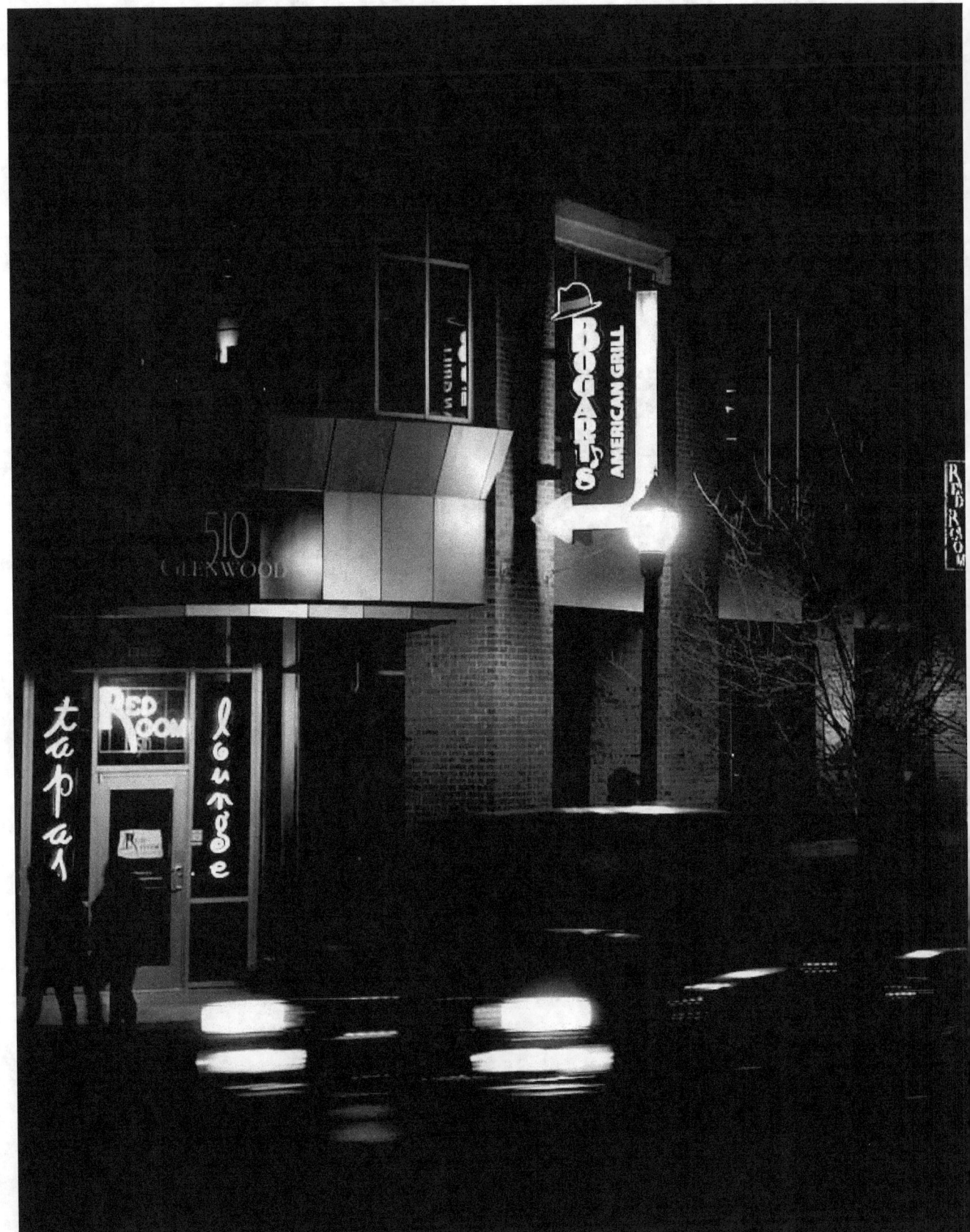

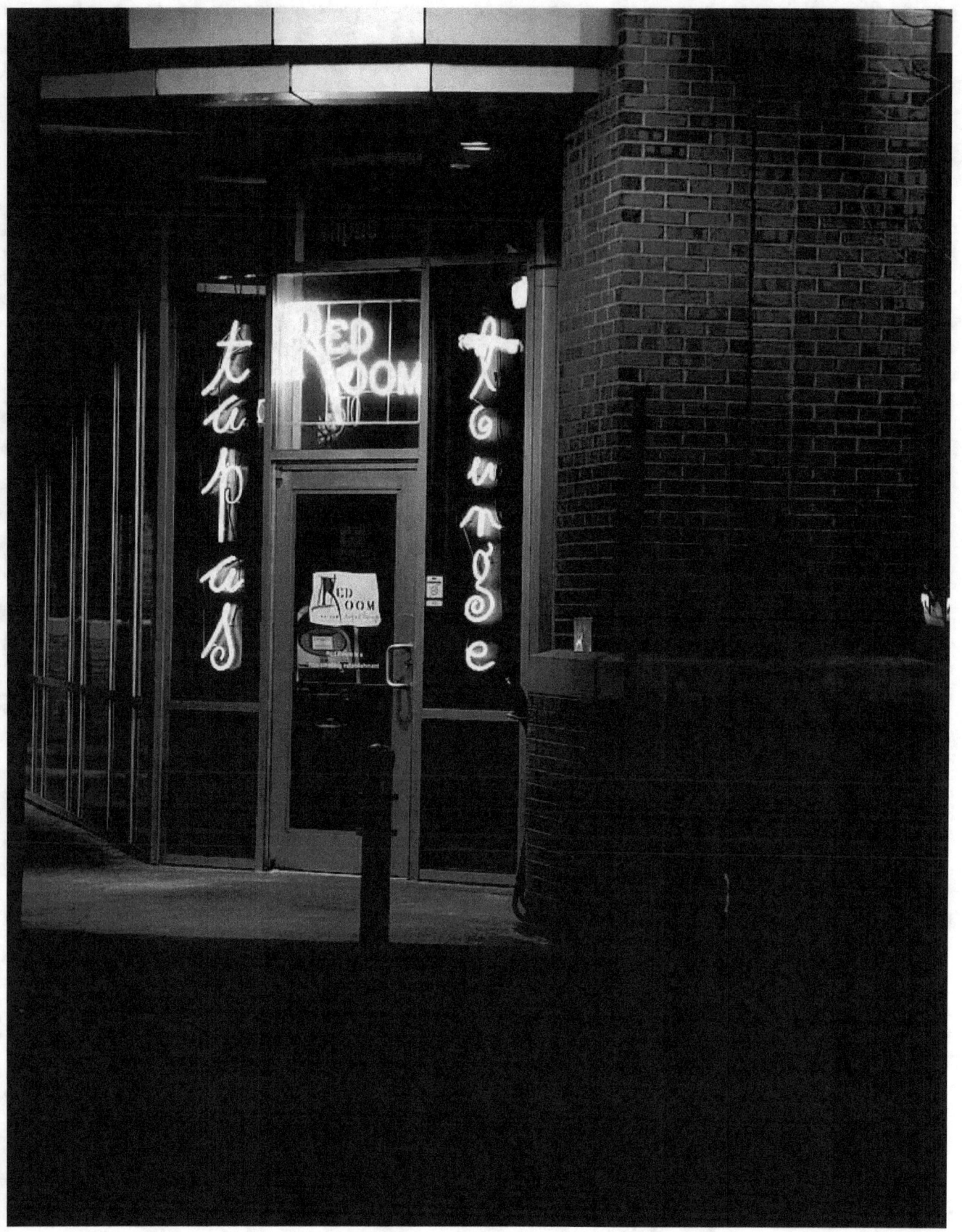

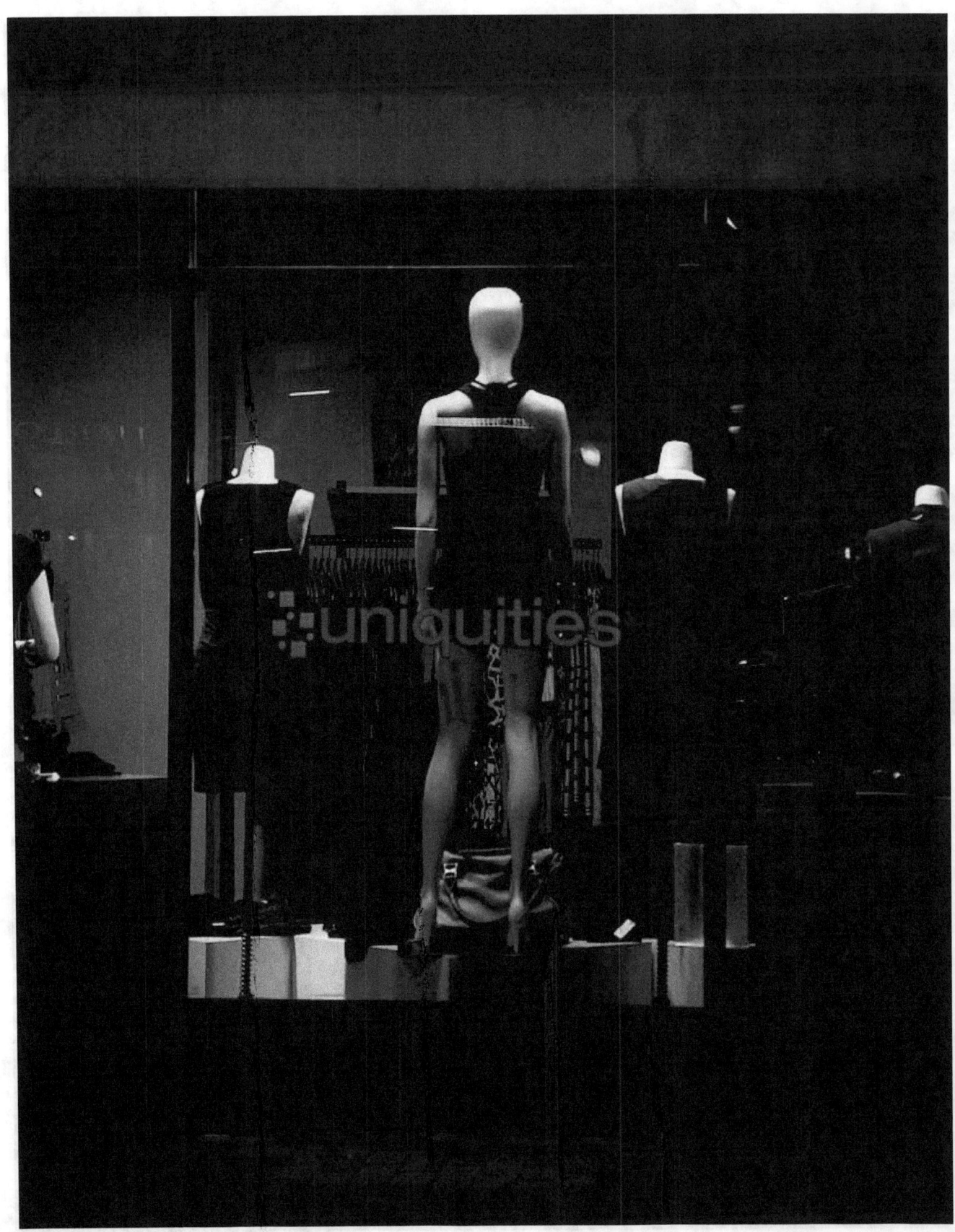

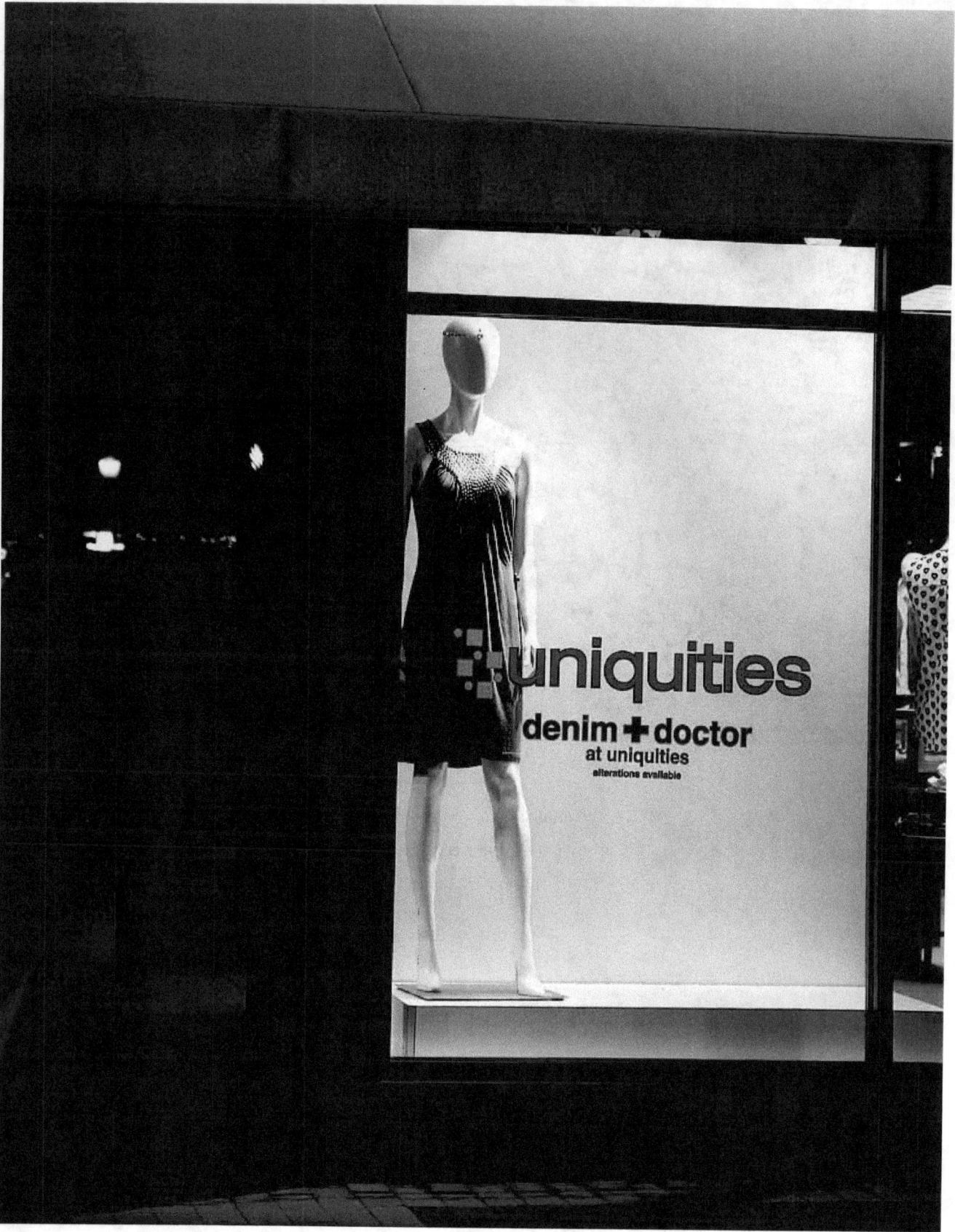

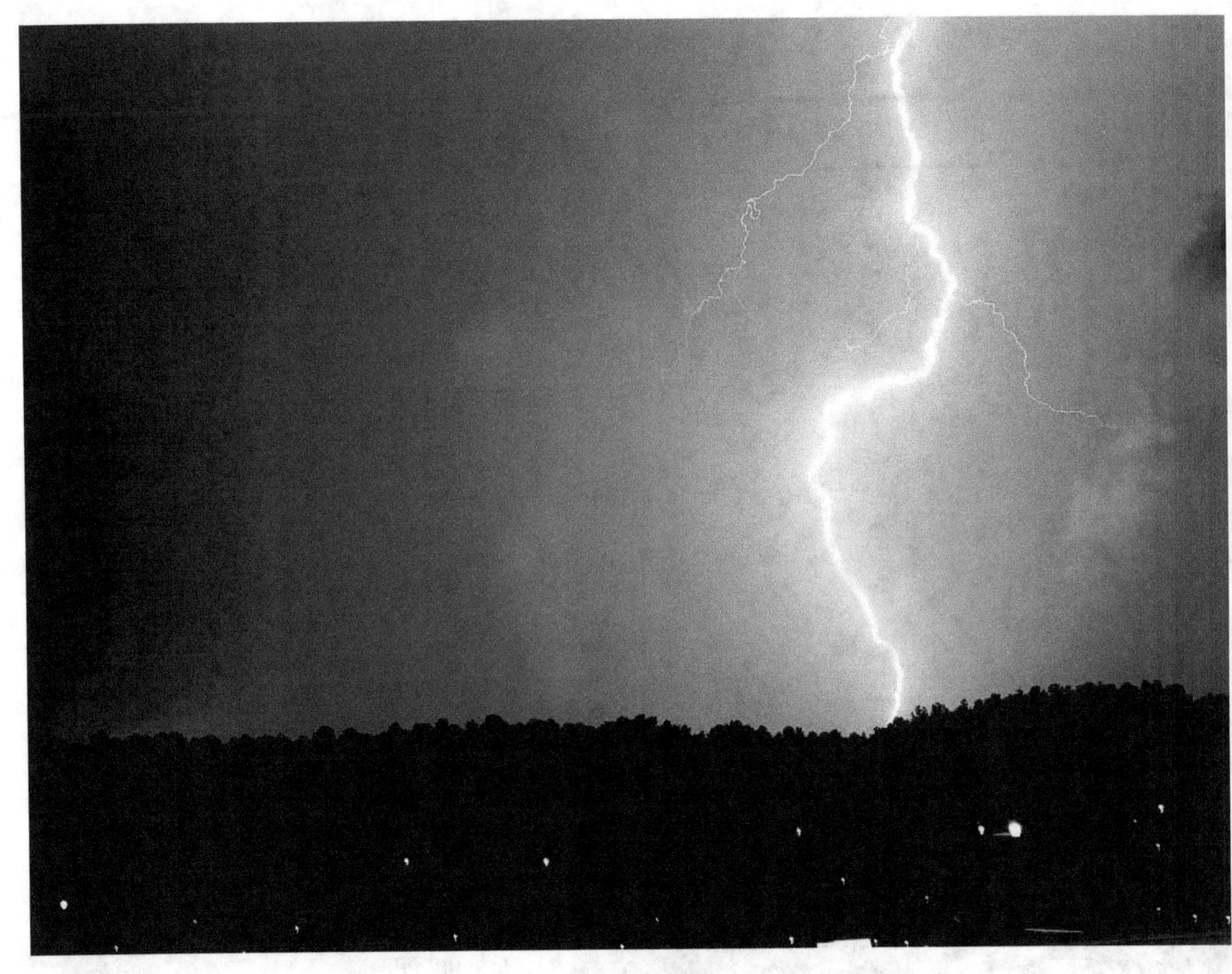

GOLD

Guilt-edged words written
In the gilt-edged pages of
Another chapter

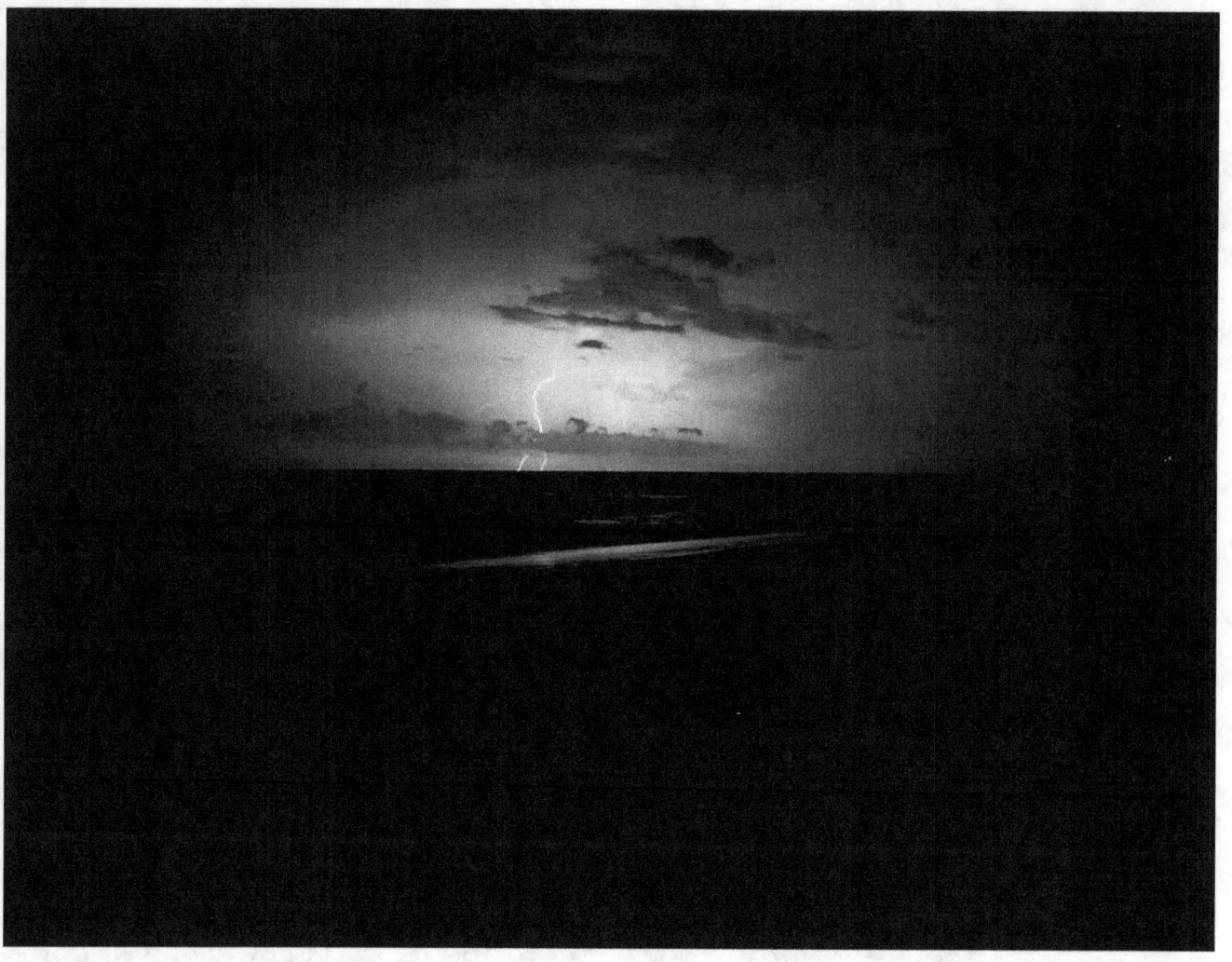

Avatar

Dredging the mud
And silt below it
The ocean sets the table
For the hungry sandpiper
The bird knows what it knows
That the ocean will provide
The bird fears what it fears
That the ocean will also devour
If given the chance
The ocean, for its part
Simply does what it does
What it has always done
What it will always do
Rake the bottom

And deposit the catch
Along the shoreline
For any who come
The birds know this
They come to visit
Take their fill then leave
To flock with others of their kind
Leaving the ocean
To do what it does
Secure in the knowledge
That the ocean will be there
To do what it has always done
Perhaps this is the reason
The waves sigh

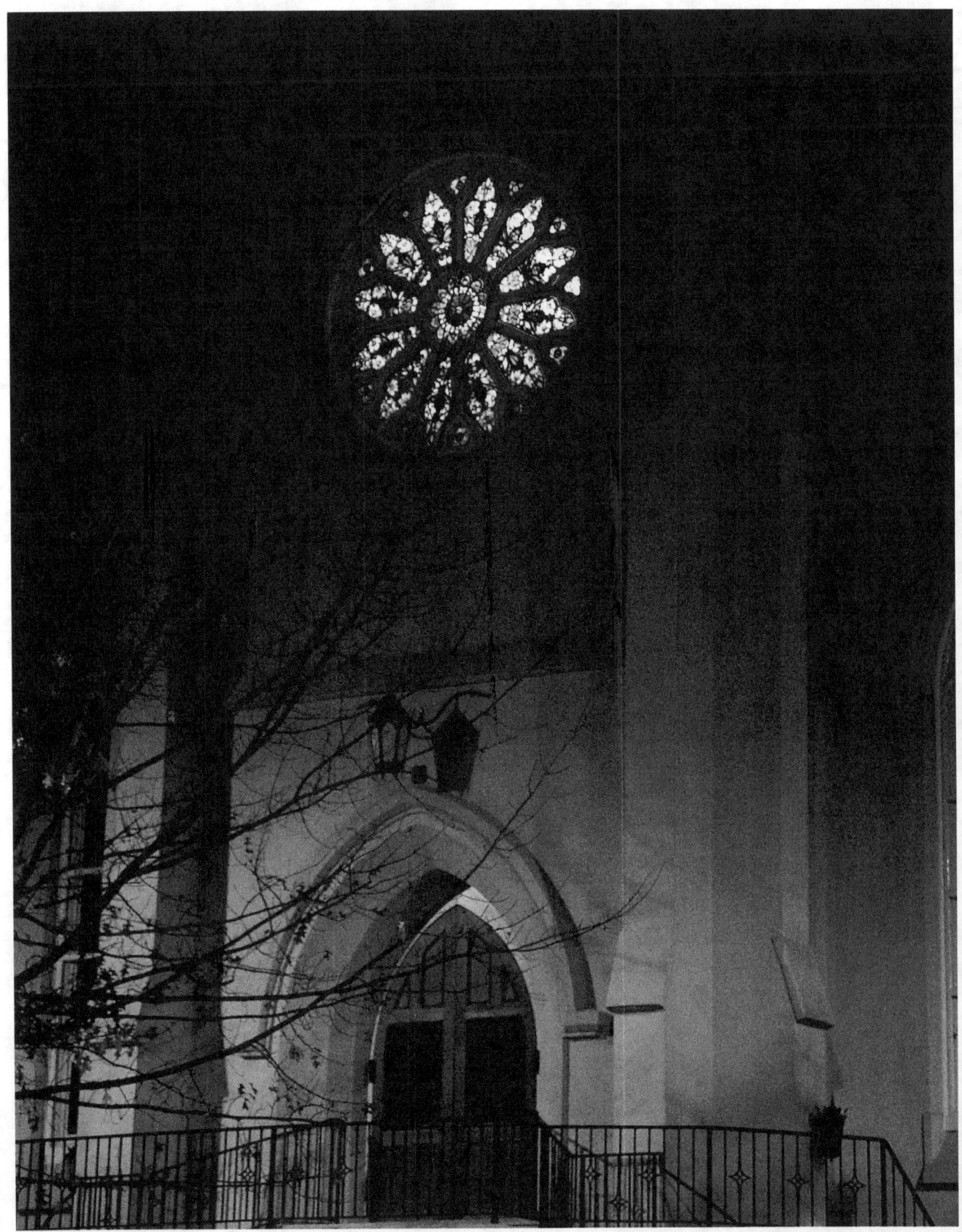

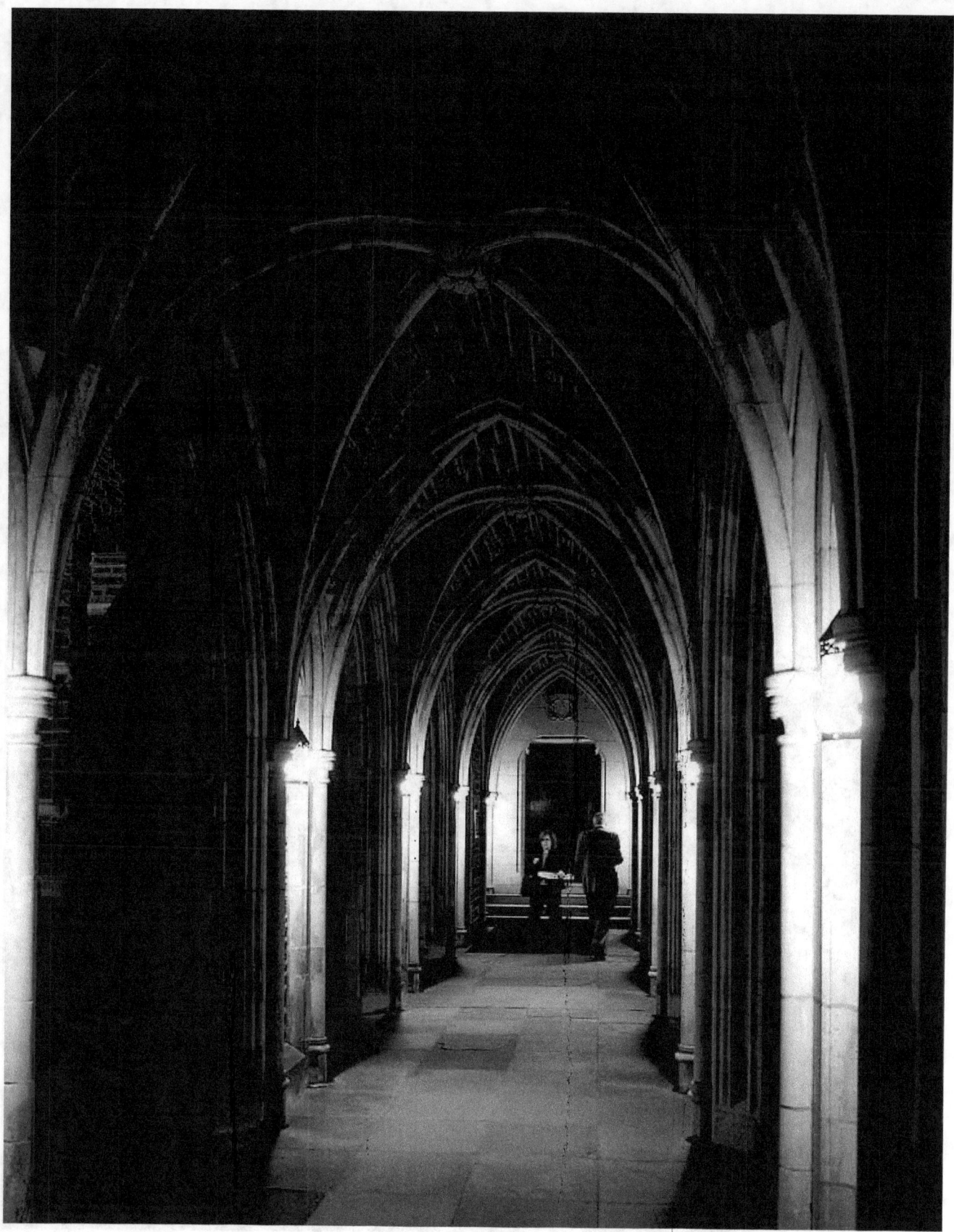

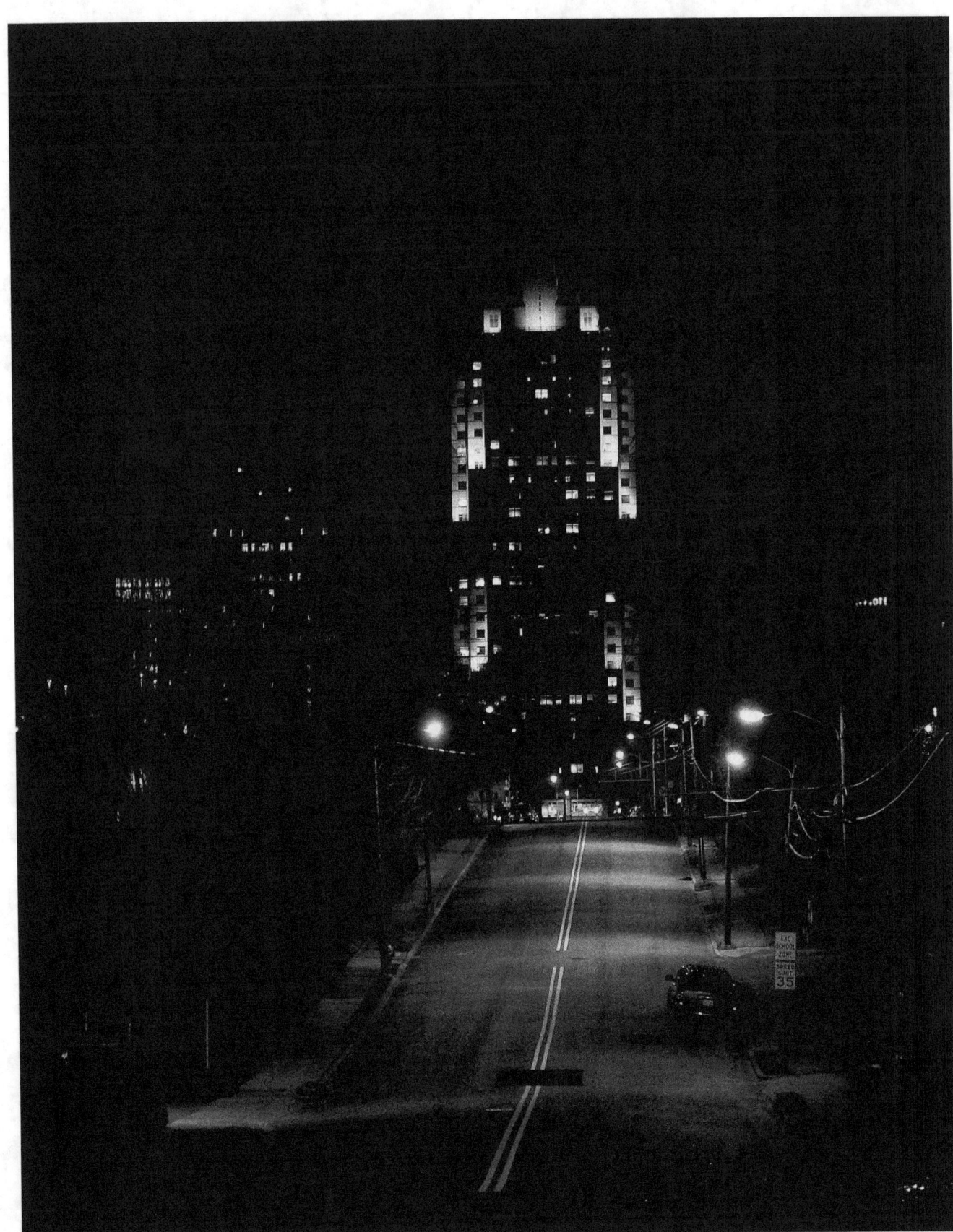

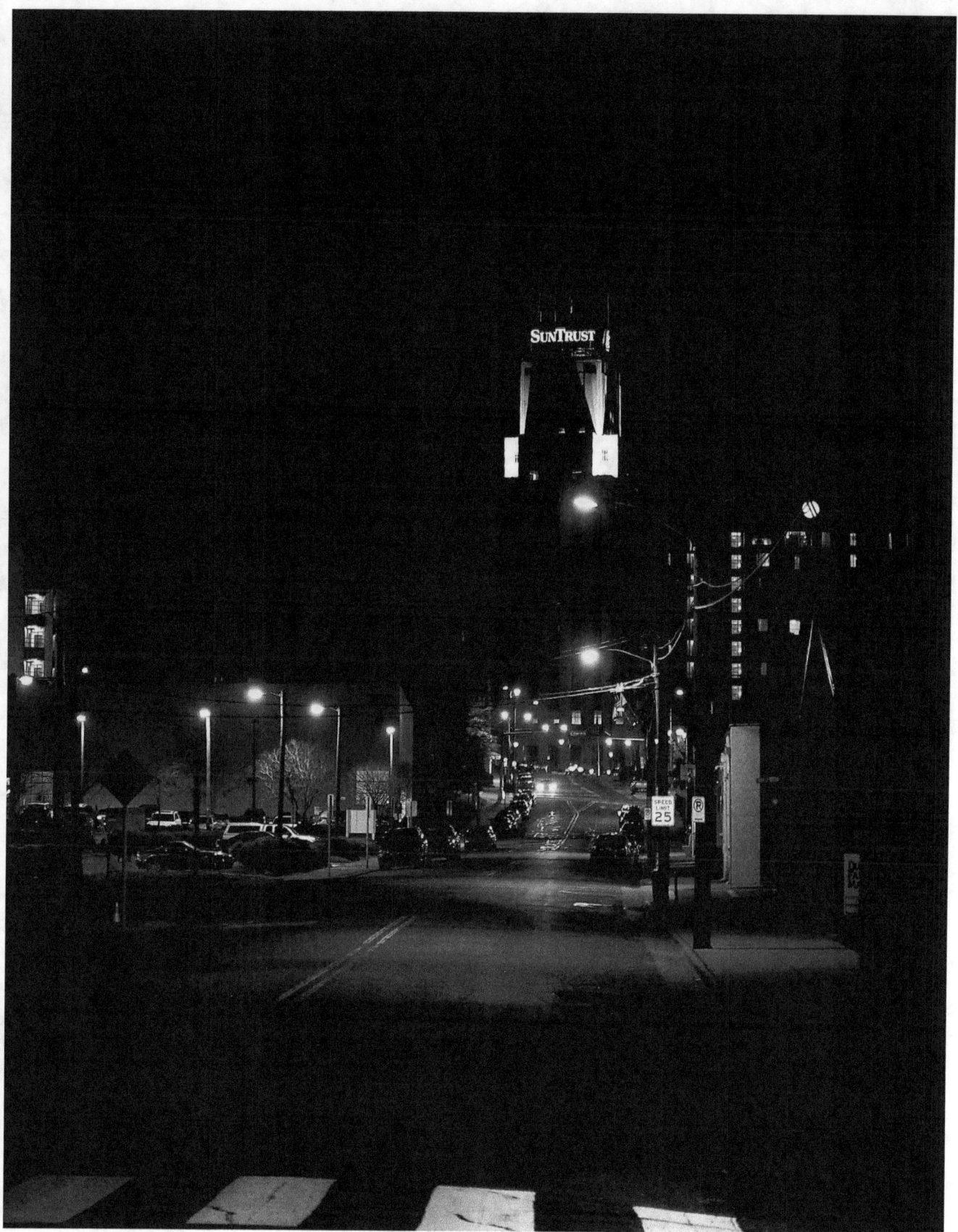

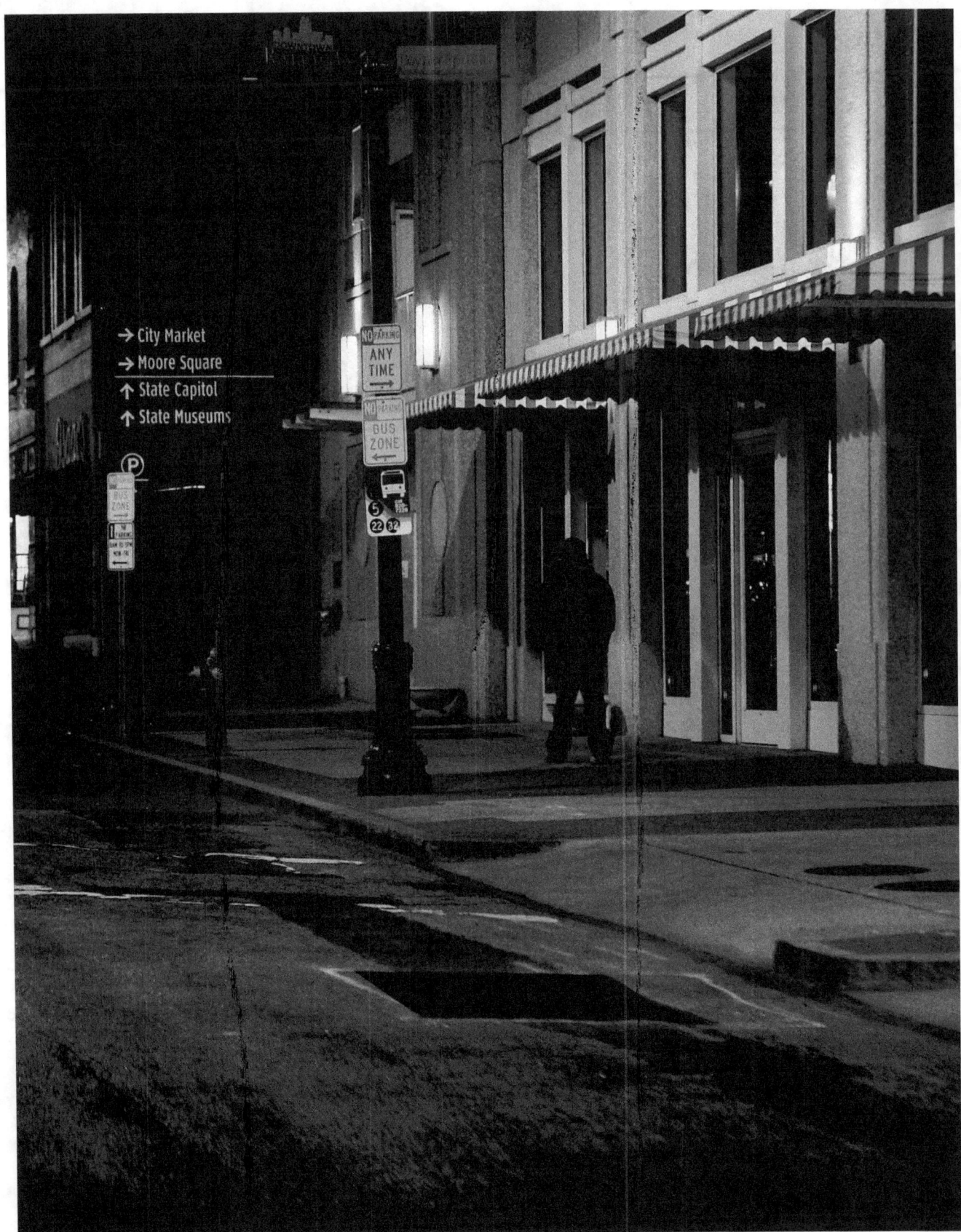

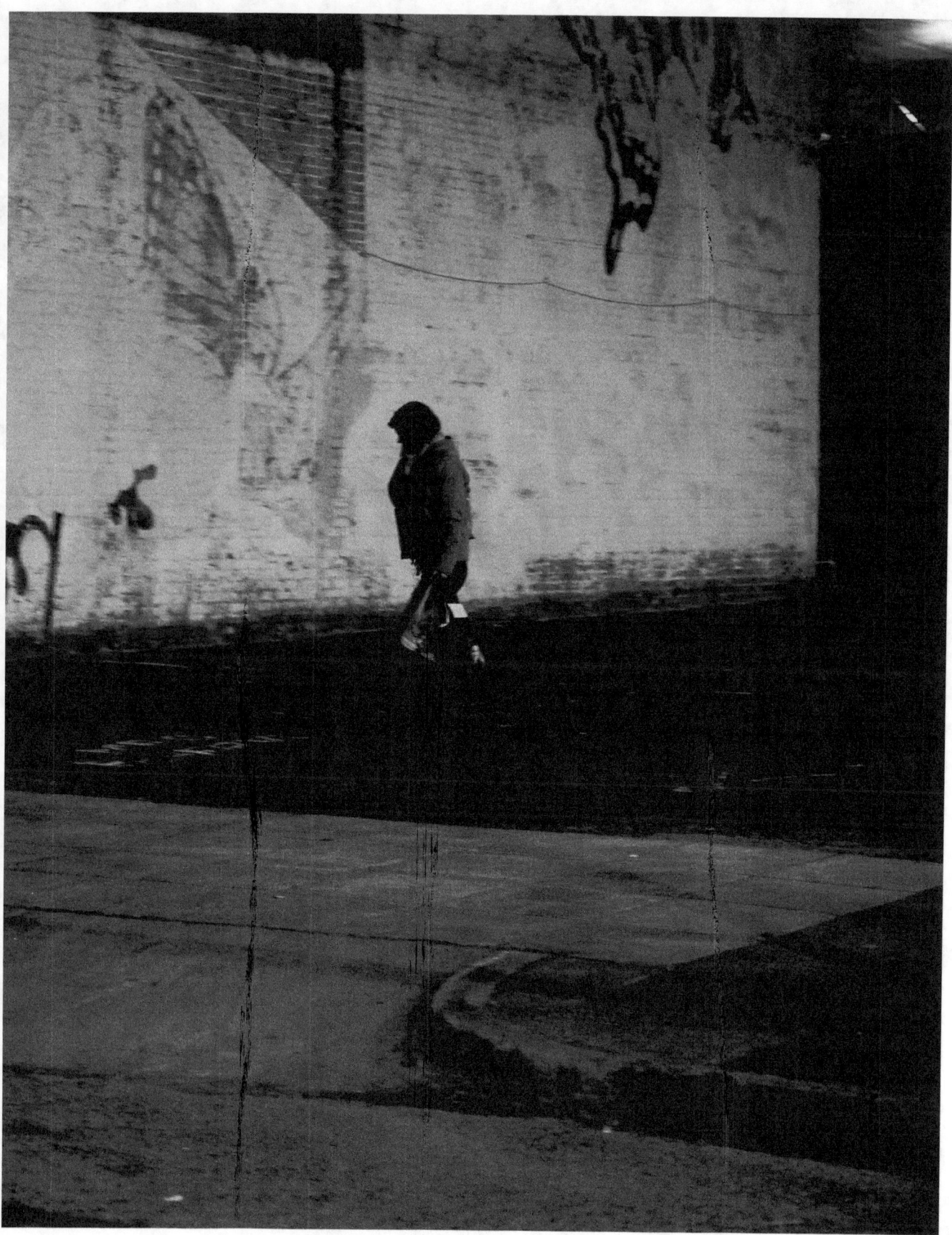

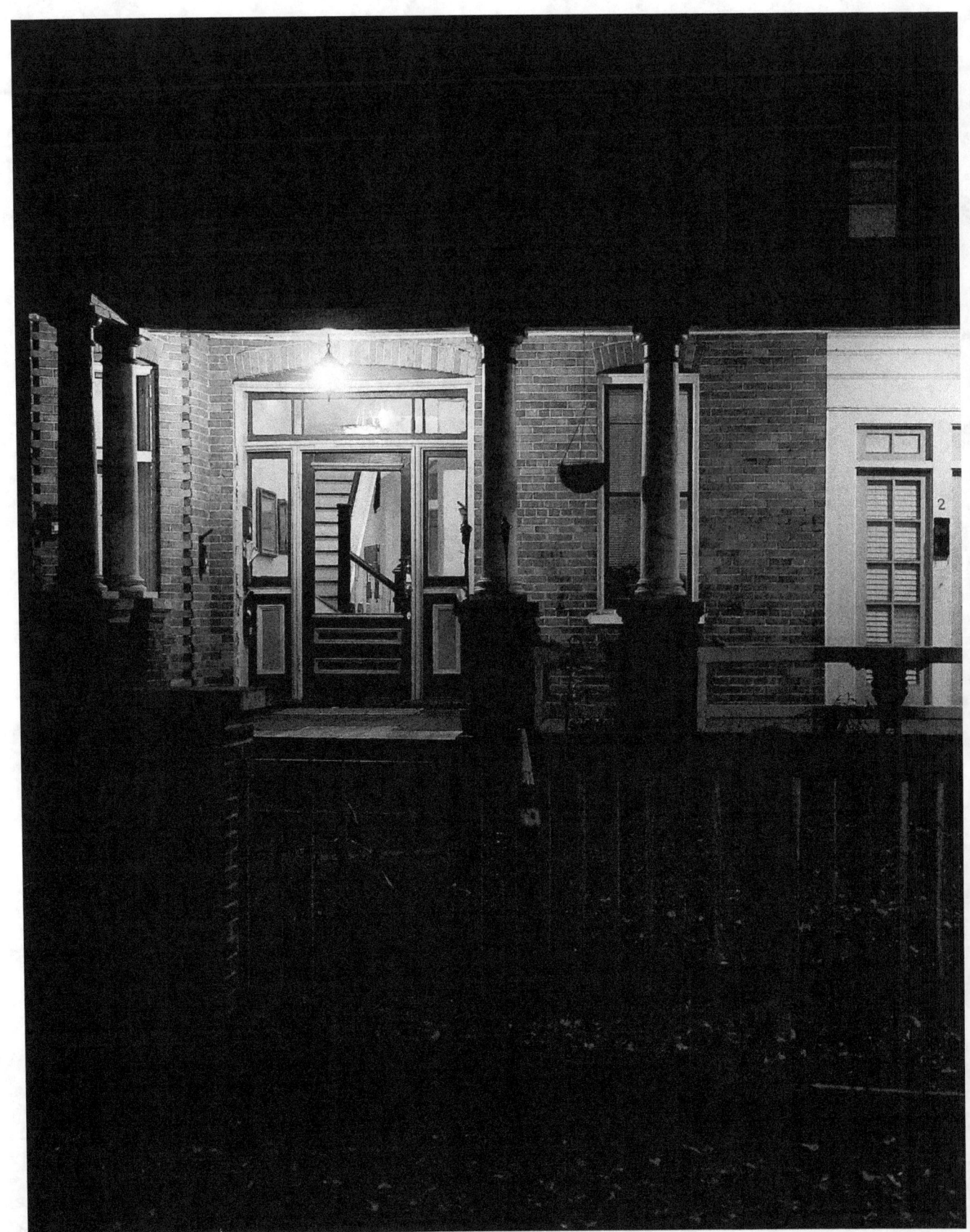

WHAT I WANT YOU TO KNOW

"Don't ask questions", you say.
"People will tell you
What they want you to know."
Fair enough, I say.
I will tell you
What I want you to know.

I love you.
It is as simple as that
It is as complex as that.

I love you, not in a way
That is convenient or neat or orderly or safe
Because love is never like that
I love you, not because
You are beautiful or charming or smart
Though you are all of these and so much more

I love you, not even because
You love me the same way
Because I know better than that

I love you the only way I know how
Always and all ways
In any way I can.
You can break my heart.
You cannot break my love.
You cannot hurt me that much.

Be happy, be well, my friend.
I will be here for you always.
This... is what I want you to know.

www.ingramcontent.com/pod-product-compliance
Lightning Source LLC
Chambersburg PA
CBHW081137170526
45165CB00008B/2700